The Consolidation
of Capitalism,
1896-1929

The Consolidation of Capitalism, 1896-1929

Readings in
Canadian Social History
Volume 4

Edited by
Michael S. Cross
and Gregory S. Kealey

McClelland and Stewart

McClelland and Stewart Limited
The Canadian Publishers
25 Hollinger Road
Toronto, Ontario
M4B 3G2

Canadian Cataloguing in Publication Data
  Main entry under title:
    The Consolidation of capitalism, 1896-1929

  (Readings in Canadian social history; v. 4)
  ISBN 0-7710-2465-7

  1. Canada – Social conditions – 1867-1918 – Addresses, essays, lectures.*
  2. Canada – Social conditions – 1918-1930 – Addresses, essays, lectures.*
  3. Canada – Economic conditions – 1867-1918 – Addresses, essays, lectures.
  4. Canada – Economic conditions – 1918-1945 Addresses, essays, lectures.
  I. Cross, Michael S., 1938-   II. Kealey, Gregory S., 1948-   III.
  Series.

  HN103.C66   971.06   C82-095337-7

Printed and bound in Canada

36,010

Contents

Abbreviations

CHR *Canadian Historical Review*
L/LT *Labour/Le Travailleur*
PAC   Public Archives of Canada

General Introduction
– The Series

The emergence of social history has been perhaps the most significant development of the last fifteen years in Canadian historical writing. Historians young and old have brought new approaches and new perspectives to Canada's past, revealing areas previously overlooked and offering new interpretations of old areas. The result has been what historian Ramsay Cook has called the discipline's "golden age." This five-volume series of readers in social history is intended to make the fruits of that "golden age" readily available to teachers, students, and general readers.

Modern social history is an approach rather than a specific subject matter. Where once social history was seen as what was left over after political and economic history was written, social history now is a "global" discipline, which can embrace politics and economics as well as the history of social groups or charitable institutions. The ideal of social history is to write the history of society, to study all of the ways in which people, groups of people, and classes of people interact to produce a society and to create social change. Such a global picture may never be drawn but its goal of an integrated history underlies recent study in Canada. The social historian, then, may write about a small subject over a limited period of time. However, that historian must be conscious of the links to the larger reality; of how local politics, say, indicate the relations of social classes, how they react with ideological assumptions of provincial politicians, how they affect local social customs.

5

It is a new field and that means its effort has been scattered. Canadian social history has embraced everything from the study of women's groups to computer analysis of population changes to the history of disease. It also has been marked by some sharp differences of opinion. The editors of this series, as practitioners and partisans, make no claim to objectivity in assessing these differences. Broadly, some historians treat social history as an extension of previous historical writing and share its assumptions about the general sweep of Canadian development: its liberal-democratic character; its fluid class structure; its peaceful and orderly growth. Others, however, break from that interpretation and argue for a different picture: a more rigid and influential class structure; a greater degree of conflict and violence; an emphasis on the working class. Which interpretation will prevail remains to be seen. The essays chosen for the series attempt to present as many viewpoints as possible, but the overall structure clearly reflects the judgement of the editors, which favours the second approach, the "working class" approach.

Rather than being structured along the traditional political divisions, the volumes in the series have been organized around dates which seemed most appropriate to social history:

I   New France to the Conquest, 1760
II   Pre-Industrial Canada, from the Conquest to the end of the imperial economic system, 1760 to 1849
III   Canada's Age of Industry, from the coming of the railway to the full flowering of industrialism, 1849 to 1896
IV   The Consolidation of Capitalism, from the beginnings of economic monopoly to the Great Crash, 1896 to 1929
V   The Emergence of the Welfare State, from the origins of large-scale state intervention to the present, 1930 to 1981.

Again, the internal divisions of the volumes have been chosen to illustrate basic themes that represent building blocks in social history. Not all themes could be included and some historians might argue with the particular choices made here. We would suggest several rationales for the selection: these themes seem important to us; the volume of writing and research on them, completed and underway, suggests that many others find them important; and they have proven useful in teaching social history.

Different periods and the availability of good literature require some variance from volume to volume. The general structure, however, is consistent. Each volume begins with an essay on the major economic developments of the period, for we work from the assumption that changing economic forms underlie most social changes. The second theme is that of social structure and social institutions, of the classes and groups of Canadian society and the way in which they interact. This theme will embrace subject matter as diverse as politics, religion, and landholding patterns.

Certain groups have emerged to centre stage historically in recent years. One is workers, the third theme in each volume. Workers and their work have been perhaps the area of richest development in historical writing in the last decade; social history has made its most profound impact in reshaping historical knowledge in this area. The fourth theme is one in which social history has had a similarly important influence, if only because interest in it is so recent. That is violence and protest, now receiving close attention from historians, sociologists, and criminologists. Violence and protest involved many Canadians and touched the lives of many more, and therefore are significant in their own right. However, they also provide a sharply defined picture of the structures and values of the society in which they occurred. The things people consider important enough to fight and protest about give us some indication of the values of particular groups. The attitudes of the leadership of society emerge in the fifth theme, social control. This theme studies the checks placed on violence and protest and inappropriate behaviour, as well as the institutions created to mould appropriate behaviour.

Along with workers, the other group to receive due attention from social history is women. No area, perhaps, was so neglected for so long as the study of women, outside of occasional writing on the suffrage movement. Recently, however, there has been a flood of literature, not just on feminism and women's organizations, but on women's productive and reproductive work. In a field devoted to creation of an integrated picture of society, this is a welcome and exciting development. Some of the trends in women's history, and some of the major achievements, are illustrated in these volumes.

The structure adopted here is offered as a useful one which will open to teachers and to students an exciting area of Canadian studies. It makes no claim to comprehensiveness; it is very much a starting point for that study. The additional readings suggested will help to move beyond that starting point and to introduce the controversies which cannot be reflected adequately in the small number of essays reprinted here. These volumes, however, do serve as a report on some approaches we have found helpful to students of social history and on some of the best literature available in this new field. More, they are collected on the premise that the investigation of social change in Canadian history, the ideas exposed and the questions raised, may allow students to understand more fully the nature of the Canadian society in which they live.

M.S. Cross
G.S. Kealey
Halifax and
St. John's,
July, 1981

Introduction
to Volume 4

Canada in the period from the end of the depression of the
1890's to the advent of the Great Depression of the 1930's has
been described by historians as "A Nation Transformed." This
great transformation touched all aspects of Canadians' lives.
The country's mood at the turn of the century was ebullient and
Prime Minister Wilfrid Laurier announced with confidence that
"The Twentieth Century belonged to Canada!"

These buoyant hopes owed much to the economic prosperity
which accompanied the wheat boom of the pre-war years and
the mineral discoveries in the Klondike and "New" or northern
Ontario. In addition, Canada received massive infusions of
American capital as the new multinational corporations began
their process of world conquest. Canada, the key to British Empire markets, became the first outpost of a sophisticated American imperialism which operated through influence rather than
domination by force. Ontario, with its head start in manufacturing, became the major beneficiary of multinational capital as
firms such as General Electric, Westinghouse, McCormack Harvester, and later the automotive companies moved to establish
plants in Canada and thus avoid Canadian and other empire
tariffs. Cities such as Hamilton expanded rapidly on the basis of
branch plant location. Ontario towns of all sizes vied with each
other to provide fatter and fatter incentives to industrial
magnates in return for the establishment of factories. Free
building sites, tax incentives, low cost services, and other lures
were offered to attract Yankee industrialists. These "robber

barons," as they were described by their progressive critics, were quick to take advantage and massive interlocking enterprises were erected in cities as varied as Sault Ste. Marie, Ontario, and Sydney, Nova Scotia.

In the Sault, American F.H. Clergue, starting with only a small power plant in 1892, built an industrial empire, the Consolidated Lake Superior Corporation, which at its peak in 1902 owned power companies, railways, steamship lines, a telegraph company, nickel, iron, and gold mines, and the Algoma Steel Company. Its decline was as precipitous as its rise and in the fall of 1903 the whole empire drowned in a sea of watered stock. Equally sensational was the career of Boston-based financier Henry Melville Whitney, who through the active support of Nova Scotia Premier W.S. Fielding consolidated Cape Breton coal mines into the mighty Dominion Coal Company in 1893. Six years later another Liberal Nova Scotia Premier, George Murray, rewarded Whitney with significant coal royalty concessions and then, with additional bounties acquired from federal Liberal Finance Minister and old Whitney friend, W.S. Fielding, the Dominion Iron and Steel Company was born. Although not as sensational a failure as Consolidated Lake Superior, DISCO too went through almost immediate corporate reorganization and Whitney was edged out before the first steel was produced. These are but two examples of one prevalent business trend in Canada's gilded age, namely the massive concentration of capital in vast firms.

Not all the buccaneers were Americans, however, and some Canadians now honour the memory of financiers such as Max Aitken, later Lord Beaverbrook, and William Mackenzie and Donald Mann, both knighted in 1911. Aitken, from his modest beginnings in New Brunswick, became the master of the corporate merger, a process by which numerous small companies were knit into an industrial giant. The end of competition was one attraction in the merger movement, but for financial operators like Aitken the real money was made in the merger itself. Here again, watered stock too often prevailed. Mackenzie and Mann were railway contractors who ultimately transformed many small lines into a third transcontinental railway in the years before World War I. The collapse of both their Canadian Northern and of the competing Grand Trunk Pacific in the winter of 1915-16 led to the establishment of the publicly owned Canadian National Railway, a product not of proud public ownership but rather of the necessity to bail the banks out of the potential huge losses caused by the bankruptcy of the railways.

Monopoly capital had other faces in Canada as well. In addition to the vast inflow of American capital through branch plant operations and the ever-increasing centralization and concentration of capital which accompanied the merger movement, there was also a significant internal reorganization of industry in this period. Although mechanization had increased throughout the nineteenth century and affected workers' lives, the rise of scientific management in the early twentieth century accomplished a significant shift in which the power and autonomy of the skilled worker on the shop floor was sharply curtailed and replaced by centralized planning under the control of engineers. The rise of the engineer to prominence in North American society provides graphic detail of the shift toward efficiency as the keynote of the period. Victorians' faith in progress gave way to the Progressives' demand for efficiency. Henry Ford's assembly line captured the imagination of the day and still provides a useful image which illuminates the transformation of the workplace.

The regional tensions implicit in the unhappy Confederation compromise re-emerged in this period with a vengeance. Capitalist development in central Canada led to a rapid deindustrialization of the Maritimes. The crisis implicit in the shift from wood and sail to iron and steam which had been weathered by the intense industrialization of the National Policy period was reversed as the nation's economy shifted focus to the centre. With the massive centralization and concentration process underway, significant Maritime centres saw their industries fail. The 1900 shift of the Bank of Nova Scotia's headquarters from Halifax to Montreal can be viewed as a major symbolic event in the region's economic demise. Although World War I momentarily halted the process, the 1920's saw a total and dismal collapse of the local economy which led to renewed regional resistance. The Maritime Rights Movement, a protest movement that blamed Ottawa for the region's decline, had little effect, however.

Meanwhile, western settlement proceeded rapidly through the agency of massive immigration. The new immigrants, many from southern and eastern Europe, were attracted by the active and often misleading promotions of Canadian immigration agents, the steamship lines, and the Canadian Pacific Railway. Many "new" Canadians spent their initial years in Canada building transcontinental railways or labouring in the mines and forests of the Canadian West. When they had saved sufficient money, they would begin to homestead. These farms became the basis of Canada's vibrant wheat economy. Yet Canadian farmers had many discontents in the first decades of the twentieth century. They viewed the CPR's western monopoly as inimical to their need for inexpensive and efficient rail transportation. They pointed with considerable justification to freight rates which were prejudicial to western grain, while favouring eastern manufacturers. Equally they detested Canada's protective tariffs, which forced them to pay high prices for manufactured products such as agricultural implements. They correctly recognized that they were financing the industrial strategy of central Canada. These and kindred complaints led to the creation of important agrarian protest movements that culminated in the post-war success of the National Progressive Party in electing sixty-four Members of Parliament in 1921. This electoral achievement was the greatest number of seats won to date by a third-party movement in Canada, and for all intents and purposes signified the end of the two-party system. A Farmer-Labour government also came to power in Ontario in 1919. Thus it should be noted that agrarian protest was not limited to the West. Ontario and Maritime farmers also entered politics vigorously in this post-war period. Generally disaffected with the trend to urban society, they feared the loss not only of their children to the growing cities but also of a rural way of life.

Labour, too, fought back against the incursions of monopoly capital. While always only representing a minority, various socialist parties emerged in the years before World War I. They enjoyed their greatest successes among resource workers in the West and ethnics in the cities. While the prevalent form of labour organization was the craft union of the skilled worker, a series of courageous attempts to create an industrial unionism rejected the exclusivity of the crafts. The Industrial Workers of the World, for example, organized all workers without regard to skill, race, ethnicity, or sex. Later, after the war, the One Big Union captured for a brief moment the aspirations and hopes of Canadian workers who demanded a better society in the aftermath of the supposed war for democracy. Peaking in the surging strike wave of 1919 that saw general strikes in many Canadian cities, the labour movement met heavy governmental repression. The RCMP, for example, owes its birth to bourgeois fears in the aftermath of the Bolshevik revolution. While achieving political victories in Winnipeg's dénouement in Manitoba and in Ontario, nevertheless the movement slid back in the 1920's into a defeatist craft exclusivism. The founding of the Communist Party of Canada in 1921 provided one path for radical workers, but far from all socialists chose this route.

Enlightened managers frightened by the post-war events and often influenced by the social gospel also began to combine the carrots of welfare capitalism with the sticks of scientific management. Industrial council schemes, lunchrooms, playgrounds, sport teams, pension plans, low mortgages, and sundry other schemes were implemented by such firms as Massey Harris and General Motors. Many of these attained considerable levels of success in the 1920's, although, ironically, industrial councils often provided the organizational basis for the industrial union drive which came in the 1930's.

The social gospel, Christianity's valiant attempt to come to grips with the evils of capitalism, occupied a central place in these decades. Reformers imbued with what one historian has described as "the social passion" worked to alleviate the worst horrors of rampant capitalism. The implicit ecumenism of the movement also led to a religious merger movement as well and in 1925, Congregationalists, many Presbyterians, and Methodists came together to form the United Church of Canada.

The social gospel and progressivism also left their imprint on the Canadian state. For while Canadian governments on all levels continued systematically to help foster capitalist growth, they began to take more seriously the requisite supervisory functions encouraged by labour and middle-class reformers. The drive for a more equitable society governed by class harmony found many advocates, some of whom, such as future prime minister William Lyon Mackenzie King, made careers out of the interaction of a concerned social science and a religious reforming conscience. King, one of the new "experts" of reform, championed an active state role in labour relations which led to the Industrial Disputes Investigation Act of 1907. The IDIA or Lemieux Act was a unique Canadian contribution to the annals of labour relations in advanced capitalist countries. Its *ad hoc* tripartite boards of labour, capital, and government, the unenforceable award, compulsory investigation and mediation, and the cooling-off period have become the main ingredients in the Canadian industrial relations system.

Initiatives came in other areas of state labour policy as well. Workmen's compensation acts were passed in most provincial jurisdictions before the war; during the war numerous manpower planning schemes were developed; after the war, partially in response to the Treaty of Versailles, most Canadian provinces passed extensive protective legislation for women and child workers. While many of these schemes proved ineffectual, they nevertheless lay the groundwork for the far more extensive state role which continued to grow especially under the later pressures of depression and war.

In addition to labour relations, however, social reform involving state participation came in many other realms. These included significant expansions of the educational system and the first real attempts to enforce compulsory education. In health it led to well-baby clinics, pasteurization of milk, public education, and, in general, a rapid growth in public health schemes. In housing it led to numerous plans to develop low-cost residences for workers and immigrants, most of which, however, failed to be implemented. Social reform engendered its own experts and from progressive concerns and social science studies grew new applied fields such as social work.

Women played prominent roles in most of these social movements. Building on their earlier activities in church and temperance organizations, they created powerful institutions such as the National Council of Women, founded in 1893. World War I brought Canadian women the vote, first in Manitoba in 1916, followed quickly by Saskatchewan and Alberta, and then by British Columbia and Ontario. In the autumn of 1917 the Borden government enfranchised the female relatives of soldiers and the next year expanded this to all adult women. In the following years the other Canadian provinces also granted women the vote so that only Quebec women were without the provincial franchise by the end of the period. World War I also brought women reformers and their male allies another major success. After years of national and provincial campaigning, temperance forces finally won the day and the new Union government imposed prohibition on Canadians in 1917. The temperance movement had played a significant role in Canadian life since the late nineteenth century through its major institutions, the Dominion Alliance and the Woman's Christian Temperance Union.

In Quebec many of these same developments were occurring,

but they were combined with a rapid growth in nationalist sentiment fueled especially by the struggles about World War I and
conscription, and by rampant nativism on the part of English
Canadians. The degree of discontent in Quebec in this period,
especially toward the end of World War I, is difficult to exaggerate. In the spring of 1918 extensive rioting in Quebec, especially
in Quebec City, led to an armed battle in which the Canadian
army fired on protesting Québécois, killing four and wounding
more than fifty. These martyrs to the Quebec nationalist cause
would be long remembered.

The essays in this volume explore many of the themes touched
upon in this brief introduction. The initial essay by Tom Traves
focuses on the theme of economic concentration and raises important questions about the particularity of Canadian capitalist
development in the shadow of American monopoly capitalism.
The relationship of immigration to Canada's economic growth
described by Donald Avery places the country's transformation
in the broader international context of the world capitalist
system. Resistance to economic exploitation also figured promi-
nently in this period and the essays by Craig Heron and Don
Macgillivray outline the different styles of class negotiation and
class conflict which occurred in Canada. The prominent role of
the Canadian state is also evident in both these essays and is explored more fully in the articles by John Weaver and Veronica
Strong-Boag. Weaver's description of the genesis of urban reform and Strong-Boag's assessment of women workers' gains by
the 1920's suggest much about the strengths and weaknesses of
the various social reform movements of the progressive period.

The first three decades of the twentieth century witnessed
rapid growth in Canada, both of population and of wealth, and
the completion of the new nation-state from sea to sea with western settlement and provincial status for Alberta and Saskatchewan in 1905. These were tangible and significant gains for the
young nation. While all Canadians clearly did not share equally
in the increasing wealth of the nation, most probably benefited
from some of the protection won by social reform and many enjoyed the domestic goods developed by new consumer-oriented
industries. Yet the tensions of this growth damaged the very core
of that nationhood. Regional resentments in the West and East,
nationalist antagonism in Quebec, nativist and racist reactions
against new Canadians, and considerable class conflict undercut

any easy national consensus. While the logic of capitalist development led to concentration and centralization, the response of the Canadian people led to tension and often to resistance.

I
Economic Overview

In his article, Tom Traves directs us to a crucial theme in the development of the Canadian economy from 1896 to 1929 – the emergence of monopoly capitalism. Traves's study, while focusing on the 1920's, provides data on the development of industrial concentration in Canada in the first half of the twentieth century. By analysing the motivations of Canadian capitalists and directing attention to the unwillingness of the Canadian state to challenge big business consolidation, Traves further demolishes many of the hoary myths of capitalist development. Competition, the free market, and significant state regulation in other than capital's interests are not evident in this period of Canadian history. One further effect of concentration, which Traves does not treat, was the ever-increasing centralization of capital in Canada. This process especially damaged the youthful industrial economy of the Maritime region, which already had experienced significant deindustrialization by the early 1920's.

A second major economic theme in this period, which was furthered by the centralization and concentration of capital, was the new dominance of American capital. Direct investment in Canada, generally in the form of branch plants, was the major vehicle of the American takeover. This direct investment was welcomed by both the Canadian state and Canadian businessmen.

While sometimes divided on issues such as tariffs, capital stood united in the realm of industrial relations. Here, the second part of the Traves article shows the strategies resorted to by

17

capital in the aftermath of the massive working-class upsurge of 1919. Welfare capitalism and company unions, which prevailed in "the torpid twenties," would nevertheless give way to industrial unionism in the Depression.

FURTHER READING:
On concentration, see Lloyd Reynolds, *The Control of Competition in Canada* (Cambridge, Mass., 1940); L.A. Skeoch, ed., *Restrictive Trade Practices in Canada* (Toronto, 1966); and Michael Bliss, "Another Anti-Trust Tradition: Canadian Anti-Combines Policy, 1889-1910," in Glenn Porter and Robert D. Cuff, eds., *Enterprise and National Development* (Toronto, 1973). On the effects of the process on the Maritimes, see Ernest Forbes, *The Maritime Rights Movement, 1919-1927* (Montreal, 1979), and David Frank, "The Cape Breton Coal Industry and the Rise and Fall of the British Empire Steel Corporation," *Acadiensis*, 7 (1977), 3-34. The literature on Americanization is very large, but see Tom Naylor, *The History of Canadian Business*, 2 vols. (Toronto, 1975); Kari Levitt, *Silent Surrender* (Toronto, 1970); and Wallace Clement, *Continental Corporate Elite* (Toronto, 1977). Other useful discussions of the specificities of Canadian capitalist development are the dated but popular Libbie and Frank Park, *The Anatomy of Big Business* (Toronto, 1973), and Jorge Niosi, *The Economy of Canada* (Montreal, 2nd ed., 1981). A useful overview of the interaction of tariffs and Americanization is Stephen Scheinberg, "Invitation to Empire: Tariffs and American Economic Expansion in Canada," in Porter and Cuff, eds., *Enterprise and National Development*.

Tom Traves is chairman of the Social Science Division at York University and is now working on railway labour relations.

Security without Regulation

by Tom Traves

In spite of the collapse of the Board of Commerce,* which crippled all hopes of achieving security through regulation, manufacturers continued to feel the need for institutional protection against the impact of rapid socio-economic change. During the 1920's the problems highlighted by the Canadian Reconstruction Association** persisted, especially the necessity to minimize the vicious effects of competition, the desire to reduce the economic losses and control the psychological unease that resulted from serious labour unrest, and the essential need to guard against the possible implementation of policies promoted by the radical new political parties spawned by the farmer and labour movements. But as the economic recession that began in the fall of 1920 lengthened into the long-expected post-war recession, and the new minority government led by Mackenzie King cast about trying to lure the votes of the radical parties following the 1921 federal election, manufacturers realized that they possessed rather limited resources to deal with the continuing crisis of industrial Canada.

Three solutions stood out as the best means to achieve environmental control and economic security. First, since manufacturers no longer counted on active government regulation to control input and output prices, they tried to increase their own

Reprinted from *The State and Enterprise: Canadian Manufacturers and the Federal Government, 1917-1931*, by Tom Traves, by permission of University of Toronto Press. © University of Toronto Press, 1979.

*Three member board appointed by Borden government in the fall of 1919 to regulate prices in a period of rapid inflation. A dismal failure, it collapsed in October 1920. (editors' note)

**Body created in March 1918 to promote the post-war interests of Canadian big business. Lasted until 1922, but clearly a failure by 1921. (editors' note)

control over such factors, either through informal price-fixing or trade associations or by more formal arrangements such as mergers. Second, since wages and salaries accounted for almost 40 per cent of their total manufacturing costs,[1] producers tried to control them by reducing industrial unrest and increasing labour productivity through the promotion of a host of so-called factory welfare programs and company union schemes. Finally, as excess capacity mounted in the face of persistent foreign competition, Canadian manufacturers demanded extensive revisions of the tariff schedule in order to guarantee the domestic market for local producers. Although active regulation was impossible, manufacturers still looked to the federal government for passive support like the tariff. But before the government could increase such protection, manufacturers had to find a way to side-step the violent objections of consumers and the low-tariff Progressive Party. Once again, following the example set during the reconstruction period, industrial Canada rallied behind the demand to appoint a tariff board in order to remove the tariff from the political arena.

THE CONTROL OF COMPETITION

As Adam Smith observed long ago, "People of the same trade seldom meet together even for merriment and diversion, but the conversation ends in a conspiracy against the public, or in some contrivance to raise prices. . . . But though the law cannot hinder people of the same trade from sometimes assembling together, it ought to do nothing to facilitate such assemblies; much less render them necessary."[2] Yet during the reconstruction period the federal government countenanced, indeed sometimes even ordered, such meetings on a regular basis. In particular, the week before the war ended, the Department of Trade and Commerce created the Canadian Trade Mission to co-ordinate and finance private efforts to establish foreign trade outlets. Led by the former chairman of the War Trade Board, Lloyd Harris, who had spent the final year of the war promoting and organizing Canadian exports to the United States, the mission set up headquarters in London to organize the post-war assault on Europe. At home, the government created a Canadian Trade Commission which regularly urged manufacturers to combine their energies to secure the greatest possible export business.

However, despite Harris's energetic efforts and his offers of extensive government credits to finance Canadian exports, he failed to drum up much business and in 1921 the government gave up on agencies such as the CTM and the CTC.[3] Individual manufacturers, however, continued to support the need for private export combinations long after the reconstruction period.

The president of the Canadian Manufacturers' Association, C. Howard Smith, put the case for private export associations most forcefully. "The individual firm is not a natural unit for international trade," he explained, "the national organization is. And now that practically every other exporting country has perfected, or is perfecting its national organization of exporters in every line of trade, Canada cannot cling to the old individualistic doctrine." Smith believed that the facts supporting his position were both "obvious and overwhelming." "Not only has [the individual Canadian exporter] nothing like the resources, the credit facilities, or the organization and the connections of great competitors with whom he must contend," Smith reported, "but he knows that he, unlike his competitors, is subject even in his foreign business to the competition of his own domestic fellow-producers." Although critics might complain that associations between fellow-producers could not fail to have serious domestic consequences, the CMA's leader brushed aside these champions of the free market with contempt. "All the old arguments," he sneered, "of the effects of such a combination upon internal trade, of the possibility of monopoly and tyranny and extortion upon domestic consumers are brought out and made to do duty whenever there is talk of forming an export trade combination in any industry." "However," he warned, "unless Canada follows the example of the United States and emerges similarly into the free air of a reasonable treatment of trade combinations, her export trade is doomed to play a very secondary part, if any part at all, in competition with the better directed and concentrated efforts of the American exporters."[4]

Despite Howard Smith's disclaimers, considerable evidence existed to support the view that export combinations to rationalize price and production schedules merely served to legitimate the activities of price-fixing rings, which already informally regulated large parts of the domestic market. By 1921, producers in over fifty industries gathered regularly as members of trade sections organized by the Canadian Manufacturers' Association. Although *Industrial Canada* described these trade associations' concerns as production costs, research, markets, trade terms and phrases, credit information, insurance, co-operative advertising and trade promotion, labour relations, and legislative matters pertaining to taxes, tariffs, and transportation, Adam Smith's caveat concerning "a conspiracy against the public" produced the greatest reaction. The CMA's leaders complained that "there are some captious critics who hold that the BE ALL and END ALL of trade organizations is to regulate prices." The association hotly denied such charges, but did acknowledge that "market conditions may be discussed with the greatest frankness. The effect on the market of what may be considered unwise sales policies may always be the subject of frank criticism, but to encourage by agreement any method of regulating prices is absolutely foreign to the Association's program."[5] To an outsider, however, the distinction between "frank criticism" and price-fixing appears a rather fine one. Certainly, by the decade's end, informal price agreements governed the sale of agricultural implements, beer, various iron and steel products, gasoline, sugar, canned goods, and textile products. More formal price and production agreements governed the output in industries producing fertilizers, leather, rubber footwear, tobacco products, and various kinds of hardware, plumbing, and heating equipment. As one trade association secretary remarked, "manufacturers up here wouldn't be bothered with an association that couldn't control prices."[6] Such price-fixing agencies ranged from price leadership by giant firms, through informal gentlemen's agreements, to formal, if not legally binding, cartel arrangements.

Price leadership was a feature common to industries dominated by a single firm that possessed sufficient resources to withstand and ultimately defeat any form of price competition. The gasoline, tobacco, and canning industries offered classic examples of such cases, for Imperial Oil, Imperial Tobacco, and Canadian Canners controlled roughly 75 to 80 per cent of their respective markets. In 1925 a special investigator for the Ontario government, G.T. Clarkson, pointed out the consequences of this domination in the gasoline industry: "It was frankly stated by officers of the other companies that, inasmuch as the Imperial Oil Company Ltd. holds a predominant position in the trade in Canada, it has been and is their custom to follow prices set by it from time to time. Such a course was upheld by them on the ground that it is a common trade practice for the largest producer in any line of business to set prices and other dealers to follow him." Given the price leaders' threats to discontinue supplying independent retailers that cut prices and the tendency in both the gasoline and canning industries to insist on exclusive "100 per cent accounts" with retail or wholesale dealers, the price leaders were able to control effectively both price and production levels within their industries.[7] Under these circumstances, government regulation to secure these ends was unnecessary.

Other industries depended on active organization rather than price leadership to regulate conditions among member firms. In many industries dominated by oligopolies, such as sugar, textiles, fertilizers, and railway supplies, informal agreements were common.[8] In the sugar industry, for example, W.F. O'Connor reported that the refiners had persisted for nearly thirty years in maintaining informal price agreements. While serving as cost-of-living commissioner in 1917, O'Connor observed: "It appears that the relations between the refineries and the wholesale grocery trade constitute resale price-fixing arrangements made by way of tacit agreement."[9] Thus when O'Connor assumed formal powers to regulate the refiners he simply confirmed the long-established traditions that prevailed in the industry. In so doing he anticipated the explanation offered by a railway uniform manufacturer who described similar arrangements during the 1930's: "We'll have to quote the same price in the end anyway, so we might as well do it at the beginning."[10]

In some cases, however, informal agreements could not be maintained and more formal arrangements were adopted. In 1924, for example, the manufacturers of rubber footwear agreed to establish prices informally, but by 1931 they felt the need to enact strong sanctions against those tempted to break ranks. Under a formal agreement adopted by the eight firms in the industry, they passed regulations establishing uniform list prices, discounts, and terms of sale, provisions were agreed on for product standardization in order to curtail rivalry in quality, and each firm agreed to the allotment of a fixed share of the market based on previous production levels. Firms exceeding their monthly quota were taxed 25 per cent of the value of their sales, although each year quotas were reviewed for adjustment. Finally, each firm posted a cash bond ranging from $10,000 to $75,000 with the trade association's secretary, and he was empowered to punish any breach of the agreement by a fine ranging from $100 to the offender's full deposit.[11] Clearly, when manufacturers agreed voluntarily to such arrangements, government support was not required, and, as R.A. Pringle discovered with the newsprint industry, when they actively opposed restraints on trade, regulation was extremely difficult.

The newsprint industry persisted in its fractious behaviour throughout the twenties, and even when disaster stared the industry in the face it was impossible to secure a general agreement to control production and prices. In 1927, with excess capacity in the industry ranging between 15 and 20 per cent, several leading firms attempted to establish an industry cartel through the creation of a joint selling agency, the Canadian Newsprint Company. However, many firms did not join the cartel, and with only 50 per cent of the industry's capacity under its control, Canadian Newsprint failed to achieve its goals and was dissolved in 1928. At that point, the Ontario and Quebec governments intervened to save their most important industry, and at their behest the Newsprint Institute was formed to prorate production and increase prices. Both governments threatened recalcitrant firms with increased royalties on timber cut on Crown lands, but International Paper, the industry's largest firm and one of its most efficient, refused to follow the premiers' orders, claiming fear of prosecution under the U.S. Sherman Anti-Trust Act. As prices declined in 1930, a leading member of the Newsprint Institute, Canada Power and Paper, offered secret price cuts and a stock bonus to secure a contract with the giant Hearst chain of newspapers. This action made a mockery of all further efforts to control competition within the industry and the Newsprint Institute collapsed. By 1932, over one-half of the industry's capacity had passed into receivership or was forced into extensive financial reorganization.[12]

The failure of the Newsprint Institute points to many of the difficulties confronting manufacturers when they attempted to control competition privately. In some industries not all producers shared the same interests. In the newsprint industry, for example, International Paper was more efficient and more diversified than most of its competitors, with the result that it saw increased competition as a chance to capture a greater share of the market rather than as a threat to its survival. Similarly, in the hosiery industry, an elaborate cartel arrangement established between 1928 and 1932 ultimately broke down because producers of unbranded goods refused to accede to the demands of brand-name producers to establish a common price for branded and unbranded hosiery alike. In other cases, persistent excess capacity across the industry made it extremely difficult to keep all parties to a trade agreement in line since there was always a powerful incentive to accept below-average prices in order to reduce the burden of fixed costs. The newsprint industry obviously suffered from such secret deals, as did the Canadian National Millers' Association, which attempted to regulate flour prices from 1920 on in the face of an industry-wide operating ratio of only 50 per cent of capacity. Finally, the big newspaper chains such as Hearst certainly proved, as did the large department stores investigated by the Royal Commission on Price Spreads in 1934, that large buyers could exert tremendous pressure on individual producers to cut prices secretly and break trade agreements in order to secure a really large order.[13]

Given the number of cases cited, it is obvious that Canadian anti-trust legislation was not regarded as a serious obstacle to attempts at industrial self-regulation. That is not to say that the federal government lacked a competition policy, to use the modern euphemism for official countenance of restraints on trade; it simply never bothered to apply the law vigorously. The principal provisions of Canadian anti-trust law had been established between 1889 and 1900, during which period the criminal code was amended to make it a criminal offence for any person to unduly limit competition to the detriment of the public welfare.[14] Apart from the problem of legally defining the public welfare and the specific nature of "undue" restraints on competition, the criminal code contained no special provisions for the establishment of the investigative machinery necessary if complex economic issues were to be brought forward for public and legal scrutiny. In 1910, under extreme pressure from agricultural groups and small-town newspapers, the Labour Minister, Mackenzie King, introduced measures to provide such machinery under the aegis of the Combines Investigation Act.[15] Upon application from any six persons who believed an injurious combine to exist, a judge could order an investigation to be started. The Minister of Labour then appointed a tripartite board, representing all the interested parties, to investigate and report its findings to the Minister, who must then publish these results. In the event of an adverse report, the combine was ordered to cease its activities or face fines and criminal charges; there was no penalty provided for past actions, although under an 1897 amendment to the Customs Act the government could reduce tariff duties on items produced by the combine or could revoke its patent rights. Between 1910 and 1919, when the Customs Act was superseded by the Combines and Fair Prices Act, administered by the Board of Commerce, only one case reached trial. This is not surprising since the procedures adopted under the 1910 legislation clearly were cumbersome, and hence subject to obstruction by skilful lawyers, while at the same time they exposed the initial complainants to retaliation by the combine or the interests connected to it.

The appointment of the Board of Commerce under the Combines and Fair Prices Act marked a major change in both the legal power and administrative procedures provided for the government's anti-trust agency. In contrast to the 1910 legislation, the new Act allowed the board to initiate investigations and to issue cease-and-desist orders where necessary. However, no prosecutions could be initiated under either the new combines law or the relevant part of the criminal code, Section 498, without the written authority of the Board of Commerce. Thus anti-trust investigations were centralized under the board's authority and the board alone was empowered to decide whether criminal charges ought to be laid. This, of course, allowed the board to distinguish between "bad" combines, which operated against the public interest, and "good" ones, which could continue.

Despite its apparent powers, the board's impact on price-fixing associations was negligible. In part, this result was attributable to sharp differences among the board's members about their proper role in anti-trust cases. From the outset, Judge Robson, the board's chairman, was distinctly unenthusiastic about attacking this issue. In October 1919 the board's secretary, W.T. White, wrote Robson several times urging that they begin to define an approach to combines policy. "I do not see much prospect of there being a great deal of work unless we tackle the Combines. I for one am eager to get at it," White declared. Robson, however, doubted the wisdom of such action: "My recollection of the Combines part of the Act is that applications have to be made to the Board through one of the Commissioners. It seems to me that it would be very difficult to inaugurate general inquiries into combines on our own initiative." Of course, the judge was mistaken, for the board's initiative was quite sufficient. As far as Robson was concerned, "the proper course will be to let the public have the idea that we are a Board which can be approached to remedy grievances after they are, by a simple formal application, laid before us."[16] Obviously, Robson regarded the Board of Commerce as a judicial tribunal, similar in character to boards established under the old Combines Investigation Act, rather than as an active regulatory agency.

By January 1920, however, commissioners O'Connor and Murdock had successfully challenged Robson's view of the matter and the board agreed to undertake a more pronounced role in anti-trust issues. Its first step, though, was its last. After issuing an order that required all parties to existing or proposed trusts, mergers, price-fixing arrangements, and other combines to identify themselves and submit evidence to demonstrate that they were not operating against the public interest, thirty-two companies and trade associations reported price-fixing arrangements covering nearly 100 commodities. At this point, however, the board was stymied, for it lacked the manpower to investigate the impact of these arrangements, while the government, for its part, refused to assist the commissioners by appointing qualified personnel at the board's request.[17]

When the Judicial Committee of the Privy Council ruled that the Combines and Fair Prices Act was *ultra vires*, Mackenzie King introduced a revised version of the Combines Investigation Act in 1923. The principal difference between the new legislation and its 1910 predecessor was a provision for the appointment of a permanent official who was empowered to investigate combines on his own initiative or at the behest of either six concerned citizens or the Minister of Labour. Like its predecessor, the new legislation provided no penalties for efforts to restrict competition. For one thing, the Prime Minister did not believe that restraint of trade was in and of itself a mean-spirited act. As King observed during the debate over this issue: "The legislation does not seek in any way to restrict just combinations or agreements between business and industrial houses and firms, but it does seek to protect the public against the possible ill effects of these combinations." Secondly, the Prime Minister fervently believed that investigation and "the power of a well-informed public opinion" were much more powerful checks to such behaviour than mere criminal prosecution. "What is the power of the criminal code to prosecute some particular person or group of persons," he asked, "in comparison with the power of spreading broadcast throughout the land accurate and true information with regard to the public interest, and which the people themselves are certain to be concerned in remedying?" Unfortunately, the people had little chance to act on such broadcasts, for in the period up to the end of the decade only seven complaints were formally investigated, of which only one, breadbaking in Montreal, concerned a manufacturer.[18]

The Combines Investigation Act of 1923 was drafted primarily to control the detrimental consequences of price-fixing arrangements between separate firms, but the Act also provided a basis for the investigation and prohibition of formal mergers that consolidated two or more firms into a single unit for the same purpose. Although it commonly was understood that the term "combine" covered mergers as well under the meaning of the 1910 legislation and its successors, in 1927 the government tidied up this point by amending the Combines Investigation Act so that "combines" formally included, *inter alia*, mergers, trusts, or monopolies.[19] However, since the first case under this legislation was not heard until 1940, the initial legislation and the amendment offered no obstacles to the progress of the greatest merger movement in Canadian history, which took place between 1925 and 1930.

In theory, monopoly provides the greatest guarantee of price and production control within any industry, and hence it provides the greatest flexibility in responding to market changes and political disruptions. Usually, the formation of price-fixing organizations provided the only means to approximate such control, but the history of such organizations was littered with broken promises and numerous failures. Under these circumstances it is hardly surprising that producers in many industries preferred to consolidate production under a single management rather than depend on the haphazard, and often less efficient, arrangements provided by trade associations and the like. While the consolidation of competing firms only occasionally produced monopoly conditions in Canadian industry, even the creation of oligopolies through mergers enhanced the prospects of continuing success for informal cartel agreements. Of course, not all Canadian mergers were forged to this end alone, or even primarily for this purpose, but the cumulative consequence of such mergers was to increase industrial concentration and decrease the likelihood of competition.

In the decade following the First World War the number and

size of Canadian mergers increased markedly. As Figure 1 indicates, following the country's first great merger movement between 1909 and 1913, activity declined sharply, but it began to increase again following the war. The 1920 recession apparently restricted further consolidations, but with the revival of the economy around 1924 a remarkable upsurge in merger activity dominated the remainder of the decade. Indeed, one study reveals that during the five years from 1925 to 1929 the number of mergers and volume of assets consolidated account for roughly 40 per cent of all such activities from the turn of the century until 1948.[20]

The origins and consequences of this merger movement have not yet been analysed in detail, but financial considerations and the restriction of competition stand out as its most important features. Promoters' profits, of course, surface as a regular feature of any merger movement, and the late twenties proved no exception. Indeed, J.C. Weldon found, as did Ralph Nelson in a similar study of American mergers, that the common stock price index was the only economic variable that correlated with measures of merger activity. Commodity price series, gross national product, and national income data showed no correlation whatsoever with consolidation data.[21] Since the disposal of securities was normally required to finance major amalgamations, this finding is not surprising.

The degree to which numerous consolidations increased the prospects of restricted competition stands out as both a cause and a consequence of the merger movement. Nearly three-quarters of all consolidations in the twenties were horizontal mergers.[22] Such amalgamations generally point to a desire to reduce competition. The formation of Canada Power and Paper in 1928 by the Holt-Gundy interests was a spectacular example of this process. After the merger of the St. Maurice, Belgo-Canada, Canada Paper, Anticosti, Laurentide, and Port Alfred paper companies into the largest paper producer in the world, the president of Canada Power and Paper explained that "The underlying reasons were principally the idea of keeping the industry from flying into a thousand parts. We felt that if the paper industry could be organized into three groups – a Quebec group, an Ontario group, and the International Paper Co. – the thing would be run in an intelligent, economical manner."[23] The consequences of such reasoning were clearly indicated by the early 1930's, when, as Table 1 reveals, significant parts of the

FIGURE 1

Number of mergers in Canada and assets consolidated, 1900-48

Number
of mergers

Assets consolidated in
millions of dollars

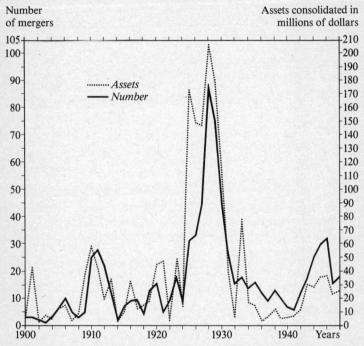

SOURCE: Compiled from J.C. Weldon, "Consolidation in Canadian Industry, 1900-1948,"
in L. A. Skeoch, ed., *Restrictive Trade Practices in Canada* (Toronto, 1966), 233, table 1.

Canadian industrial economy operated under near monopoly or oligopoly conditions.

In conclusion, it seems quite clear that Canadian manufacturers had private means to control competition in the event that government regulation failed to protect them from the vicissitudes of the marketplace. Gentlemen's agreements to fix prices, trade association agreements to fix price and production quotas, and formal mergers all provided an alternative or, after 1920, a substitute for public regulation. However, such private solutions were not always effective. The history of Canadian Canners Limited, for example, demonstrates this point in a dramatic way. In 1893 nine canning companies formed a trade association, the Canada Packers Association, to carry out joint promotional campaigns, but a few years later they extended their cooperation to establish a Dominion Syndicate, which acted as their common marketing agent. By 1903, however, competition from independent canners proved so strong that Canadian Canners Consolidated was organized to amalgamate the Dominion Syndicate and most of the independents, about thirty firms in all. During the first great merger movement seventeen more independents were absorbed and the new consolidation was christened Dominion Canners. Entry into the industry was fairly easy, however, because capital costs were low, and independent competition continued to pester Dominion so that in 1915 it became necessary to form yet another joint marketing agency, Canadian Canners Limited, which was controlled by Dominion Canners. In 1923 this arrangement was formalized and Canadian Canners was incorporated to purchase the assets of Dominion Canners and twenty-nine other independent firms.[24]

It is notable that during this period the federal government passed several amendments to strengthen the anti-trust sections of the criminal code and appointed no less than three agencies to monitor private efforts to control competition against the public interest. Despite these bows to the virtues of free enterprise, however, no action was ever taken to limit these successive attempts at price and production control in the canning industry. One report prepared for the Board of Commerce noted that "if a combination is allowed to swallow up its rivals by fair means or foul and unfairly keep all competition out of the field, it is almost certain to become uneconomic, careless and inefficient and will charge too much for its services, whether its profits be large or whether they be small." "The canning business," the

TABLE 1
Control of Output in Selected Manufacturing Industries

	Cumulative percentage of output controlled by				
	1 firm	2 firms	3 firms	4 firms	5 firms
Automobiles	40	65	89		
Ammunition, explosives, ammonia, chlorine	100				
Agricultural implements				75	
Brewing (Ontario and Quebec)		60			
Cement	90				
Copper	53		93		
Canning (fruit and vegetables)	67	83			
Cotton yarn and cloth	48		79		
Electrical equipment (heavy)			100		
Fertilizer			70		
Lead	91				
Meat packing	59	85			
Milling					73
Nickel	71				
Oil	55				
Pulp and paper					90
Rubber footwear	39	50	61	72	
Silk (real)	23	42	61		
Silk (artificial)	66	100			
Sugar					100
Tires					65
Tobacco	70	90			
Zinc	74				

SOURCE: Lloyd G. Reynolds, *The Control of Competition in Canada* (Cambridge, Mass., 1940), 5, table 1.

report concluded, "offers a most tempting field for such unfair throttling of competition."[25] So it did, but Canadian anti-trust laws provided scant protection for consumers, other producers, or any of the other elements of the "powerful public opinion" to which Mackenzie King regularly appealed.

THE CONTROL OF LABOUR COSTS

Labour costs reflected the influence of many factors, including the general level of economic activity, the size of the labour market, labour productivity rates, the impact of unionization, and the cost of lost production due to strikes, lockouts, or individual absenteeism. Manufacturers could not hope to control macro-economic variables, but they did possess both the capacity and the desire to limit the labour unrest that cost them many anxious moments and a good deal of money in the post-war decade. In retrospect, the union movement's decline in size, militancy, and effectiveness during these years prompted one historian, Stuart Jamieson, to describe the period as "the torpid twenties," but during the reconstruction era manufacturers neither anticipated such results nor felt free to leave labour issues to chance. All the indicators at the time pointed to very different conclusions. During the war, union membership had increased from a low of 143,000 in 1915 to 378,000 in 1919, and labour unrest increased at least as fast as union activity. In 1919, uprisings in Winnipeg and Vancouver, accompanied by smaller clashes in other important labour centres such as Calgary, Edmonton, Victoria, Prince Rupert, Regina, Toronto, Kirkland Lake, Montreal, and Cape Breton, produced social chaos and political hysteria. As Jamieson pointed out, "1919 was a peak period of labour unrest, with numbers of strikes, workers involved and man-days lost far exceeding any previous year in Canada's history. And, in proportion to the country's total paid labour and to total union membership, it has never been reached since . . . ." The next year was much the same. Although strikes generally were smaller in size and shorter in duration, there were nearly as many walkouts as the year before, 310 compared to 322 in 1919.[26] Under these conditions it is hardly surprising that producers, alone in their own factories or together at Canadian Manufacturers' Association meetings, gave long and hard thought to their employees' attitudes, working and living conditions, and politics.[27]

Changes in technology and the emergence of large corporations produced an urgent need for major reforms in industrial relations policies after the turn of the century. Although Gregory S. Kealey has argued that during the 1880's and 1890's "craftsmen employed their monopoly on skill and experience to dictate terms to their employers in an amazing array of areas which in modern parlance gave to these late nineteenth century craftsmen a high degree of workers' control of production,"[28] the subsequent development of the assembly line and mass production techniques destroyed this pattern in all but a few industries. As production functions became routine and were hived off from entrepreneurial functions in the main office, the social distance between employer and employee increased dramatically,[29] and industrial conflict intensified as manufacturers tried to force their workmen to adjust their production patterns to the rhythm of the assembly line. Manufacturers' attitudes towards their workmen hardened with each conflict. "Under the factory system," complained the *Monetary Times*, "many employers fail to recognize an essential difference between machines and the human labor by which they are operated; kindly interest and consistent devotion have been replaced by indifference and distrust. The outcome has been strikes, lockouts and riots."[30]

These attitudes, however, were counter-productive. The new production schedules required industrial labourers to perform assembly line work with increased intensity and attention to detail, but such changes in work habits by skilled and unskilled workers alike demanded more sophisticated managerial techniques and attitudes than had prevailed in the past.[31] During the 1920's the CMA tried to encourage these attitudes by promoting the spread of new ideas about industrial relations. As one reformer, CMA president S.R. Parsons of British American Oil, indicated, these policies might help "to regain an attitude akin to that which prevailed in the seventeenth century when there was a glory and a pride in trade and craft which has been largely lost out of our industrial life." However romantic, these sentiments reflected an attempt by Canadian manufacturers to confront the problem of industrial alienation. As a Massey-Harris official observed, perhaps somewhat hopefully, "it is not too much to say that in Canadian industry the old point of view that labor was simply a commodity is a thing of the past. The employees are thought of and treated not as cogs in the industrial machine but as human beings; and it is becoming recognized more and more by the best type of manufacturer that the proper function of industry is to produce men no less than goods."

The CMA leaders believed that the formation of co-operative works councils and improvements in working conditions and benefits were the best ways to achieve this goal. The association's Industrial Relations Committee argued "that the real solution and the only solution of the so-called problem of industrial relations is the development of a spirit of mutual good-will and cooperation instead of antagonism."[32] The committee recommended that manufacturers establish works councils, based on Mackenzie King's Colorado plan in the United

States and the Whitley plan in Great Britain, as joint manage-
ment-labour forums to discuss subjects such as "wages, production, hours of labor, conditions of the plant, and suggestions to
improve processes of manufacture." Ultimately, the CMA hoped
that "such councils [would] awaken the interests of employees
and make them feel that the prosperity of the individual plant
adds to their own welfare."[33]

Such councils, of course, were little more than company
unions.[34] To make the idea more attractive to workmen and to
increase their stake in the success of the scheme, the CMA recommended that employers introduce many "factory welfare"
measures in conjunction with the co-operative councils. At this
time, factory welfare measures included "workingmen's clubs,
physical culture, education, industrial training, religious work,
music, social gatherings, profit sharing, stock purchase plans,
domestic education, health (bathing facilities and lunch rooms),
insurance and beneficial organizations, savings plans, financial
aid, and the general promotion of close relations between
employer and employee."[35] In order to justify these improvements among themselves, some manufacturers pointed out
that they had "been brought to a realization that, in order to obtain 100 cents on the dollar paid to the employee, consideration
had to be given to the mental and physical condition of the
human unit of organization . . . . To say the [improvements] are
costly is to falsify. The results that accrue more than equalize
and justify the cost of upkeep."[36]

The impact of these proposals on industrial circles is indicated
by a survey conducted for the Ontario Department of Labour in
1928. From a sample of 300 firms employing 185,000 workers, it
was found that 61 per cent of the firms had pension schemes of
various kinds; 35 per cent had group insurance plans; 26 per cent
of the firms, covering half of the employees, had insurance
schemes other than group insurance; 25 per cent had bonus
systems of some kind; 15 per cent had employee stock purchase
plans; and 21 per cent of the firms surveyed, employing 48 per
cent of the workers, had works councils and shop committee
schemes in operation.[37]

H.C. Pentland regards the spread of these tactics as a consequence of the separation between ownership and management
functions within the modern corporation. The new professional
managers were more detached and could "more readily appreciate the advantages of good communication in an on-going con-

cern divorced from the life-cycle of any particular individual."
As a result, they were "better equipped for the work of getting
joint-councils established and making them operate." This view
seems well founded. As noted, the CMA Industrial Relations
Committee, which promoted these ideas so vigorously, was
always dominated by representatives from bigger companies,
which often employed specialized industrial relations officers.[38]
This point is also borne out by the results of the Labour Department survey which indicated clearly that larger firms, employing
a disproportionately large number of industrial workers, tended
to establish works councils more frequently.

The spread of factory welfare schemes reflected an important
change in manufacturers' ideas about motivating their work
force. At one time, employers generally had agreed with the view
that "It was flaws in the character of workingmen – unwillingness to work or save or educate themselves – which held them
back, not any failure of the system."[39] The growth of the
American industrial engineer F.W. Taylor's scientific management movement, however, and the development of the "science"
of industrial psychology began to undermine this image of the
industrial worker. As more and more manufacturers confronted
the problem of industrial alienation, managers struggled to
come to terms with the need to broaden their interpretation of
the worker's conception of self-interest. The human engineering
techniques associated with the scientific management and factory welfare movements represented a serious effort to provide
social as well as economic incentives for increased production.
As the Massey-Harris official observed, "employees are thought
of and treated not as cogs in the industrial machine but as
human beings."[40]

The spread of such reformist views encompassed an increased
toleration, and sometimes even a demand, for more comprehensive social welfare policies from all levels of government. Factory welfare schemes alone could not ensure greater social cohe-
sion or increased productivity. Obviously, the worker had a life
beyond the factory walls. Sooner or later, general social problems became industrial problems. The housing crisis, for example, was typical of such concerns. *Industrial Canada*, the CMA
journal, reported a study which "after painting the picture of
slum conditions prevailing in our cities in lurid hues, declares
that even revolution in its full physical significance would be

justified in the light of such revelations."[41] Although the Toronto branch of the CMA had actively supported the first sizable low-cost housing project in Canada in 1913,[42] the lack of adequate housing remained obvious. By the end of the war the situation had become alarming. "In Toronto we have over 40,000 houses that have been condemned," declared Thomas Roden, a senior CMA executive member, "and yet [they] have been reinhabited, and similar conditions exist in other parts of Canada. That is a condition that we should not allow to exist. It was that condition that brought about the downfall of Russia, the indifference of the guiding classes to these conditions." The solution to this persistent problem, however, seemed beyond the capacity of the private sector. Therefore the CMA proposed another approach: "Private enterprise seems unable if not unwilling to shoulder the risk and expense of erecting enough houses to fill the present need and, in the emergency, the Government itself should do something to solve the problem."[43]

This proposal, along with the CMA's generally favourable view of a state health insurance system and an old-age pension plan, indicates clearly the CMA's growing realization that state-sponsored social welfare reforms were desirable. *Industrial Canada* put the issue bluntly:

> The whole system of state insurance must be grafted onto society in order to buttress the capitalist state. This includes more than securing compensation for accidents; it means out-of-work benefits, care for the health of the family, old age pensions, and even something in the way of death benefits and funeral expenses. To obstruct, as a class, the enactment of these ameliorative measures, is short-sighted. . . .[44]

The development of such views, however, never completely displaced traditional attitudes which characterized the work force as selfish and short-sighted. Nor were all manufacturers swept away with enthusiasm at the birth of the social welfare state. As Reinhard Bendix has noted, reformist arguments were sufficiently ambiguous that it was "easy for employers to feel with equal sincerity either that the old symbols of the struggle for survival were as valid as ever or that the new emphasis upon the attitudes of workers constituted a major change which redeemed the attitudes of the past."[45] For every defence of social reform it was easy to find a contrary opinion. Arthur Hatch, a Stelco executive who once served as the CMA president, complained:

> Our statute books are clogged now with hundreds of acts that are not only useless but mischievous. They make it harder and more expensive for people to live and to do their work without bestowing any benefits or furnishing any really necessary safeguards. They add immensely to the cost of Government. Many of the laws are designed to dissipate capital and distribute it in socialist schemes that will do more harm than good. Instead of this mass of legislation we need a few good and simple laws, severely, but justly, administered.[46]

Hatch and similar-minded manufacturers objected most vociferously to workman's compensation, unemployment insurance, and minimum wage and compulsory arbitration measures.

These manufacturers objected to workman's compensation benefits and proposals for unemployment insurance plans on much the same grounds. The workman's compensation plan, they argued, failed to tax the workers who benefited from the scheme, and it was subject to the escalating demands of labour unions which persistently argued for higher rates of compensation. Furthermore, the plan often encouraged malingering, they claimed.[47] Unemployment benefits would also provide "an invitation to stop work." Such schemes, the manufacturers declared, obscured the real solution to the distress of the unemployed, which was more jobs through increased economic development. Moreover, experience in other countries, such as England, revealed that "the principle of insurance is lost sight of, and under political exigencies the schemes degenerate into the mere distribution of public monies among the unemployed regardless of whether they have contributed or not."[48]

Although it rejected proposals for a minimum wage law for adult males, the CMA did accept the principle of such regulations for women and minors. However, this legislation was appealing because it protected fair-minded employers from unscrupulous competitors who heartlessly exploited the most vulnerable segment of the work force. Such legislation, manufacturers pointed out, was social, not economic, and was justifiable on humanitarian grounds alone. The principle could not be applied across the whole labour market, however. In all but exceptional cases competitive values had to prevail over sentiment. Moreover, the CMA objected that once minimum wages were imposed for all workers, the government which initiated them would be most unlikely to lower them, even if economic conditions deteriorated, for fear of defeat by hostile voters.[49]

The CMA lodged a similar objection against proposed compulsory arbitration laws. "Employers have learned by bitter experience," *Industrial Canada* claimed, "how unreliable is the third, or presumably disinterested party, in a commission. Instead of being a non-partisan, fair-minded judge, he is too often a political appointee who promptly sides with the employees and becomes their advocate rather than their judge." The heart of the CMA's objection in this case, however, was that "the application of the compulsory arbitration principle to general industry constituted an unwarranted interference with an employer's management of his own business."[50]

These objections suggest two levels of analysis concerning manufacturers' attitudes towards the social welfare state. First, despite objections by some of their contemporaries that social reforms buttressed rather than weakened the capitalist order, many manufacturers feared that successive governments would side with their employees at the employers' expense. Ultimately, such costs might become antithetical to the long-run interests of capital. This points to questions about the nature of the capitalist state itself. Second, it is important to note that the difference between acceptable social welfare measures and unacceptable reforms lay in the fact that the former did not interfere with the traditional prerogatives of the employer to run his own shop as he saw fit and did not tax manufacturers as a special occupational group. This distinction suggests the basis of a psychological interpretation of the manufacturers' attitudes. For factory legislation of the kind described clearly struck at the heart of a code of ethics, long formalized in a series of popular myths and symbols, which manufacturers were prepared to defend fiercely. Whatever the economic costs, workman's compensation, unemployment insurance, and minimum wage and compulsory arbitration laws all tampered with the manufacturer's traditional right to deal with his employees as the market or his conscience dictated. Robert E. Lane has argued that such tampering was psychologically intolerable:

While regulation came to businessmen with a relatively low

price tag, it nevertheless was burdensome and exacted a toll of
anxiety, frustration, and dejection beyond all relation to the
economic cost. The reason for this, of course, is that men re-
spond to a variety of motives and are moved by needs and
desires not measured along economic parameters. . . .
[Regulation], the events which prompted it, and the rationale
which supported it, impinged on such motives and thwarted
such needs. First, the regulation challenged the businessman's
belief system, profaned his idols, and depreciated his myths.
As the literature of anthropology testifies, such an attack is
painful and disruptive to any community. Second, it
denigrated the businessman himself, lowered his status in the
community, and allocated to him a role subordinate to the
one he had enjoyed. In this way it attacked what might be
termed the business ego, psychologically a most traumatic experience. Third, it frustrated men by depriving them of
choices to which they had become accustomed, choices
associated with dealing with unions, paying for overtime, and
advertising and pricing their products. Finally, it aroused new
anxieties and developed uncertainties in a time already tense
with doubt and foreboding. It exacerbated one of the defects
of a mobile, free, and indeed, "contract society."[51]

To what extent, then, did manufacturers believe that a few
factory and social welfare reforms could constitute an effective
response to industrial alienation? One is tempted to dismiss such
measures as blatant hypocrisy. After all, companies with the
worst industrial relations records in the country often claimed
the most enlightened views regarding the need for reforms.[52] Yet
as Reinhard Bendix has noted, "when ideologies are formulated
to defend a set of economic interests, it is more illuminating to
examine the strategy of argument than to insist that the argument is selfish."[53] In this case, the strategy of argument is quite
revealing. By the end of the war spokesmen in the CMA, the CRA,
and even in the Prime Minister's office accepted the apparently
undeniable fact that large-scale enterprise and capitalist social
relations created a profound sense of alienation from work and
from the prevailing social system among the industrial working
class. Given their unwillingness to reject economies of scale or
change property relations, manufacturers opted to support the
factory welfare movement. Problems that derived from systemic
contradictions were thus transformed into "industrial relations

problems" amenable to managerial solutions. Questions of
power and wealth gave way to answers stressing human engineering and communication techniques. While H.C. Pentland
once noted that "feudal employers understood better than capitalist ones that human motivation is a complex thing in which
economic motives may play a minor part,"[54] the ideology, if not
always the practice, of labour relations had begun to change.
Together with stable prices, wage changes, declining unemployment, and apathetic union activity, this change helped produce
"the torpid twenties" after the seething reconstruction period.

NOTES

1. Dominion Bureau of Statistics, *Canada Year Book, 1922* (Ottawa,
   1924), 420-1. This figure is based on wages and salaries as a
   percentage of the net value of manufactured products, excluding
   material costs.
2. Smith, *The Wealth of Nations* (New York, 1937), 128.
3. Peter E. Ryder, "The Imperial Munitions Board and Its Relationship to Government, Business and Labour" (Ph.D. thesis, University of Toronto, 1974), 151-61; O. Mary Hill, *Canada's Salesman
   to the World: The Department of Trade and Commerce* (Montreal, 1977), 184-5.
4. *Industrial Canada* (May, 1923), 50-1.
5. *Ibid.*, (July, 1923), 139; *ibid.*, (November, 1921), 71, editorial.
6. Lloyd G. Reynolds, *The Control of Competition in Canada* (Cambridge, Mass., 1940), 8, table 2, quotation on p. 21.
7. *Ibid.*, 12-15, Clarkson report to the government of Ontario, 11
   January 1926, quoted in note 9. The canning industry is discussed
   in T.D. Traves, "Some Problems with Peacetime Price Controls:
   The Case of the Board of Commerce of Canada, 1919-20," *Canadian Public Administration*, 17, 1 (1974), 92.
8. Reynolds, *Control of Competition*, 15-16.
9. Canada, Department of Labour, *Labour Gazette* (June, 1917),
   482-7. Sugar prices had also been fixed as far back as the 1880's.
   See Michael Bliss, "Another Anti-Trust Tradition: Canadian Anti-
   Combines Policy, 1889-1910," *Business History Review*, 47
   (1973), 42.
10. Quoted in Reynolds, *Control of Competition*, 16, note 23.
11. *Ibid.*, 18-19.
12. This case is discussed most fully in V.W. Bladen, *An Introduction
    to Political Economy* (Toronto, 1956), Chapter 7; and H.V.
    Nelles, *The Politics of Development* (Toronto, 1974), 443-53.

13. Reynolds, *Control of Competition,* 21-2, 26-7. For a discussion of the department stores, see Richard Wilbur, *H.H. Stevens* (Toronto, 1977), Chapter 4.

14. A survey of Canadian anti-trust policy can be found in J.A. Ball, *Canadian Anti-Trust Legislation* (Baltimore, 1934); Maxwell Cohen, "The Canadian Anti-Trust Laws – Doctrinal and Legislative Beginnings," *Canadian Bar Review,* 16 (1938); Bliss, "Another Anti-Trust Tradition"; and Reynolds, *Control of Competition.*

15. Bliss, "Another Anti-Trust Tradition."

16. PAC, Board of Commerce Files (BCF), vol. 1, file 1-1, White to Robson, 30 October, Robson to White, 23 October 1919.

17. For a more detailed discussion of this issue, see Traves, "Some Problems," 90.

18. King quoted in D. Gordon Blair, "Combines, Controls or Competition?" *Canadian Bar Review*, 31 (1953), 1094; and in F.A. McGregor, "Preventing Monopoly – Canadian Techniques," in E.H. Chamberlain, ed., *Monopoly, Competition and Regulation* (London, 1954), 371; Reynolds, *Control of Competition* 155, note 30.

19. J. Edgar Sexton, "Mergers under Canadian Combines Law," *Western Ontario Law Review*, 2 (1963); and W.G. Phillips, "Canadian Combines Policy – The Matter of Mergers," *Canadian Bar Review*, 42 (1964).

20. J.C. Weldon, "Consolidation in Canadian Industry, 1900-1948," in L.A. Skeoch, ed., *Restrictive Trade Practices in Canada* (Toronto, 1966), 233, table 1.

21. For a detailed discussion of the 1909-13 merger movement, see A.E. Epp, "Cooperation among Capitalists: The Canadian Merger Movement, 1909-13" (Ph.D. thesis, Johns Hopkins University, 1973). Nelson, *Merger Movements in American Industry, 1895-1956* (Princeton, 1959); Weldon, "Consolidation in Canadian Industry," 236-7, table 2.

22. Weldon, "Consolidation in Canadian Industry," 263, table 13.

23. Quoted in Reynolds, *Control of Competition*, 174, note 3. See also Bladen, *Introduction to Political Economy*, 189-90.

24. *Ibid.*, 174-5, note 3.

25. BCF, vol. 12, file 2-33, Report on the Canadian Industry, prepared by W.T. Jackman.

26. Stuart M. Jamieson, *Times of Trouble: Labour Unrest and Industrial Conflict in Canada, 1900-66* (Ottawa, 1968), Chapter 4: "The Torpid Twenties," 158, 185, 186.

27. Throughout this period, the CMA's Industrial Relations Committee was composed of representatives of some of the biggest companies in the country. In 1919, for example, the committee was composed of spokesmen for Goodyear Tire and Rubber, the Steel Company of Canada, Massey-Harris, Vulcan Iron Works, the British American Oil Company, and Canadian General Electric.

28. Kealey, "The Honest Workingman and Workers' Control: The Experience of Toronto Skilled Workers, 1860-1892," *L/LT*, 1 (1976), 32.
29. T.W. Acheson, "Changing Social Origins of the Canadian Industrial Elite, 1880-1910," in Glenn Porter and Robert Cuff, eds., *Enterprise and National Development* (Toronto, 1973), 78.
30. Cited in Michael Bliss, *A Living Profit* (Toronto, 1974), 75. See also Craig Heron and Bryan D. Palmer, "Through the Prism of the Strike: Industrial Conflict in Southern Ontario, 1901-14," *CHR*, LVIII (1977).
31. Reinhard Bendix, *Work and Authority in Industry* (New York, 1963), 204.
32. *Industrial Canada* (July, 1918), 151 (Parsons); *ibid*. (January, 1927), 112 (Massey-Harris); *ibid*. (July, 1922), 156-7 (IRC).
33. *Ibid*. (July, 1920), 173, Report of the Industrial Relations Committee. For a discussion of King's work and ideas, see W.L.M. King, *Industry and Humanity* (Toronto, 1973), with an introduction by David Jay Bercuson; and Paul Craven, "The Invention of the Public: Mackenzie King and the Problem of Order," unpublished paper read to Sociology Department Colloquium, University of Toronto, 26 January 1977.
34. For a revealing case study, see Bruce Scott, "A Place in the Sun: The Industrial Council at Massey-Harris, 1919-1929," *L/LT*, 1 (1976).
35. Stephen J. Scheinberg, "Progressivism in Industry: The Welfare Movement in the American Factory," Canadian Historical Association, *Historical Papers* (1967), 184-5.
36. *Industrial Canada* (June, 1918), 65-6.
37. *Ibid*. (June, 1929), 147.
38. Pentland, *A Study of the Changing Social, Economic and Political Background of the Canadian System of Industrial Relations* (Ottawa, 1968), 100.
39. Bliss, *A Living Profit*, 63. Bliss (pp. 69-71) also provides a description of earlier factory welfare schemes which began around the turn of the century.
40. Bendix, *Work and Authority*, 204.
41. *Industrial Canada* (November, 1920), 59.
42. Bliss, *A Living Profit*, 70.
43. *Industrial Canada* (July, 1918), 196-7; *ibid*. (June, 1918), 40.
44. *Ibid*. (July, 1930), 152; *ibid*. (July, 1929), 145-6; *ibid*. (April, 1919), 130: Judson Gennel, "State Insurance as a Means to Contentment," reprinted from the *Michigan Manufacturer*.
45. Bendix, *Work and Authority*, 296.
46. *Industrial Canada* (July, 1924), 146.
47. *Ibid*. (July, 1924), 108; *ibid*. (June, 1917), 203. For the history of this dispute, see Michael Piva, "The Workmen's Compensation Movement in Ontario," *Ontario History* (1975).

48. *Industrial Canada* (December, 1919), 45; *ibid.* (July, 1930), 152-3.
49. *Ibid.* (April, 1922), 50.
50. *Ibid.* (November, 1919), 44; *ibid.* (July, 1929), 146.
51. Robert E. Lane, *The Regulation of Businessmen* (Hamden, Conn., 1966), 19-20.
52. See *Industrial Canada* (October, 1922), 47, for a discussion of the British Empire Steel Corporation's views.
53. Bendix, *Work and Authority*, 199.
54. Pentland, "The Development of a Capitalistic Labour Market in Canada," *Canadian Journal of Economics and Political Science*, 25 (1959), 454.

II
Social Structure

Although always a nation of immigrants, Canada experienced particularly rapid immigration in the period between the end of the depression of the 1890's and the outbreak of World War I. The Laurier and pre-war Borden years witnessed the fulfilment of the National Policy promises. Rapid industrial development in the nation's heartland was matched by an orgy of western railroad building and land settlement. The new immigrants served the developing capitalist economy in three ways. First, as Donald Avery describes here in detail, they provided the labour power on which the railroads depended and without which the mineral and lumber corporations could not have existed. Second, this rural, resource proletariat subsequently moved on to the land and provided the consumer and producer goods markets for central Canadian manufacturers of everything from clothing to ploughs and combines. Third, with the advance of western settlement the new settlers began to raise the crops which were so crucial to Canada's role in the international economy.

Traditionally, much of the literature on ethnicity in Canada has been self-congratulatory. Deprived immigrants, driven from their homelands, arrive in Canada, the land of opportunity. As Avery's article demonstrates there was often more to the story than the hard-work-leads-to-success story generated by the popular mythology. Immigration, especially of non-Anglo-Saxons, engendered considerable controversy and occasional violence. Like the nineteenth-century Irish who built Canada's early canals and railways, the Ukrainians, Jews, Poles, Italians, and other eastern and southern European immigrants, as well as Asian immigrants, often met with suspicion, hostility, and racism. This story is now being chronicled by Canadian historians who are also, for the first time, beginning to chart the history of Canada's ethnic population from the point of view of the immigrants themselves.

FURTHER READING:

On nativism, see Howard Palmer, *Patterns of Prejudice: A History of Nativism in Alberta* (Toronto, 1982). On the response to Asian immigrants, see W.P. Ward, *White Canada Forever: Popular Attitudes and Public Policy Toward Orientals in British Columbia* (Montreal, 1978); Ken Adachi, *The Enemy That Never Was* (Toronto, 1976); and Hugh Johnston, *The Voyage of the Komagata Maru: The Sikh Challenge to Canada's Colour Bar* (Delhi, 1979). A useful collection of essays covering many aspects of Canadian ethnic history is Jorgen Dahlie and Tissa Fernando, eds., *Ethnicity, Power and Politics in Canada* (Toronto, 1981). The Multicultural History Society of Ontario has published much useful material, for example, the special issue of *Polyphony* (1982) on Finns in Canada, edited by Varpu Lindstrom-Best. On radical immigrants in Canada, see Donald Avery, *Dangerous Foreigners: European Immigrant Workers and Labour Radicalism in Canada, 1896-1932* (Toronto, 1979). For interesting studies of one ethnic group, the Italians, see the Canadian essays in George E. Pozzetta, ed., *Pane E Lavoro: The Italian American Working Class* (Toronto, 1980), and in Robert F. Harney and J. Vincenza Scarpaci, eds., *Little Italies in North America* (Toronto, 1981).

Donald Avery teaches in the History Department of the University of Western Ontario and has published broadly in the field of ethnic radicalism.

Canadian Immigration Policy and the "Foreign" Navvy, 1896-1914

by Donald Avery

Two of the most important factors determining the rate and pattern of Canadian economic growth during the period from 1896 to 1914 were the expansion of the railway system and the massive influx of immigrants. Throughout both the Laurier and Borden eras, the agricultural and industrial sectors of the economy required abundant new supplies of labour, both skilled and unskilled. As a result there was a strong commitment to the idea of an "open door" immigration policy, particularly on the part of the entrepreneur. But the question of labour supply was not simply economic; it had had consequential and, at times, explosive cultural and racial overtones. Indeed, the debate over which groups should be admitted to the country constituted one of the most important aspects of the social history of this entire period. Whose influence would prove to be decisive in determining the character of the Canadian population – the big businessman, driven by the logic of economic growth and power, or the Canadian nationalist, determined to admit only those immigrants capable of easy assimilation into the existing population?

Nowhere was the clash of ideologies more pronounced than in the question of wholesale importation of immigrant railroad labourers, commonly referred to as "navvies." By exploring the social and economic conditions connected with the employment of navvies, the underlying attitudes of the Anglo-Canadian, par-

From Canadian Historical Association, *Historical Papers* (1972), 135-56. Reprinted by permission.

ticularly those of the managerial class, towards the unskilled immigrant worker are revealed.

There is no doubt that the connection between the railroad construction and immigration was direct and immediate. The opening up of the Prairies, and the resultant demand not only for feeder lines but additional transcontinentals to move the bountiful harvests, acted as a tremendous catalyst for railway building.[1] This was, of course, a process that worked both ways. As has so frequently been the case in Canadian history, railway construction preceded settlement.[2] During the period under review, the railway aspect of the railway-settlement symbiosis took precedence. Colonization railroads were clearly seen as a means of placing settlers in developing regions.[3] In this process immigrants would satisfy several needs: they would serve as a source of labour in the construction of the roads; their crops would provide an additional revenue base; and ultimately their labour could be utilized in developing industries.[4] Moreover, from the point of view of immigration policy, work on railroad construction gangs would be a means of initiation whereby the newcomers could adapt to the Canadian environment.[5]

In their stated policies, both the Laurier and Borden governments clearly gave priority to the recruitment of agricultural settlers.[6] This meant that immigration officials tended to see the recruitment of foreign labourers to work on railway construction as an aspect of the settlement process. But while the federal policy may have given priority to agricultural immigrants of an "acceptable" ethnic group, the urgent demands of the railroads for cheap and readily available labour created a serious problem. If the immigrant settler was only interested in railway construction work until he became established, if he was, in consequence, only a temporary member of the industrial labour force until a better opportunity presented itself, then the unskilled labour market would be very unstable. Yet one of the vital ingredients of rapid industrialization is the existence of what Professor H.C. Pentland has called a capitalistic labour market:

> By a capitalistic market is meant one in which the actions of workers and employers are governed and linked by impersonal considerations of immediate pecuniary advantage. In this market the employer is confident that workers will be available whenever he wants them; so he feels free to hire them on a short term basis, and to dismiss them whenever

there is a monetary advantage in doing so. . . . labour to the employer is a variable cost. . . . From a broader point of view, the capitalistic labour market represents a pooling of the labour supplies and labour needs of many employers, so that all may benefit by economizing on labour reserves.[7]

To maintain such a market in Canada, it was necessary to do much more than import large numbers of unskilled immigrants. In addition, these immigrants had to be of a type prepared to seek employment in the low-paying, exacting jobs associated with labour-intensive industries. Implicit in this argument was the idea that a permanent proletariat might not be a bad thing.

The ethnic composition of the railroad proletariat was to change substantially during the 1896-1914 period. The Irish Catholic navvies, who had been so important in building the railroads of the nineteenth century, were no longer available in sufficient quantity. The great wave of Irish immigration had subsided. Indeed, during the period 1901-1911, the number of Irish immigrants coming to Canada numbered only 10 per cent of those coming from England and 25 per cent of those coming from Scotland.[8] It is also worth noting that in occupational terms, during this period there were more farmers, farm labourers, and mechanics coming from Ireland than there were general labourers.

In terms of numbers, English and Scottish immigrants could have provided the necessary replacement for the Irish navvies.[9] This was particularly true between 1904 and 1914 when approximately 995,107 immigrants, or 41 per cent of the total number of emigrants leaving Great Britain, came to Canada.[10] This alteration of the pattern of British emigration flow away from the United States and towards Canada was greeted with considerable enthusiasm by immigration officials.[11] This favourable reaction was magnified by the belief that the quality of the British immigrants was improving.[12] But if these immigrants were attractive to government officials, large employers of unskilled labour were not so impressed. Few of these British immigrants were in the category of unskilled labour – only 15.6 per cent as compared to 51.5 per cent for the European immigrants who arrived in the same decade, 1901-1911.[13] Moreover, many of the British immigrants who came over as navvies proved to be very troublesome.

One of the most celebrated incidents of this nature occurred in

1897 when the Canadian Pacific Railway was preparing to expand its Crow's Nest Pass line, an endeavour for which it required a large supply of labour. On this occasion, an attempt was made by Immigration officials to find work on the Crow's Nest Railway for some 1,000 Welsh farmers and farm labourers who wanted to settle in western Canada.[14] The project was very much in keeping with the settlement-railroad arrangement. The initial income of the immigrants would be supplemented, and the railway companies would be provided with a large pool of unskilled labour. The CPR was immediately interested.[15]

But the arrangement was not a success, largely because the Welsh workers were not prepared to tolerate the low wages or the camp conditions. Their ability to focus public attention on their plight proved embarrassing to both the CPR and the Canadian government.[16] Indeed, the incident created such a stir in Britain that James A. Smart, Deputy Minister of the Interior, warned the CPR president that unless the situation was rectified "immigration to Canada could be very materially checked."[17] But Thomas Shaughnessy, the president of the CPR, was not a man easily cowed or intimidated. In a very blunt letter, he rejected the validity of the complaints and expressed his disdain for the British labourer:

> Men who seek employment on railway construction are, as a rule, a class accustomed to roughing it. They know when they go to the work that they must put up with the most primitive kind of camp accommodation. . . . I feel very strongly that it would be a huge mistake to send out any more of these men from Wales, Scotland or England. . . . it is only prejudicial to the cause of immigration to import men who come here expecting to get high wages, a feather bed and a bath tub.[18]

The sentiments that Shaughnessy expressed were shared by many Canadian entrepreneurs; they wanted hardy, malleable labourers whose salary requests would be "reasonable," who were not unionized, and who could not use the English-Canadian press to focus public attention on their grievances.[19] Shaughnessy also articulated a certain bias held by many Canadian entrepreneurs, and many western Canadians, that the British labourer was not suited either physically or psychologically to the conditions on the frontier.[20]

Even many of the Immigration officials manifest distinct reservations about recruiting British labourers. In 1897, for instance, when the matter of bringing British navvies into the country to aid in the construction of the Crow's Nest Railway was first being discussed, W.F. McCreary, the Winnipeg Commissioner of Immigration, indicated his objection to the project: "The English are no use whatever on the railroad, or, in fact, for that matter, almost any place else."[21]

It is evident that many employers discriminated against British immigrants, a situation which disturbed many in the old country.[22] In 1907, the editor of the *East Anglian Daily Times* complained to Sir Wilfrid Laurier that the Grand Trunk Railway had refused jobs to several immigrants "because they were Englishmen."[23] Although Laurier denied that such discrimination existed, studies of the employment practices of railroad construction companies have revealed that the charge had appreciable substance.[24]

The source of labour supply which would most perfectly accommodate the capitalistic labour market was to be found in the Orient. In this region the supply of unskilled labourers was unlimited. Asiatics, moreover, of all immigrant groups, could be cast more easily into the role of a permanent proletariat.[25] There had, of course, always been a direct connection between transcontinental railroads and the importation of Oriental labourers. Sir John A. Macdonald had been prepared to override the sustained and vociferous objections of British Columbia that no Chinese be employed on the road gangs building the CPR.[26] According to Macdonald, the shortage of white construction workers necessitated a choice for the people of British Columbia: "either you must have this labour or you cannot have a railway."[27] To make the decision more acceptable the Prime Minister emphasized that these Chinese navvies were only a temporary addition to the labour force. Hence there need be "no fear of a permanent degradation of the country by a mongrel race."[28] Yet it is significant that, contrary to this prediction, most of the Chinese remained in British Columbia. By 1891 they constituted about one-tenth of the total population of the coast province.[29]

The Oriental worker was regarded by many businessmen associated with labour-intensive industries as the ideal worker for an expanding economy.[30] But from the point of view of both Canadian workers and Canadian racial nationalists, the Chinese immigrant in particular was regarded as highly undesirable.[31] Both groups agreed that the social behaviour of the Chinese was deplorable, that they lived in overcrowded and filthy conditions, and that they were "a non-assimilating race."[32] To organized labour, however, the matter was even more crucial; not only would the Chinese presence create a mongrelized nation, but it would also produce an autocratic economic and political system:

> They [the Chinese] are thus fitted to become all too dangerous competitors in the labour market, while their docile servility, the natural outcome of centuries of grinding poverty and humble submission to a most oppressive system of government renders them doubly dangerous as the willing tools whereby grasping and tyrannical employers grind down all labour to the lowest living point.[33]

What is important about the involved subject of Chinese immigration is that even as the exclusionist forces were gaining in strength, the voice of the business groups was still heard loudly and clearly in Ottawa.[34] The CPR and other railroad companies continued to agitate for an "open door" arrangement allowing Asiatic labourers into the country, and strenuously opposed any increase in the head tax.[35] It is also apparent that the CPR continued to employ a considerable number of Orientals and established arrangements with emigration organizations such as the Canadian Nippon Supply Company not only to import Japanese labourers, but also to control them while they were in the employ of the railway company.[36] But perhaps of even greater significance was the fact that the state-supported Grand Trunk Pacific was also seriously contemplating importing Oriental labour. In December 1906 a tentative agreement was made between the representatives of the Canadian Nippon Company and E.G. Russell, purchasing agent of the Grand Trunk Pacific.[37] Public statements by prominent officials of the GTP served to confirm the belief that the railway company intended to import Asiatic workers. In March 1907, Frank Morse, vice president and general manager, was quoted as saying that "no transcontinental had yet been constructed without the assistance of oriental labour."[38] In September, while the ashes of Vancouver's Chinatown smouldered, the general manager of the Grand Trunk, Charles M. Hays, gave a provocative analysis of the labour requirements of the transcontinental:

We will employ the kind of immigrants on the line that the Government allows into the country. Am I opposed to the entrance of oriental labour, you ask? Well, you need cheap labour, don't you, and why should we reject the oriental if we cannot get the supply we require from any other source?[39]

Hays might also have added that the rising cost of labour was a major consideration for the Grand Trunk. Indeed, with the extensive industrial activity, particularly the appreciable railway construction, wages for unskilled labour had soared. Between 1903 and 1907, the daily wage of white navvies in British Columbia had increased from $1.50 to as high as $3.00. The advance was even more spectacular for Oriental navvies; for this group the daily wage had advanced from $1.00 to $2.50.[40] According to the 1908 Royal Commission appointed to inquire into the methods by which Oriental labourers had been induced to come to Canada, the impact of these high wages was to render ineffective the hitherto prohibitive head tax.[41] The situation had been, therefore, very conducive for Asiatic immigration.[42]

Naturally the railway companies welcomed this state of affairs; for the Laurier government, however, the situation was fraught with grave danger. This was dramatically shown by the Vancouver riots of September 1907 and the subsequent growth of the Asiatic Exclusion League.[43] In 1908, the Dominion government responded to the protests emanating from British Columbia with two Orders-in-Council: the first excluded immigrants from coming to Canada other than by continuous journey from their country of birth or citizenship; the second stipulated that immigrants from India had to have $200 in their possession upon landing in Canada.[44] These Orders-in-Council complemented the celebrated Gentlemen's Agreement between Canada and Japan of December 1907. This arrangement had provided that control of Japanese immigration, especially from the labouring classes, would rest with the Japanese government.[45]

These developments, however, did not mean that railroad entrepreneurs such as Charles M. Hays had discarded the notion that Oriental labourers should be imported; nor did the arrangements of 1907-08 mean that the Laurier government would be unresponsive to future suggestions that the regulations be relaxed. This was illustrated in 1909 when Charles Hays once again proposed an "open door" immigration policy.[46] Laurier's rationale for rejecting this overture was neither radical nor economic. He took his stand on purely political grounds:

> The condition of things in British Columbia is now such that riots are to be feared if Oriental labour were to be brought in. You remember that in our last conversation upon this subject I told you that if the matter could be arranged so that you could have an absolute consensus of McBride, the dangers would probably be averted, but with the local government in active sympathy with the agitators the peace of the province would be really in danger and that consideration is paramount with me.[47]

The fact that in the 1908 federal election the Liberals had lost five out of the seven seats they had previously held in British Columbia clearly weighed heavily with Laurier.[48] He was also no doubt influenced by the mounting evidence that both the federal and provincial Conservatives would in the future make even greater use of the "yellow peril."[49]

By 1907, therefore, the Canadian railroad companies had reached an impasse with regard to a cheap labour supply. British workers were clearly unsuitable as an industrial proletariat, while Oriental labourers could not be imported in sufficient quantities for ethnic and cultural reasons. The response of the Canadian "captains of industry" to the situation was to turn increasingly towards central and southern Europe for their "coolie labour." Yet, this approach also embarrassed the Dominion government; by 1907 the idea had become popular in Canada that southern Europeans were of "inferior stock," inclined towards crime and immorality.[50] A distinction was made, however, between southern Europeans and central Europeans; the latter group, it was widely believed, were superior in a racial sense, as well as having preferable cultural qualities which were derived from their agrarian way of life.[51]

This bias against southern Europeans had been evident in the immigration priorities established during Clifford Sifton's term as Minister of the Interior, 1896-1905.[52] In 1897, for example, W.F. McCreary, Commissioner of Immigration, had prevailed upon the Minister of Railways, Andrew Blair, to exert "mild" pressure upon the CPR to desist from importing Italian navvies from the United States.[53] According to McCreary, the Italians and many other southern Europeans were birds of passage, coming into the country with no intention of settling on the land or making any positive contribution.

In contrast, encouragement had been given to railway companies by the Dominion government to employ central European settlers. The railway companies had found this group appealing because "they ask no light-handed work . . . they have been obedient and industrious."[54] This docility was perhaps not surprising, for in 1900 James A. Smart, the Deputy Minister of the Interior, had made it very clear to his subordinates that the central European settler-labourer should be discouraged from adopting collective bargaining tactics. "They should be told when they need work they had better take the wages they are offered."[55]

The 1901 strike of the maintenance-of-way employees, "the humble and unlettered trackmen," provided an example of how the foreign worker was regarded by the CPR.[56] The strike also revealed the extent to which the Dominion government was willing to accommodate the company. The CPR was bent on smashing the strike; it refused to co-operate with representatives of the strikers and denounced the president of the Brotherhood of Railway Trackmen as a "foreign agitator."[57] It also set about recruiting strikebreakers both in Canada and from the United States. These tactics placed the Laurier government in a very awkward position.

The attempt by the Canadian Pacific to use the Winnipeg Immigration officers "not only to recruit scabs" but to coerce the Galician and Doukhobor workers threatened to destroy the credibility of the Immigration Branch with both the immigrants and organized labour.[58] But Commissioner J. Obed Smith of the office refused to accommodate the company despite pressure from the CPR.[59] His predecessor, W.F. McCreary, however, held a different view. He informed Clifford Sifton that the consequences of strained relations with the CPR "would be disastrous for Canadian immigration ventures."[60]

Ultimately it was the McCreary attitude which prevailed. The CPR was allowed to import "four or five hundred pauperized Italians" from the United States in contravention of the Alien Labour Law.[61] This Act, passed in 1897, forbade companies from bringing contract labour into Canada, or in any way encouraging or assisting the importation of alien workers.[62] By the time of the strike, however, the Dominion government was not directly responsible for the enforcement of this legislation;

rather, enforcement depended upon individual action before the courts.[63] Mackenzie King, the Deputy Minister of Labour, brought the Alien Labour Act to the attention of the CPR president, but the Dominion government otherwise ignored the situation.[64] During the next three years, the Canadian Pacific continued to import Italian navvies from the United States and actually developed a scheme whereby these men were supplied on a regular basis by an organization operating out of Montreal.[65]

By 1904 there were between 6,000 and 8,000 destitute Italian labourers in Montreal. Urged by Montreal civic officials, the Montreal Trades and Labour Council, the Montreal Italian Immigration Society, and the Italian consul in the city, the Laurier government was finally forced to act.[66] A Royal Commission was established under the chairmanship of Judge John Winchester, which ultimately indicted the CPR in a scathing fashion.[67] Yet no attempt was subsequently made to strengthen the Alien Labour Law.[68] If anything, the trend was in the opposite direction.

Between 1906 and 1908 actual construction on the various sections of the Grand Trunk Pacific and the National Transcontinental was initiated; the "new" railway boom was about to begin.[69] In keeping with the optimism of the period, in 1907, Frank Morse, the vice president and general manager of the Grand Trunk Pacific, stated that his company needed 20,000 navvies and suggested that the Laurier government consider advancing the fares of these men in order to expedite recruitment.[70] Given the attitude which had developed towards British and Oriental navvies it is not surprising that in this situation the contractors of the Grand Trunk Pacific and National Transcontinental now turned towards southern Europe for the fulfilment of their labour needs. Their recruitment program, however, ran counter to the prejudices which had developed among Immigration officials, and in the country at large, against the admission of immigrants from this region. The Immigration Branch was primarily interested in agricultural immigrants who could be temporarily utilized in railroad construction work. They were prepared to adopt a tough line against the indiscriminate entry of "inferior" immigrants simply to meet the short-term needs of railway contractors. Hence, they attempted to enforce rigorously the continuous journey and money reserves regulations.[71]

From the point of view of railroad contractors, the Scandinavian and Galician settler-labourers favoured by the Immigration officials had several disadvantages.[72] In the first place, these settler-labourers would only be available during the late spring and summer, quitting in August in order to harvest their crops.[73] Moreover, these immigrants were sufficiently thrifty that they quickly established themselves full time on the land, and so moved out of the labour market. In contrast, the Italian labourers were not interested in settling on the land; in fact, many of them returned at the end of the construction season to the United States or to Italy. The Italians also preferred to remain aloof from other ethnic groups, "to form companies and board themselves, building little camps for that purpose, as they can do so for less than $4.50 per week."[74] They often followed the practice of working with the contractor through headmen or *padrone*.[75] Both the *padrone* system and the isolation of the camps held advantages for the contractor. Their internal discipline made the Italian labourers a reliable group, while their lack of contact with Canadian workers, especially with Canadian trade unions, tended to minimize the danger of a strike occurring.[76]

In the clash between the Immigration Branch and the railroad companies, the federal politicians were inclined more often than not to support the interests of the companies. When the need arose, the "open door" could usually be achieved by the large employers of labour through their political leverage. This was clearly indicated in the period 1910-13 when Liberal and Conservative ministers acceded to the demands of the railway contractors for a relaxation of regulations pertaining to the immigration of navvies. During 1910, both the CPR and the Grand Trunk Pacific exerted pressure on the government to admit "railroad labourers . . . irrespective of nationality." The Grand Trunk contractors further insisted that they had to have southern Europeans who were "peculiarly suited for the work."[77] After Laurier had been approached by Duncan Ross, a lobbyist for the construction firm of Foley, Welch & Stewart, during his "famous" 1910 tour of western Canada, the Dominion government capitulated on the issue.[78] By this time, of course, the prestige of the Laurier government was riding on the rapid completion of the Grand Trunk Pacific.[79] In this situation, neither the cause of Canadian racial purity, nor the opposition of organized labour, nor the objections of the Immigration Branch, nor the combined opposition of Frank Oliver, the Minister of the Interior, and William Lyon Mackenzie King, the Minister of Labour, could offset the influence of the railway contractors. Mackenzie King vividly described the mood of the Laurier cabinet:

> Oliver is strong in his opposition to labour being brought into the country for work on railroads that ultimately is not going to be of service for settlement and favours making restrictions on virtually all save northern people of Europe. I agree with him, but we are about alone in this, others preferring to see railroad work hurried.[80]

The coming to power of the Conservatives in 1911 did not significantly disrupt the government-contractor relationship; indeed, the ability of the business lobby to influence immigration policy decisions was again clearly revealed in 1912. In that year the Immigration officials resumed their attempts to limit the number of southern Europeans entering Canada as railway navvies in response to increasing public complaints that those immigrants "constituted a serious menace to the community."[81] However, the Minister of the Interior, Robert Rogers, was too good a politician to offend powerful vested interests. When it was brought to his attention by both Donald Mann of the Canadian Northern, and Timothy Foley, one of the leading contractors of the Grand Trunk Pacific, that the restrictions were unnecessary and indeed harmful, Rogers overruled his subordinates.[82] The result was the free entry of alien navvies.[83]

The admission of large numbers of southern Europeans, particularly Italian labourers, showed that the long-standing goal of bringing into the country only the settler-labourer type of immigrant had been displaced by a policy of importing an industrial proletariat. Immigration statistics reveal that the percentage of unskilled labourers, as compared to the total male immigrants entering Canada, had increased from 31 per cent in 1907 to 43 per cent in 1913-14.[84] In contrast, the percentage of agriculturalists decreased from 38 per cent in 1907 to 28 per cent in 1914.[85] Similarly, the ethnic aspects of immigration policy revealed that there was a steady advance in the percentages of central and southern European immigrants from 29 per cent in 1907 to 48 per cent in 1913-14.[86]

Economic priorities were paramount in determining the attitude of the successive Dominion governments towards the industrial utilization of the immigrant navvy. Completion of the Grand Trunk Pacific and the Canadian Northern was of such crucial importance that the Ottawa authorities seemed prepared to allow railroad contractors a free hand in the operation of the construction camps. This *laissez-faire* stance was adopted despite abundant evidence that working conditions were not only unsanitary but also hazardous.[87] The *Annual Reports* of the Department of Labour showed that the number of fatal accidents associated with the operation and construction of railroads was unusually high. Between 1904 and 1911, for example, out of a total of 9,340 fatal industrial accidents in Canada, 23 per cent were related to the railway industry.[88] Even these statistics do not tell the true story. It was not until 1912 that the Dominion government required contractors receiving public funds to register fatalities occurring in their camps.[89] Even with this provision there was some question as to whether the number of recorded deaths of foreign labourers were always accurate: " 'Oh, some Russian is buried there' was the passing remark that commonly designated an unkempt plot in the vicinity of an erstwhile camp."[90] The human and economic consequences of the high rate of accidents connected with railroad construction were also illustrated in a report written by J. Bruce Walker, Commissioner of Immigration, in 1910. Walker reported that one of the reasons for the shortage of labour in the National Transcontinental construction camps around Fort William was that many Galician and Polish labourers would not accept construction jobs because "the majority of men now engaged in rock work are afraid of it on account of the numerous accidents."[91]

The contractors were also given a free hand with respect to the standards of accommodation provided in the construction camps. Although there was an obligation on the part of the head contractor, who accepted federal funds, to provide for the basic needs of the men, contractual arrangements and actual practice seemed often to have been at variance.[92] Controversy over unsanitary conditions in navvy camps, of course, has had a long history in Canadian railway construction.[93] In 1897 the CPR had been charged with mistreating a group of Welsh navvies, and complaints continued to reach the attention of the federal government throughout the period under review.[94] In October 1910, the Edmonton Trades and Labor Council made representation to the Minister of Labour about the improper treatment of construction workers employed by the Grand Trunk Pacific.[95] The Council pointed out the disgraceful condition of the camps, the prevalence of typhoid fever within the camps, the inadequacy of the food and accommodation supplied to the men while en route to the job site, and the delays occurring in the payment of wages. Frank Plant, an official of the Department of Labour, was dispatched to Alberta to investigate the charges and submit a report. Plant noted some abuses, but, in general, he exonerated the company and its leading contractors, especially Foley, Welch & Stewart.[96] With respect to the living conditions within the camps, Plant noted that the accommodation was adequate and the food generally wholesome. None of those interviewed, he optimistically reported, had had "any grievance as to treatment, food or accommodation."[97]

Critics of the contracting companies were not so easily satisfied. It was alleged in labour circles that the government inspectors visited the bush camps only infrequently and spent most of their time "at the end of steel," close to civilization.[98] It was further alleged that the men were often intimidated by the power of the head contractor, who "along the grade . . . is supreme . . . not unlike a Tartar chieftain."[99] The prospect of being dismissed, miles from settlement, was enough to deter most men.[100] And for the foreign worker, who was often unable to communicate in English, who was manipulated by an "ethnic straw-boss," and who had a basic mistrust of state officials, the government inspector simply did not offer a viable channel of protest.[101]

Conditions in the railroad construction camps of the Grand Trunk Pacific and the National Transcontinental continued to be an issue until the outbreak of war. In 1913, for example, another raft of complaints led to an investigation of the Foley, Welch & Stewart camps. Once again, however, the company was exonerated.[102] This conclusion brought an angry response from militant elements in the labour movement. According to the *Eastern Labor News*, "the false statements made as to living conditions . . . and given wide publicity in the capitalist press, will wisen up the workmen so that they will vote for a man to represent themselves, and not for the lying parasites who will always be against them."[103]

The failure of government officials to redress their grievances turned many alien construction workers in the direction of radical labour. By 1912, the growing labour radicalism in the construction camps was a source of concern to many of those who had immediate contact with these foreign workers.[104] What made it appear even more ominous was the fact that neither the companies involved, nor the federal or provincial governments, nor the institutionalized churches, nor even the Trades and Labor Congress seemed prepared to assume responsibility for the physical and spiritual needs of the alien navvy.

The problem faced by the churches in relation to the foreign workers stemmed from insufficient resources and faulty organization.[105] The energies of the Presbyterian and Methodist churches, in particular, were consumed by the thousands of immigrants who were located on homesteads or in urban ghettos.[106] The failure of the established churches in coping with the foreign workers was responsible for the formation of the Reading Camp Association, in 1899, by a young Presbyterian minister, the Reverend Alfred Fitzpatrick.[107] Fitzpatrick's concern was not specifically religious; rather, he was interested in Canadianizing the men by teaching them the English language and introducing them to the native "ideals of citizenship, and . . . life."[108] The Reading Camp Association attempted to elicit the support of the businessmen-philanthropists, especially those associated with railways and mining operations. By 1912, the Association was supported financially by all three transcontinental railways, as well as by leading members of the Toronto business community.[109] Writing in 1919, one business contributor rationalized his support for the Association in these words:

> I am not very strong on Religious matters but my business training tells me that the work you are doing will go a long way to educate foreigners and rough fellows out on our Frontier and after all that is where the trouble in the Industrial World is most ready to break out or I might say that is amongst men of this type that the I.W.W. and Bolsheviki find their ground for sewing [sic] their seed, therefore I am pleased to help support the work.[110]

While a segment of the business community, out of enlightened self-interest, was prepared to support at least some basic Canadianization work among the alien labourers, appeals by the Association to the federal government had failed. The Association was "slapped . . . over the back with the British North America Act, and referred . . . back to the provinces."[111] Most of the provinces were likewise indifferent to the appeals of the Association, assuming, perhaps, that responsibility for these workers rested with the Dominion government.[112] From Fitz-patrick's perspective, this rejection was all the more frustrating because neither level of government, federal or provincial, had implemented Canadianization programs among the immigrant workers in the industrial camps.[113]

The Canadian Trades and Labor Congress also seemed quite unconcerned about the plight of the foreign navvy during most of the period under study. The Congress seems to have con-cerned itself mainly with the introduction of restrictive immigra-tion measures designed to safeguard the job security of Cana-dian workers.[114] But even in this effort the TLC directed its efforts mainly against British skilled mechanics and Orientals. In 1911, however, the Congress began to display a greater inter-est in the problems of the alien worker. A resolution was passed at the annual convention calling for the services of the TLC solici-tor to be extended to the unskilled labourers in the construction camps "so as to prevent these workers from being intimidated by contractors and local law enforcement agencies."[115]

One explanation for the greater interest shown by the TLC at this stage was to be found in the growing influence of the Indus-trial Workers of the World among the unskilled workers.[116] The IWW threat revealed itself in various strikes among the construc-tion workers employed by contractors of the Grand Trunk Pacific and the Canadian Northern.[117] One of the most serious strikes occurred in 1912 among the 7,000 navvies engaged in the construction of the Canadian Northern Railway. Although the strike only directly affected one company and did not extend be-yond the borders of British Columbia, the incident had a num-ber of wide-reaching implications. An article in the *British Co-lumbia Federationist* of April 5, 1912, hailed the walkout as "an object lesson as to what a movement animated by an uncompro-mising spirit of revolt . . . can accomplish among the most heterogeneous army of slaves that any system of production ever assembled together."[118] In a later edition, the *Federationist* noted that the ethnic antagonisms which the railway contractors had utilized in dividing the men had been laid aside: "Cana-dians, Americans, Italians, Austrians, Swedes, Norwegians, French and Old Countrymen all on strike . . . a hint to King Capital to look for some other country more healthy for him to exploit labourers in than this."[119] Initially there seemed to be a reasonable chance for an IWW victory, but increasingly the position of the employers improved as the power of both provincial and federal governments was brought to bear on the dispute. The high degree of class unity exhibited by the workers in the early stages of the strike was eroded by the ability of the contractor to hire "scab" labour from employment agencies in Vancouver and Seattle.[120]

The *British Columbia Federationist* alleged that the McBride government had rushed detachments of provincial police to the railway camps not only to protect the strikebreakers, but also to arrest the strike leaders on trumped up charges.[121] There certainly appeared to be little evidence that the police had been dispatched to protect the strikers from the violence of professional thugs employed by the contractors.[122] The Borden government soon revealed its willingness to co-operate with management. Despite the objections of organized labour, few contractors had difficulties circumventing the Alien Labour Law in their efforts to import navvies from the United States. There is evidence that Donald Mann of the Canadian Northern and Timothy Foley, one of the principal contractors, had prevailed upon Robert Rogers, the Minister of the Interior, to issue instructions allowing certain regulations to be waived by officials of the Immigration Department.[123] Furthermore, the Dominion government refused to consider a union request that a conciliation and arbitration board be established. The official reason given for this refusal was that railroad construction belonged to "a class of labour to which the provisions of the Industrial Disputes Investigation Act could only be applied by the mutual consent of the employers and employees."[124]

Time worked against the strikers. As the *Federationist* so succinctly stated, "the threat of hunger makes cowards of us all."[125] That the strike had been broken was clearly indicated in September when the Canadian Northern announced that most of the men had returned to work, and "the places of the others had been filled."[126]

In the peak years between 1911 and 1914, an estimated 50,000 workers were engaged annually in the construction of the various transcontinentals and provincially chartered railways.[127] The abrupt cessation of most of these projects, due to the unsettled international situation of 1914, meant that a high percentage of these labourers became unemployed.[128] The foreign navvy, whom the railroads had relied upon to supply the cyclical demands for construction labour, found the transition most difficult. Many navvies emigrated to the United States but large numbers of destitute men, unfamiliar with Canadian society, drifted into the cities and towns. Hence they became a focal point of racial tension and labour radicalism. Under the banner of economic growth, the Laurier and Borden governments had given a high priority to railroad construction. The amount of new track laid was impressive but the social costs were high.[129]

NOTES

1. Morris Zaslow, *The Opening of the Canadian North* (Toronto, 1971), 199-223; O.D. Skelton, *The Life and Letters of Sir Wilfrid Laurier* (Toronto, 1921), 415-18; W.L. Morton, *Manitoba: A History* (Toronto, 1957), 275-8, 298-300; James B. Hedges, *Building the Canadian West: the land and colonization policies of the Canadian Pacific Railway* (New York, 1939), 34, 47, 129-30, 140-2, 390-1; G.R. Stevens, *Canadian National Railways* (Toronto, 1963), II, 12-19, 54-5.
2. H.G.J. Aitken, "Defensive Expansionism: The State and Economic Growth in Canada," in W.T. Easterbrook and M.H. Watkins, *Approaches to Canadian Economic History* (Toronto, 1967), 203-10.
3. Zaslow, *Canadian North*, 167-71, 180-1, 187-94, 215-22; Hedges, *Building the Canadian West*, 129-30, 140-1.
4. This point has been developed by the authors cited in note 1.
5. PAC, Immigration Branch (IB), f. 39145, W.F. McCreary, Commissioner of Immigration, Winnipeg, to Andrew G. Blair, Minister of Railways and Canals, 21 June 1897; *Sessional Papers*, 1900, no. 25, pt. 2, 111, 147; *ibid.*, 1902, no. 25, pt. 2, 122, 139; *ibid.*, 1903, no. 25, pt. 2, 111; *ibid.*, 1904, no. 25, pt. 2, 98-100.
6. *Canada – A Handbook of Informaton for Intending Emigrants* (Ottawa, 1874); *Sessional Papers*, 1896, no. 13, pt. 7, Annual Report of the High Commissioner, Sir Charles Tupper; House of Commons, *Debates*, 1897, 4067; *Sessional Papers*, 1913, no. 25, pt. 2, 77; *ibid.*, 1914, no. 25, pt. 2, 80, 106; *Debates*, 1914, 1612; Norman Macdonald, *Canada: Immigration and Colonization 1841-1903* (Toronto, 1968), 148, 197; John W. Dafoe, *Clifford Sifton in Relation to His Times* (Toronto, 1931), 132-44; W.T.R. Preston, *My Generation of Politics and Politicians* (Toronto, 1972), 216-17; Skelton, *Life of Laurier*, 46-7; Karl Bicha, "The Plains Farmer and the Prairie Frontier, 1897-1914," *Proceedings of the American Philosophical Society*, 109, 6 (1965), 414-35.
7. H.C. Pentland, "The Development of a Capitalistic Labour Market in Canada," *Canadian Journal of Economics and Political Science*, XXV (November, 1959), 450, 460.

8. Lloyd Reynolds, *The British Immigrant* (Toronto, 1935), 32-45; *Sessional Papers*, 1902-15, Report of the Superintendent of Immigration.

9. Immigration from France is not discussed in this paper for two reasons. In the first place, the total number of French immigrants between the years 1900 and 1914 was only 25,273. Moreover, in terms of occupation, only 15 per cent of the male immigrants arriving in the period 1906-14 were placed in the general labourer category. *Report of the Royal Commission on Bilingualism and Biculturalism*, Book IV, 238-9; *Sessional Papers*, 1907-08 to 1915, Report of the Superintendent of Immigration.

10. Rowland Berthoff, *British Immigration in Industrial America, 1790-1950* (Cambridge, 1953), 21; Reynolds, *The British Immigrant*, 299.

11. Reynolds, *The British Immigrant*, 21; *Sessional Papers*, 1907-08, no. 25, pt. 2, 67, 85; *ibid.*, 1911, no. 25, pt. 2, 75, 95; *ibid.*, 1912, no. 25, pt. 2, 70, 94.

12. *Ibid.*

13. Reynolds, *The British Immigrant*, 46.

14. PAC, IB, f. 39501, Memorandum, James A. Smart (Deputy Minister of the Interior), 1897.

15. *Ibid.*

16. *Ibid.*, James A. Smart to Thomas Shaughnessy, 26 October 1897.

17. *Ibid.* In October 1897 the Canadian agent in Cardiff, Wales, W.L. Griffith, informed Smart that as a result of the statements appearing in the press "matters are very ugly here. The people are prepared to mob me." Griffith to Smart, 25 October 1897.

18. *Ibid.*, Thomas Shaughnessy to James A. Smart, 27 October 1897.

19. Martin Robin, "British Columbia: The Politics of Class Conflict," in Robin, ed., *Canadian Provincial Politics* (Scarborough, 1972), 29-30. Similar American studies have revealed the same trend: Neil Betten, "The Origins of Ethnic Radicalism in Northern Minnesota, 1900-1920," *International Migration Review*, IV, 2 (Summer, 1970), 51, 55; Melvyn Dubofsky, *We Shall Be All: A History of the Industrial Workers of the World* (Chicago, 1969), 320-1. This trend has also been described from the ethnic perspective by Joseph Kirschbaum, *Slovaks in Canada* (Toronto, 1967), 69-76.

20. Dafoe, *Clifford Sifton*, 148-52, 322; Reynolds, *The British Immigrant*, 41-5, 72-3; Carl Berger, *The Sense of Power* (Toronto, 1970), 181, 260; Edmund Bradwin, *The Bunkhouse Man* (Toronto, 1972), 94, 211.

21. Basil Stewart, *'No English Need Apply' or, Canada as a Field for the Emigrant* (London, 1909), 25-40; G.F. Plant, *Overseas Settlement: Migration from the United Kingdom to the Dominions* (London, 1951), 59-60; *Special Report on Immigration, dealing mainly with co-operation between the Dominion and Provincial Governments and the movement of people from the United King-*

dom to Canada, Arthur Hawkes, Commissioner (Ottawa, 1913), 10, 20-2.

22. PAC, Sir Wilfrid Laurier Papers, 125151, editor, *East Anglian Daily Times*, Ipswich, to Laurier, 8 May 1907.

23. *Ibid.*, 125152, Laurier to editor, *East Anglian Daily Times*, 10 May 1907; Bradwin, *The Bunkhouse Man*, 94, 211; Stevens, *Canadian National Railways*, II, 194-5; PAC, IB, f. 571672, no. 1, W.D. Scott to Lord Strathcona, 11 January 1907.

24. PAC, IB, f. 39501, W.F. McCreary to James A. Smart, 30 October 1897.

25. Royal Commission on Chinese Immigration, 1885, "Evidence," 55-7, 85, 95; Report (Gray's Section), lxix; Berger, *The Sense of Power*, 231; Charles J. Woodsworth, *Canada and the Orient* (Toronto, 1941), 35-8.

26. Woodsworth, *Canada and the Orient*, 29; Margaret Ormsby, *British Columbia: A History* (Toronto, 1959), 280.

27. *Debates*, 1882, 1477; Andrew Onderdonk, the chief contractor of the British Columbia section, had informed Macdonald in 1882 that unless he was allowed to import Chinese coolies, the CPR would not be finished for another twelve years. PAC, Macdonald Papers, 144771, A. Onderdonk to John A. Macdonald, 14 June 1882. Eventually Onderdonk brought over 10,000 Chinese into British Columbia. Pierre Berton, *The Last Spike* (Toronto, 1971), 204.

28. *Debates*, 1883, 1905.

29. Woodsworth, *Canada and the Orient*, 41.

30. See note 25.

31. Royal Commission on Chinese Immigration, 1885, "Evidence," 48, 83, 125, 140; *Debates*, 1883, 904; *ibid.*, 1884, 975-6.

32. Royal Commission on Chinese Immigration, 1885, "Evidence," 46.

33. *Ibid.*, 156.

34. The Laurier government received numerous letters from large employers of labour, both agricultural and industrial, particularly when in 1903 it was proposed to increase the head tax to $500.

35. Laurier Papers, 5749, Sir William Van Horne, president of CPR, to J.C. McLagan, editor of Vancouver *World*, 17 July 1896; *ibid.*, 41460, Thomas Shaughnessy to Laurier, 26 February 1900; *ibid.*, 71362, D. McNicoll, general manager, to Laurier, 31 March 1903.

36. *Report of the Royal Commission Appointed to Inquire into the Methods by which Oriental Labourers have been induced to Come to Canada* (Ottawa, 1908), 5, 13, 18, 54. PAC, W.L.M. King Papers, C-29731, C-29478.

37. *Report of the Royal Commission . . . Oriental Labourers*, 15, 19; *Sessional Papers*, 1909, no. 36, Report of the Deputy Minister of Labour, 111-12; King Papers, C-30258-30259.

38. *The Bruce Times*, 7 March 1907; PAC, IB, f. 594511, no. 1.

39. Montreal *Daily Herald*, 28 September 1907; PAC, IB, f. 594511, no. 2. For an account of the anti-Asiatic riots, see Ormsby, *British Columbia: A History*, 350-1.
40. *Labour Gazette*, VII (1906-1907), 261; *Sessional Papers*, 1911, no. 36, Reports of the Deputy Minister of Labour, 95.
41. *Sessional Papers*, 1911, no. 36, 95.
42. *Ibid.*
43. Ormsby, *British Columbia: A History*, 350-1. Extensive correspondence on the activities of the Asiatic Exclusion League are to be found in the correspondence between W.W.B. McInnes and Laurier during 1907 and 1908. Laurier Papers, 129162, 131593, 131596, 134026, 136303, 136615.
44. John Duncan Cameron, "The Law Relating to Immigration to Canada, 1867-1942" (Ph.D. thesis, University of Toronto, 1942), 265-9; R. MacGregor Dawson, *William Lyon Mackenzie King, 1874-1923* (Toronto, 1958), 164; Woodsworth, *Canada and the Orient*, 82-94, 103, 289; Khushwant Singh, *A History of the Sikhs, 1839-1964* (Princeton, 1966), 160-75.
45. The negotiations with the "Gentlemen's Agreement" are fully documented in the Laurier Papers, the King Papers, and the Rodolphe Lemieux Papers in PAC.
46. Laurier Papers, 160620-160621, Charles Hays to Laurier, 4 October 1909; *ibid.*, Hays to Laurier, 10 November 1909; Stevens, *Canadian National Railways*, II, 226-7.
47. Laurier Papers, 160983, Laurier to Hays, 12 November 1909. There are indications that in 1912 the GTP approached the British Columbia government requesting their assent to the importation of Chinese navvies. The McBride government refused. A.W. Currie, *The Grand Trunk Railway in Canada* (Toronto, 1957), 412.
48. Woodsworth, *Canada and the Orient*, 94. Although Laurier's biographer, O.D. Skelton, stressed the fact that "Laurier sacrificed British Columbia's seats rather than compete with Mr. Borden in concessions to the exclusionists," it was quite apparent that there were limits to this sacrifice. Skelton, *Life of Laurier*, 348.
49. Woodsworth, *Canada and the Orient*, 96-9; Ottawa *Free Press*, 23 September 1910; *Vancouver Province*, 6 October 1910; *Debates*, 1911, 286, 9815-9850.
50. Allan Smith, "Metaphor and Nationality in North America," *CHR*, LI, 3 (September, 1970), 250. J.S. Woodsworth, *Strangers Within Our Gates* (Toronto, 1911), 159. John Higham, *Strangers in the Land: Patterns of American Nativism, 1860-1925* (New Brunswick, N.J., 1955), has provided an excellent study of American bias against southern European immigrants.
51. This point was made in countless letters from Immigration officials, especially in PAC, IB, f. 594511, nos. 1-6.
52. Sifton appears to have had a very low opinion of Italian immigra-

tion, PAC, Clifford Sifton Papers, 90315, Sifton to Smart, 17 November 1901.

53. PAC, IB, f. 39145, no. 1, W.F. McCreary to A.G. Blair, 21 June 1897.

54. *Ibid.*, f. 60868, no. 1, C.W. Speers, Travelling Immigration Inspector, to Frank Pedley, Superintendent of Immigration, 24 January 1900.

55. *Ibid.*, f. 39145, no. 1 James A. Smart to W.F. McCreary, 5 June 1900.

56. John Wilson, *The Calcium Light: Turned on by a Railway Trackman* (St. Louis, 1902), Introduction.

57. *Ibid.*, 42.

58. PAC, IB, f. 39145, no. 1, J. Obed Smith, Commissioner, to Frank Pedley, 24 June 1901; *ibid.*, Smith to J.W. Leonard, General Superintendent, Western Division, CPR, 25 June 1901; *Inland Sentinel*, cited in Wilson, *The Calcium Light*, 51; *The Voice*, cited *ibid.*, 51.

59. PAC, IB, f. 39145, no. 1, J. Obed Smith to Frank Pedley, 26 June 1901.

60. Sifton Papers, 83178, W.F. McCreary to Clifford Sifton, 3 July 1901. McCreary was a Winnipeg lawyer who had been very active in civic affairs during the 1880's and 1890's. After three years as Commissioner of Immigration (1897-1900) he was elected for the federal constituency of Selkirk. *The Canadian Guide*, 1903 (Ottawa, 1903), 111. It does appear, from both his stand in 1901 and his previous attempts to work in a co-operative fashion with the CPR, that McCreary regarded the support of the CPR as very important to the cause of the Liberal Party.

61. PAC, IB, J. Obed Smith to Frank Pedley, 26 June 1901.

62. W.D. Atkinson, "Organized Labour and the Laurier Administration: The Fortunes of a Pressure Group" (M.A. thesis, Carleton University, 1957), 20-35; Martin Robin, *Radical Politics and Canadian Labour* (Kingston, 1968), 54-5.

63. Robin, *Radical Politics*, 55; H.A. Logan, *Trade Unions in Canada* (Toronto, 1948), 483, 488.

64. Mackenzie King to Thomas Shaughnessy, 3 July 1901, cited in Wilson, *The Calcium Light*, 46.

65. PAC, IB, f. 39145, no. 1, J. Obed Smith to W.D. Scott (the new Superintendent of Immigration), 7 May 1903; Royal Commission to Inquire into the Immigration of Italian Labourers to Montreal, and alleged fraudulent practices of employment agencies, *Report* (Ottawa, 1904), 19.

66. PAC, IB, f. 28885, no. 2, Chevalier Honore Catelli, president, Montreal Italian Immigration Society, to Dr. A.D. Stewart, 15 April 1904; Catelli to Stewart, 29 April 1904; Dr. Peter Bryce, Immigration Medical Inspector, to James A. Smart, 23 April 1904;

Sessional Papers, 1906, no. 36, Report of the Deputy Minister, 88.
67. Royal Commission to Inquire into the Immigration of Italian Labourers, 72.
68. Logan, *Trade Unions in Canada*, 483, 488.
69. Stevens, *Canadian National Railways*, II, 159-63, 172-83, 214-17.
70. *The Bruce Times*, 7 March 1907; PAC, IB, f. 594511, no. 2, Frank Morse to Acting Superintendent of Immigration, L.M. Fortier, 15 October 1907. Morse had been hired as general manager of the GTP by Charles Hays, and apparently the choice was disastrous. Stevens, *Canadian National Railways*, II, 224. Peter Veregin, the Doukhobor leader, publicly announced his intention to try and recruit 10,000 Russian railway labourers as an illustration of his good will toward the Canadian government. University of Toronto Archives, James Mavor Papers, James Mavor to George Cox, Toronto, 12 April 1907. It is significant that by the period 1910-14 some 50,000 navvies were also required annually. *Labour Gazette*, XII (July, 1911-June, 1912), 721. See also Monthly Reports Pertaining to Railroad Construction, 1910-14.
71. Extensive correspondence by Immigration officials on this problem of restriction is located in PC, IB, f. 594511, nos. 2-6; *Sessional Papers*, 1911, no. 25, pt. 2, 104; *ibid.*, 1914, no. 25, pt. 2, 144. What also troubled Canadian Immigration officials was the difficulty of deporting "undesirable" non-naturalized Slavic and Italian labourers who entered Canada from the United States. PAC, IB, f. 594511, no. 3, F.H. Larned, Acting Commissioner-General, Immigration and Naturalization, to W.D. Scott, 16 June 1906.
72. In 1908, W.D. Scott had taken considerable exception to the ethnic groups the Grand Trunk Pacific was attempting to import into Canada. PAC, IB, f. 594511, no. 2, W.D. Scott to J.T. Davis, 4 May 1908.
73. PAC, IB, f. 571672, no. 1, Blake Robertson, Immigration Special Inspector, to Frank Oliver, 10 October 1907.
74. *Ibid.*
75. *Ibid.* The *padrone* system has been extensively discussed in American studies on the subject of Italian immigration. Maldwyn Jones, *American Immigration* (Chicago, 1961), 190-2, provides a succinct explanation of how the system worked. Royal Commission to Inquire into the Immigration of Italian Labourers, 19, provides a vivid description of how the *padrone* Herocle Cordasco operated.
76. Bradwin, *The Bunkhouse Man*, 110-11; *Proceedings before the Royal Commission on Industrial Relations*, 1919 (Department of Labour, Library, Ottawa), Edmonton hearings, 12, 52; *ibid.*, Cobalt hearings, 1757, 1764.
77. PAC, IB, f. 594511, no. 3, W.D. Scott to D. McNicoll, vice presi-

dent, 6 July 1910; *ibid.*, J.O. Reddie, GTP, to W.D. Scott, 1 April 1910.

78. Laurier Papers, 182131, Duncan Ross to Laurier, 27 February 1911: PAC, IB, f. 594511, no. 3, W.W. Cory, Deputy Minister of the Interior, to W.D. Scott, 16 July 1910.

79. PAC, IB, f. 594511, no. 3, W.J. Bartlett, secretary, Winnipeg Trades and Labour Council, to Frank Oliver, Minister of the Interior, 3 August 1910. Attorney General W.J. Bowser of the British Columbia government, in September 1911, charged the Immigration Branch with consciously violating the Alien Labour Law by allowing railway companies to import navvies from the United States (Montreal *Daily Star*, 5 September 1911; Vancouver *News Advertiser*, 7 September 1911).

80. PAC, The King Diary, 10 January, 1911.

81. PAC, IB, f. 594511, no. 3, Report, J.M. Langley, Chief of Police, to Mayor Alderman, City of Victoria, B.C., 28 August 1911; *ibid.*, no. 5, J. Bruce Walker, Commissioner of Immigration, to W.D. Scott, 12 March 1912.

82. *Ibid.*, no. 5, Donald Mann to W.D. Scott, 27 August 1912; *ibid.*, Timothy Foley to Robert Rogers, 27 March 1912. Three-quarters of the total construction mileage was awarded to Foley Brothers in their many different partnerships. They were an American contracting company which had had considerable experience with both the CPR and the Canadian Northern. Stevens, *Canadian National Railways*, II, 176.

83. PAC, IB, f. 594511, no. 5, Memorandum, office of the Minister of the Interior to W.W. Cory, Deputy Minister of the Interior, 2 April 1912. John D. Cameron, "The Law Relating to Immigration," 278.

84. Statistics tabulated from *Sessional Papers*, 1907-08, no. 25, pt. 2, Report of the Superintendent of Immigration; *ibid.*, 1915, no. 25, pt. 2, Report of the Superintendent of Immigration.

85. *Ibid.*

86. *Ibid.* For the railway contractors the outbreak of conflict in the Balkans meant that many of their Bulgarian navvies rapidly returned to Europe. *The Christian Guardian*, 12 November 1912.

87. There was quite a difference of opinion between the account included in labour newspapers such as *The Voice* and the official reports of investigators sent out by the Department of Labour and the Immigration Branch.

88. Statistics tabulated from *Sessional Papers*, 1913, no. 36, Report of the Deputy Minister of Labour.

89. *Ibid.*, 12.

90. Bradwin, *The Bunkhouse Man*, 153, 200, 212.

91. PAC, IB, f. 594511, no. 3, J. Bruce Walker to W.D. Scott, 16 February 1910.

92. Bradwin, *The Bunkhouse Man*, 81, 144-53, 200, 206. The Department of Labour had the responsibility of enforcing the Fair Wages Regulation (1900), which established certain employment practices applicable to employers who were receiving either a federal subsidy or guarantee. Dawson, *William Lyon Mackenzie King*, 70-1; *Sessional Papers*, 1907, no. 36, Report of the Deputy Minister of Labour, 64-7.

93. Partial accounts of camp conditions are included in Berton, *The Last Spike*, 110, 194-205, 275-9; Terry Coleman, *The Railway Navvies* (London, 1965), 66, 80; Currie, *The Grand Trunk*, 28-9.

94. PAC, IB, f. 39501, no. 1, James A. Smart to Thomas Shaughnessy, 26 October 1897. In 1906 a series of complaints were submitted by a party of Scottish navvies concerning the construction camps of the Grand Trunk Pacific. *Ibid.*, f. 751672, no. 1, Lord Strathcona, High Commissioner, to Frank Oliver, 5 December 1906.

95. *Sessional Papers*, 1912, no. 36, 88-100.

96. *Ibid.*

97. *Ibid.*

98. Bradwin, *The Bunkhouse Man*, 206, 216.

99. *Ibid.*, 198, 206-13.

100. *Ibid.*

101. *Ibid.*

102. *Sessional Papers*, 1914, no. 36, 58.

103. *Eastern Labour News*, 24 May 1913.

104. Bradwin, *The Bunkhouse Man*, 234.

105. *Ibid.*, 219-20. In this study the author has restricted his analysis to the Methodists and Presbyterians. Certainly the role of the Catholic Church in the bush camps among the Roman Catholic and Greek Catholic navvies would be a study of considerable importance.

106. Apparently the Methodist Church spent a quarter of a million dollars on its missions among the foreigners between 1896 and 1914. George Emery, "Methodists on the Canadian Prairies, 1896-1914" (Ph.D. thesis, University of British Columbia, 1970), 346. The Presbyterians were also very much committed. See Presbyterian Church in Canada, "Report of the Board of Home Missions," Acts and Proceedings of the General Assembly, 1900-1914 (United Church Archives). W.G. Smith, *Building the Nation: The Churches' Relation to the Immigrants* (Toronto, 1920), 65-77, 122-3, 176, 193.

107. PAC, Frontier College Papers, 1919 (known as the Reading Camp Association until 1919), A. Fitzpatrick to H.H. Fudger, president, Robert Simpson Co., November, 1919; Alfred Fitzpatrick, *University in Overalls* (Toronto, 1923), x, 13; Bradwin, *The Bunkhouse Man*, 14-17.

108. Frontier College Papers, 1912, A. Fitzpatrick to Dr. M.E. Church,

2 December 1912; *ibid.*, 1919, A. Fitzpatrick to H.H. Fudger, 19 November 1919.

109. *Ibid.*, 1912, A. Fitzpatrick to James Hales, 31 July 1912; *ibid.*, Fitzpatrick to J.B. Skeaff, manager, Bank of Toronto, 29 July 1912.

110. *Ibid.*, 1919, Wallace Robb, president of the Cannuck Supply Co., Montreal, 14 November 1919.

111. *Ibid.*, A. Fitzpatrick to R.H. Grant, Minister of Education, Ontario, 17 December 1919.

112. Ontario had been the first province to provide financial assistance, with amounts ranging from $25 in 1900 to $1,750,000 in 1912. *Ibid.*, A Fitzpatrick to R.H. Grant, 17 December 1919. In 1919 both Saskatchewan and Alberta indicated that they would provide $250 each. *Ibid.*, August Ball, Deputy Minister of Education, Saskatchewan, to Fitzpatrick, 5 November 1919; *ibid.*, John Ross, Deputy Minister of Education, Alberta, to Fitzpatrick, 1 February 1919.

113. Numerous authors urged government to move in this direction, most notably Woodsworth, *Strangers Within Our Gates*; J.T.M. Anderson, *The Education of the New Canadian* (London, 1918); Smith, *Building the Nation*; Bradwin, *The Bunkhouse Man*; and, of course, Fitzpatrick, *University in Overalls*.

114. Bradwin, *The Bunkhouse Man*, 134; *Proceedings of the Twenty-sixth Annual Session of the Trades and Labor Congress of Canada* (1910), 41. PAC, IB, f. 594511, no. 3, L.M. Fortier, Acting Superintendent of Immigration, to P.M. Draper, 1 September 1910.

115. *Proceedings of the Twenty-seventh Annual Session of the Trades and Labor Congress of Canada* (1911), 83.

116. Bradwin, *The Bunkhouse Man*, 234; Logan, *Trade Unions in Canada*, 299. An excellent account of the success achieved by the IWW among the unskilled labourers is Dubofsky, *We Shall Be All*, 24, 26, 151.

117. Stevens, *Canadian National Railways*, II, 194-5.

118. *British Columbia Federationist*, 5 April 1912, 1.

119. *Ibid.*, 8 June 1912, 1.

120. *Ibid.*; *The Western Wage Earner* (April, 1909), 4.

121. *British Columbia Federationist*, 29 June 1912, 1; *ibid.*, 22 June 1912, 1.

122. *Ibid.*

123. PAC, IB, f. 594511, no. 3, Donald Mann to W.D. Scott, 26 August 1912; *ibid.*, Timothy Foley to Robert Rogers, 27 March 1912.

124. *Labour Gazette* (August, 1912), 191.

125. *British Columbia Federationist*, 6 May 1912.

126. *Labour Gazette* (July, 1912), 79.

127. *Ibid.* (February, 1912), 721. See monthly reports, *Labour Gazette* (July, 1910-July, 1914).

128. In September 1914 the *Labour Gazette* reported that railway construction had "somewhat halted upon the advent of war . . . ." *Ibid*. (September, 1914), 332. Throughout the next twelve months continual reports were made on the number of unemployed navvies who had gravitated to cities such as Winnipeg, Edmonton, and Vancouver. *Ibid*. (October, 1914-September, 1915).

129. The amount of railway mileage in Canada more than doubled between 1896 and 1914. By 1921, only taking the Canadian Pacific system and the railways owned by the Dominion government, there were 35,452 miles of track. Stevens, *Canadian National Railways*, II, 17, 519.

III
The Working Class

In the first decades of the twentieth century, Canadian workers met monopoly capital head-on at their workplaces. The strength of the labour movement in the nineteenth century had been based on the skill and pride of the artisan. In the early twentieth century the process of mechanization, well underway in the second half of the nineteenth century, combined with new notions of managerial prerogative, which were ideologically termed "scientific management," to destroy the skilled workers' strength. Faced with the option of retreating into the ever-narrowing defence of craft unionism or turning to broader conceptions of working-class unity implicit in socialism and explicit in revolutionary industrial unionism, Canadian workers moved simultaneously in both directions. Many workers joined the various socialist movements of the day and embraced trade-union forms such as the Industrial Workers of the World (IWW) or later the One Big Union (OBU), which tried to organize all workers. Other skilled workers, however, such as most of the Hamilton moulders and machinists described here, turned instead to their craft union and to patterns of exclusion to preserve their privileged status in the labour market. While disastrous as a long-term strategy for the labour movement, this tactic often worked for individual workers. These two strategies, which appear as quite separate now, were not so clearly perceived by the workers of the period and many mixed elements of each. Historical writing which has starkly pitted the "central Canadian," conservative, craft-oriented Trades and Labor Congress against the western, radical, and industrial unionist IWW and OBU makes too much of this distinction. As the failed Hamilton machinists' strike of 1916 suggests, skilled workers could also rise to the challenge of monopoly capitalism. Indeed, their brother metal trades workers provided key leadership to many of the strikes in the militant struggles of spring and summer 1919. The defeats of that year, however, heralded the demise of narrow craft unionism which would succumb in the 1930's to the final successful drive of mass production workers to create industrial unions appropriate to monopoly-capital economic organization.

FURTHER READING:

On the Canadian trade-union movement in this period, see Robert Babcock, *Gompers in Canada* (Toronto, 1974); Stuart Jamieson discusses strikes during the twentieth century in *Times of Trouble* (Ottawa, 1968). On various aspects of western radicalism, see A. Ross McCormack, *Reformers, Rebels, and Revolutionaries: The Western Canadian Radical Movement, 1899-1919* (Toronto, 1977); David J. Bercuson, *Confrontation at Winnipeg: Labour, Industrial Relations and the General Strike* (Montreal, 1974); and Bercuson, *Fools and Wisemen* (Toronto, 1978). Among studies of the material conditions of Canadian workers are Terry Copp, *The Anatomy of Poverty: The Conditions of the Working Class in Montreal, 1897-1929* (Toronto, 1974), and Michael J. Piva, *The Condition of the Working Class in Toronto, 1900-1921* (Ottawa, 1979). For general discussions of the Canadian working-class experience, see Gregory S. Kealey, "Labour and Working-Class History in Canada: Prospects in the 1980s," *L/LT*, 7 (1981), 67-94; David J. Bercuson, "Through the Looking-Glass of Culture: An Essay on the New Labour History and Working-Class Culture in Recent Canadian Historical Writing," *L/LT*, 7 (1981), 95-112; and Bryan Palmer, "Classifying Culture," *L/LT*, 8/9 (1981/2), 153-83.

On general labour policy in the period, see Paul Craven, *"An Impartial Umpire": Industrial Relations and the Canadian State 1900-1911* (Toronto, 1980). On Maritimes' workers, see David Frank and Nolan Reilly, "The Emergence of the Socialist Movement in the Maritimes, 1899-1916," *L/LT*, 4 (1979), 85-113;

Nolan Reilly, "The General Strike in Amherst, Nova Scotia, 1919," *Acadiensis*, 9, 2 (1980), 56-72; and Ian McKay, "Strikes in the Maritimes, 1901-1914," *Acadiensis* (forthcoming).

Craig Heron is a member of the York University Department of History and is working on a book comparing the experiences of Hamilton, Sydney, and Sault Ste. Marie steel workers.

The Crisis of
the Craftsman:
Hamilton's Metal Workers
in the
Early Twentieth Century

by Craig Heron

I

"When you speak of 'skill,' do you mean 'ability'? What you term 'skill' or 'ability' might in reality be only dexterity." It was spring of 1916, and a panel of Royal Commissioners was seated in Hamilton's court house to hear evidence on unrest in the city's munitions industry. An unidentified machinist in the audience had just disrupted the proceedings by requesting permission to question his employer, who was on the witness stand. "Let us presume," the worker went on, "that a man comes into your employ who soon becomes proficient in operating a machine, from the fact that he is very bright, and becomes a piece worker, earning even more than your skilled men, such as toolmakers, would you call him a 'skilled' man?" Without waiting for a reply, the angry machinist turned to address the whole court room:

> I have seen men right in this shop who, by reason of doing the one thing day after day and week after week, the operation has become a part and parcel of their lives. . . . I have seen these piece workers move with the automatic precision and perform a certain operation with unerring facility. Yet you term these men 'skilled.' They are not skilled, . . . they have

From *Labour/Le Travailleur*, 6 (1980), 5-48. Abridged by author. Reprinted by permission.

become automatons. Their work requires no brain power, whereas the toolmaker requires both brain and brawn. He must have constructive ability. And you, sir (he continued with a wave of his arms towards the witness), know nothing about that.

The worker sat down to loud applause from "many tool-hardened hands." The voice of Hamilton's beleaguered craftsmen had been heard.[1]

In recent years labour historians have been increasingly fascinated with the lively history of the skilled stratum of the nineteenth-century working class, the artisans. Often colourful, articulate, tough-minded men, these craftsmen were not only leading actors in the emergence of a working class in the early years of the century; when they gave up their self-employed status and entered the "manufactory" to practise their craft under one employer's roof, they brought with them the accumulated traditions, values, and institutions of the pre-industrial era. A vibrant artisanal culture therefore continued to thrive in late nineteenth-century industry, where the skills of these men were indispensable to many sectors of production.

Artisanal culture had much broader dimensions than life in the workshops where the craftsmen toiled. They were confident of the social worth their skills bestowed upon them and expected to lead dignified, respectable lives. Central to their outlook on the world was a gritty spirit of independence and determination to resist subordination. In the workshops, and in society generally, they demanded for all men and women the maximum of personal liberty and freedom from coercion and patronage, and politically they became the staunchest proponents of egalitarian democracy. From employers they expected no interference with their traditional craft practices, which controlled the form and pace of production. Their "manhood," they insisted, demanded such treatment. The principal institutions of collective self-help which promoted and defended this artisanal life were, of course, their craft unions.

All of these social and ideological phenomena, however, rested on the craftsmen's continuing shop-floor power, and by the end of the nineteenth century that power was being challenged by employers who saw these men and their mode of work as serious obstacles to larger corporate strategies. This essay will concentrate simply on the workplace crisis facing these craftsmen, without further reference to its implications for working-class ideology, politics, and social life. It will deal with the skilled men in one Canadian city, Hamilton, Ontario, and, more specifically, with that city's largest group of craftsmen at the turn of the century, the metal workers. An analysis of the clash between artisanal culture and industrial capitalist rationality will bring into focus the ambivalence of the artisanal legacy for the working class in the early twentieth century. On the one hand, these workingmen battled valiantly against the more dehumanizing, authoritarian tendencies of modernizing industry; they levelled an intelligent and impassioned critique at the process of change in Canadian industrial life. On the other, in fighting back, they failed to transcend the sense of proud exclusiveness which their traditionally privileged position in the workplace engendered. For the most part, the response of these workers to the industrial age ushered in with the rise of corporate capitalism in Canada was an attempt to defend their shop-floor prerogatives, not to lead a broader working-class revolt. Craft pride tended to override class solidarity.

This essay will move from a description of the state of the two largest metal-working crafts at the end of the nineteenth century, the moulders and the machinists, to a discussion of the efforts of employers to transform their factories into more efficient, centrally managed workplaces, and finally to an assessment of the response of the craftsmen to these new conditions.

II

Metal-working shops, especially foundries, machine shops, and agricultural implement works, had predominated in Hamilton's industrial structure since the mid-nineteenth century. Particularly important were the stove-manufacturing shops, whose size and production made the city a national leader in the industry. The leading stove foundry, the Gurney-Tilden Company, was described in 1892 as "the largest industry of their kind in the Dominion."[2] It was in this industrial setting that Hamilton's artisans worked the metal into the wide range of products that won for Hamilton the epithet "The Birmingham of Canada."

Of the two most prominent groups of craftsmen in the city, the moulders could lay claim to the deepest roots in pre-industrial society. In fact, moulders liked to trace their ancient traditions to the biblical figure Tubal Cain. From their skilled hands came metal castings as diverse as stoves, machinery castings, and ornamental iron and brass work. Technological change had almost completely bypassed the foundry, which remained down to the end of the nineteenth century a classic "manufactory" of highly skilled craftsmen working in one employer's shop. A turn-of-the-century article in *Iron Age* emphasized that the craft "is learned almost entirely by the sense of feeling, a sense that cannot be transferred to paper. It is something that must be acquired by actual practice. A sense of touch plays such an important part in the construction of a mold that without it it is impossible to construct a mold with any reasonable expectation of success."[3] This sense was what craftsmen liked to call the "mystery" of their trade. With a few tools and the knowledge under his cap, the moulder prepared the moulds to receive the molten iron or brass. A mould began with a "pattern," usually wooden, in the shape of the finished casting, which was imbedded in sand. Preparing and "ramming" the sand (that is, pounding it firmly with iron-shod poles) required great care and precision so that when the pattern was drawn out a perfect mould remained to hold the molten metal. If a cast product was to have a hollow space, the moulder inserted a "core," a lump of specially prepared sand that had been carefully shaped and baked hard at the coremaker's bench (originally moulders made their own cores, but gradually a division of labour emerged). Once cool, the casting was shaken out of the sand and cleaned, to be ready for any finishing processes. The size of the objects to be cast ranged so widely that the moulder might work on a bench or prepare his moulds in great stretches of sand on the foundry floor.[4] "The jobs he undertook," recalled one observer of Canadian foundries, "were varied in the extreme, a single job sometimes entailing days of careful labor, and the work being given a finish in which the maker took pride."[5]

That pride also fed on the physical demands of the work, which was notoriously heavy, dirty, and unhealthy. One Hamilton moulder described the city's foundries as "the darkest and rottenest places in Hamilton, and so stuffy that you can hardly breathe." He claimed the shop he was working in was so dark "that he had had to use a torch to see what he was doing." Ontario's factory inspectors repeatedly criticized foundry working conditions for the thick, smoky air, the extremes of heat and cold, and the heavy, dangerous tasks required. An American study also found abnormally high rates of death by respiratory diseases among foundry workers.[6]

Passing from the foundry to the machine shop in, say, the Sawyer-Massey agricultural implement works was to cross the great divide of the Industrial Revolution, from the more primitive methods of handicraft to the clatter of complex machinery. Machinists were a much newer group of craftsmen, whose role in industry was little more than a century old by 1900; yet, despite their position at the centre of the machine age, they too had developed a workplace culture in the artisanal mode. When the peripatetic Royal Commission on the Relations of Labour and Capital opened its hearings in Hamilton early in 1888, an elderly machinist named William Collins appeared. A retired artisan with British training, Collins described himself as "a general workman": "I learned the whole art or mystery of mechanics – that is, so far as human skill, I suppose, could accomplish it, either wood, iron, brass, blacksmithing, or anything; I am one of the old school."[7] He was, in fact, a relic of that period in the late eighteenth and early nineteenth centuries when a millwright, as he was then known, was a highly valued mechanic whose manual skills and ingenuity in the construction of machinery made possible the mechanical innovations of the Industrial Revolution in Britain. By mid-century, however, the typical British machine-builder was less in the Collins mould and more often a skilled operator of metal-working machinery. The introduction of steam-powered devices, especially lathes and planers, had brought the old craft into a new, technically more sophisticated phase,[8] where an engineer or machinist would use a mechanized cutting tool to shape metal objects – anything from machinery parts to gun barrels – usually in manufacturing firms or railway shops. The tools of the trade might be any number of simple lathes, drills, planers, shapers, or slotters, as well as various devices for careful measurement of the cut.

Although William Collins might regret that mechanization had been "detrimental to the interest of the employé, inasmuch as the introduction of machinery reduced the labour required,"[9] individual manual skill did not disappear since most machine shop work still required the careful, trained hands of the craftsman. Machine tools simply facilitated precision.[10] Another Hamilton machinist, Joseph James Whiteley, emphasized before the same Royal Commission that running his planer demanded expertise: "There is no man who can run a machine properly after three years apprenticeship. I served my time seven years at Whitworth's, of Manchester, the finest shop in the world, and I found I had something else to learn."[11] Craft pride, in fact, was nurtured by the confidence that "the industrial world depended for its success largely on the skill and technical knowledge of the machinist."[12]

The indispensable skills of these craftsmen in the metal trades gave them a functional autonomy on the shop floor that curbed employer interference with their established work routines. But their craft unions were the effective bastions protecting their workplace traditions. Both the moulders and the machinists constructed elaborate trade-union constitutions that stipulated all rules and procedures covering recruitment into the craft through apprenticeship, wage or piece rates, hours of work, and daily work load. The full-time organizers who enforced the customary practices of the craft were in the service of the craft unions, which were taking a new lease on life with the return of prosperity in the late 1890's. Craft unionists were setting about to consolidate their workplace prerogatives within powerful continental organizations affiliated to the American Federation of Labor.[13] In Hamilton the Iron Molders' Union, Local 26, founded in 1860, was recognized as one of the strongest labour organizations in the city by the turn of the century.[14] The machinists had two weaker unions: the British-based Amalgamated Society of Engineers, dating back to 1851, and the International Association of Machinists, Lodge 414, first organized in 1900.[15]

These then were the two main groups of artisans comprising Hamilton's skilled metal workers. In the last half of the nineteenth century, the moulders and machinists were quite often employees of different firms, but by the turn of the century they more frequently worked in separate departments of larger corporations, where artisanal customs soon came into sharp conflict with the new imperatives of modern industry.

III

The 1890's marked a turning point in the work world of moulders and machinists. Over the next thirty years a transformation within metal-working factories swept away the artisanal culture of these workers which had flourished in the preceding decades. Technological and managerial innovations undermined and ultimately destroyed a work environment in which skilled craftsmen with indispensable expertise had presided over the pace and organization of the labour process.

The driving force behind this process of change sprang from the new shape of economic life in Canada. By the 1890's Hamilton's industrial life was being integrated into national and international markets which involved stiffer competition for the city's firms and the rise of increasingly large corporate enterprises. Hamilton not only participated in the Canadian merger movement in the pre-war decade, with the creation of such firms as the Steel Company of Canada and the Canadian Iron Corporation; it also opened its floodgates to branch plants of American giants like International Harvester and Canadian Westinghouse. These developments certainly increased both the scale of the average workplace in the city and the economic clout of employers and, perhaps more important, generated a sharpened concern about protecting profits against more powerful competition. Some of the city's oldest metal shops, especially the stove foundries, were particularly hard-pressed in this new environment.

With their eyes fixed on profit margins, corporate managers in Hamilton attacked labour costs on two fronts. The first, aggressive anti-unionism, was ultimately the prerequisite for the second, the restructuring of the work process. The shop-floor power of craftsmen that was consolidated in their unions was a constant threat to corporate planning of production. Before 1900 individual employers, and occasionally groups of them, challenged unions in the city with varying degrees of success, but after the turn of the century anti-unionism became a cornerstone of labour relations for the largest Hamilton firms. The city's two largest employers of skilled metal workers, in particular, had well-established reputations as union-busters before their arrival in Hamilton. International Harvester's predecessor companies had such an anti-labour record, dating from the 1880's, that the Hamilton labour movement mounted a vigorous and ultimately successful campaign to prevent the city fathers from granting the Deering company a bonus to locate in Hamilton.[16] Similarly in 1903 George Westinghouse, president of both the Canadian and American companies, engaged in a much publicized exchange with the American Federation of Labor president, Samuel

Gompers, over the question of unionizing his staff; he made it quite clear that this was one corporation which would tolerate no workers' organizations in its plants.[17] The Westinghouse management in Hamilton never departed from that position.

The strikes in Hamilton's metal-working plants over the three decades from the 1890's to the 1920's fell into a pattern of union resurgence and employers' counter-attack, in three periods of peak prosperity: 1899 to 1906, 1911 to 1913, and 1916 to 1919; and in most cases employers sought to use a strike as an occasion to drive out the union. Hamilton industrialists also participated in schemes to weaken the negotiating power of unions, like legislative restraints and promotion of immigration;[18] but probably more energy was directed to weakening the appeal of trade unionism through company-sponsored welfare programs, which not only weaned workers away from reliance on the benefit schemes of the unions but also promoted loyalty to the corporation. Profit-sharing, benefit and pension schemes, and recreation programs were introduced at the Steel Company of Canada, International Harvester, Canadian Westinghouse, Sawyer-Massey, and other large firms in the city before World War I and with new enthusiasm immediately after the war. In 1912 International Harvester and Canadian Westinghouse even undertook to pre-empt the social functions of trade unions and to promote craft pride within the confines of the company by inaugurating banquets of their most skilled machinists, the tool-makers. Seven years later International Harvester went so far as to launch an industrial council as an alternative form of "industrial democracy" to trade unionism. These corporations evidently saw themselves locked in a battle for the allegiance of their workers.[19]

Only the stove foundries provided a significant exception to this pattern of anti-unionism in Hamilton's metal-working industries. The similarity of the production process in this branch of moulding encouraged the stove founders to standardize their employment practices through a common front in their relations with their workers. Between 1902 and 1908 they abandoned their long-standing hostility to unions and began formal, province-wide collective bargaining with the International Molders' Union to produce common labour practices and wage rates in all shops.[20] The economic slump of 1907-09 and intensified competition from the United States, however, encouraged a return to the older, antagonistic form of labour relations. A strike of all the moulders in Hamilton's stove foundries in 1909[21] did not prevent the elimination of union controls in these shops until the resurgence of the union in the latter years of World War I. This branch of moulding, however, was obsolescent, as sheet metal increasingly replaced cast iron in household stoves.[22] Slowly this pocket of strength for the unionized craftsmen in the foundry trade dwindled into insignificance. The stove foundrymen's accommodation with the moulder's union, moreover, remained the exception, and employers in the city's metal-working factories made eradication of craft unionism among their workers the bulwark of their management strategies.

IV

Employers were not simply attempting to eliminate unions in order to push their workers harder; they were equally concerned about having the flexibility to reorganize the work process in order to rid themselves of their reliance on testy, independent-minded craftsmen whose union regulations kept the supply of new men and the pace of work strictly under control. After 1900 Hamilton employers' strategies fit into an emerging consensus about factory management in Canada. During the decade before World War I Canadian companies succumbed to the North American mania for more "system" in industrial organization.[23] The fascination with "systematic" management began to reach full flower in Canada after 1911, when American writers, notably Frederick W. Taylor and his school of "scientific management," were catching great public attention. These new management specialists advocated complex procedures for establishing "scientific" norms for the speed of work based on stop-watch measurement, along with incentive wage payment systems that both rewarded the fast worker and punished the laggard. A key tenet of the Taylor system was the centralization of all control over the production process in the hands of the managers through planning, routing, scheduling, and standardization.[24] The Canadian business press generally applauded these new plans. *Industrial Canada* concluded in 1914: "The experience of manufacturers seems to be that scientific management decreases a staff while it increases its efficiency. . . . Reports from firms on this continent show that scientific management has become practical."[25] Clearly, new ideas were in the air about how to run a factory.

Managers in Hamilton's metal-working industries used three

related tactics to pursue their goals of tightening their grip on the labour process, speeding up production, and reducing labour costs. Wherever possible the chief elements in a reorganization of production in the city's foundries and machine shops became narrowing the work of the skilled, upgrading labourers to become "handymen" who specialized in only one fragment of the process, and introducing new machinery. Since the restructuring of the labour process moved at different paces in the foundries and the machine shops, we will consider each in turn.

Foundrymen were well aware that skilled moulders could not be completely eliminated from the foundry. The machinery and jobbing shops in particular still needed the well-rounded craftsman who could prepare enormous castings for hydroelectric generators or any number of other diverse products. Wherever possible, especially in the stove foundries, the moulders' tasks were specialized. A moulder's work could be rigidly confined to the specific tasks requiring his expertise, while other repetitive or purely physical labour could be divided up among less skilled, lower-paid workers. Foundry work had always involved sundry unskilled labourers and moulders' helpers, at one time known as "bucks" or "berkshires," as well as a small stock of men whose experience was in small, non-union shops and who never served a proper union apprenticeship. All of these men would develop some familiarity with foundry practice without ever attaining full craftsmanship.[26]

International Harvester's Hamilton operation made full use of such unskilled help, especially new European immigrants, by organizing them into "gangs," each of which would perform one step in the moulding process. "The usual system," explained the *Canadian Foundryman*, "is to divide the help in the foundry into ramming, finishing and coring gangs." The gangs could also be organized side by side to stimulate increased production through competition. "Each man made part of a machine," reported the local union president, James W. Ripley, in 1910, "and they had to work like Trojans to keep up. No ordinary mechanic could work that way, because he could not stand the pace. . . . The foreigners were rugged men, but even they did not last long." The company also hired women to work as coremakers. A reporter who visited their workroom in 1907 was struck by the accelerated pace of production: "the girls were working apparently for dear life."[27] Both immigrants and female labourers came to their jobs without any well-established customs of what constituted a "fair day's work" in the foundry, and both groups tended to leave the work force quickly.

This kind of subdivision of the moulder's tasks, however, was really only made possible by increased mechanization of foundry work. In particular, it required the introduction of the moulding machine. A 1908 article in *Canadian Machinery* described the advantages of this new device over the foibles of human producers:

> The molding machine is purely and simply a mechanical molder and differing from its human competitor can work the whole twenty-four hours without stopping, knows no distinctions between Sundays, holidays and any ordinary day, requires as its only lubricant a little oil, being in fact abstinent in all other matters, has no near relatives dying at awkward moments, has no athletic propensities, belongs to no labor organization, knows nothing about limitation of output, never thinks of wasting its owner's time in conversation with its fellow machines. Wars, rumors of war and baseball scores, have no interest for it and its only ambition in life is to do the best possible work in the greatest possible quantity.[28]

Actually, there was no one single machine, but rather a range of machinery with different applications. The earliest were hand-operated devices: the "squeezer," which pressed or "rammed" the sand into the mould by the use of a lever, and the stripping plate, which was used to draw the pattern out of the mould. Experiments began in the late 1880's to apply power to these processes and to combine the ramming and pattern-drawing; a further refinement was known as "jolt ramming" whereby the mould was dropped sharply by pneumatic pressure to pack the sand. Each year the American Foundrymen's Association convention featured more and more complex equipment on display. As well as specific devices for preparing the mould, North American foundrymen were soon fitting up their shops with a host of new labour-saving equipment: mechanical sand-mixers, conveyors to move the sand around the shop, tumbling barrels and pneumatic hammers and chippers for cleaning the castings, pneumatic ramming devices, and electric travelling cranes which could carry the iron to the mould or move moulds or castings easily.[29] The impact of all these additional devices was to lighten some of the burdensome work in the foundry and to reduce the time necessary for many of the ancillary tasks to the main arena of moulding.

Mechanization might have meant lighter work, but it also resulted in more castings per day. An Ontario factory inspector found that the men who operated the new machines had "to go lively, as the machines are generally speeded up to the limit." Margaret Loomis Stecker, a contemporary American student of moulding machinery whose sympathies lay with mechanization, noted that

> molding machines, instead of being labor-saving devices in the sense that they made easier the work of the molder, often necessitated a material increase in effort by the man who operated them. Though time was actually saved in making any mold, the fact that more molds were produced meant that there was more sand to shovel, more molds to lift, more molds to pour, more castings to shake out.

She concluded that "the molding-machine operator became himself a mere machine, with none of the variety to his work which characterized the skilled handworker."[30]

Hamilton's foundries were not slow to adapt. The two biggest, International Harvester and Canadian Westinghouse, were, in fact, pioneers in the field. Henry Pridmore, a leading manufacturer of moulding machines, had begun his experiments in 1886 in the McCormick Harvester works in Chicago where the company introduced the new machinery in a successful attempt to drive out the local moulders' union. A company executive later boasted: "Their great foundries and their novel molding machinery were the admiration of the iron world." Not surprisingly then, a visitor to the new Hamilton Harvester plant's foundry in 1904 discovered moulding machinery in each moulder's stall.[31] The Canadian Westinghouse plant was similarly in the vanguard of managerial innovation. The superintendent of its foundry was David Reid, "one of the most prominent foundrymen of America." His extensive American experience had included managing a foundry where he had been responsible for some major restructuring of the work process: "By introducing modern methods here, such as molding machines, and dividing labor, whereby the molder practised the art of molding and nothing else, the melt was increased from 12 or 15 tons daily to between 50 and 60 tons."[32] Reid's influence, however, was not restricted to the Westinghouse foundry; in 1905 he became the president of the Associated Foundry Foremen of America, a scion of the American Foundrymen's Association, and launched a Hamilton branch. The purpose of the organization was "education" for better foremanship, and its meetings were devoted to discussions of more efficient foundry practice.[33]

Mechanization in other machinery foundries in Hamilton seems to have proceeded quickly. Gartshore-Thompson and the Berlin Machine works were mechanized as early as 1908, Bowes-Jamieson by 1911, and Brown-Boggs, Dominion Steel Castings, and the Hamilton Malleable Iron Company by 1913.[34] The stove foundries showed some interest in the new machinery as well. Although this was not an arena where the moulding machine had been expected to make much impact,[35] the committee of the American Stove Founders' Defense Association which investigated the new technology in 1908 concluded that "All stove patterns can be molded with some form of machine or device now in use."[36] These discussions coincided with the 1909 assault of Ontario's stove founders on the moulders' union. That year the *Spectator* reported that stove manufacturers wanted to determine the value of the moulding machines and that "if they cannot secure the co-operation of the moulders in trying them out, they will have to use other labor." The strike-bound Gurney-Tilden Company introduced its first mechanical devices – a compressed-air moulding machine and several squeezers – along with Italian labourers, and soon precipitated a strike of their scab moulders, who promptly joined the union.[37] By the 1920's most of the city's foundries had introduced a full range of mechanical devices. The machinery at the Hamilton Stove and Heater Company so impressed a foundry trade journalist in 1920 that he burbled, "Verily, the molding machine only requires to be taught to talk, when it will be perfect." By 1928 the *Canadian Foundryman* could gloat over the sweeping changes since the pre-war years:

> Twenty years ago an unskilled man in the foundry would not have been permitted to handle even a slick, being only allowed to assist in the ramming of big jobs perhaps, lifting or similar work. Now unskilled labor can step into an up-to-date foundry and within a few days perform a task equal to that of the skilled molder, due to present day equipment.[38]

There was, nonetheless, a continuing need for the manual skill of expert moulders. An article on the Otis-Fensom Elevator Company's Hamilton plant pointed out that "within most cases only a few pieces being required at one time from one pattern, good mechanics and the old system of hand moulding seems [*sic*] preferable." As the depression began to lift in the mid-1920's foundrymen undertook extensive discussions about where to find the skilled help they required now that the apprenticeship system was in disarray. It seems, however, that skilled moulders were needed in relatively small numbers.[39]

By the 1920's, therefore, the role of the artisan in the foundry had been reduced to only those few tasks which could not be turned over to machines and handymen. Skilled workers had certainly not been banished from the industry, and their union survived down to the end of World War I on the basis of their continuing importance in the production process, however much that may have been eroded and confined. But they no longer wielded their artisanal control mechanisms for setting the pace of production as they had thirty years before. As early as 1909, Josiah Beare, a young union moulder in Hamilton, told a workmate: "Jim, I have worked too hard in my time; the pace is set too fast for the average man to keep up, and I am a nervous wreck;" he died six weeks later of "heart trouble."[40]

The technology and management of machine shops went through a similar, perhaps even more dramatic evolution. In the second half of the nineteenth century the arms and sewing machine industries had been in the forefront of technological experimentation in British and North American machine shop work. One of the most important developments had been the turret lathe, a machine mounted with a cluster of tools which could be applied to a piece of work in a sequence of operations without adjusting the material in the lathe (though until these processes were automated, the workman's manual skill was still required). The other great innovation was the milling machine, a device with a set of rotating cutting tools for planing, curving, or otherwise shaping the metal, which required less individual skill in the hands of the operator. From the 1890's onward, in response to the mass production demands of, first, bicycle manufacturers and, later, automobile makers, the tendency in mechanical innovation was for increasingly sophisticated, specialized tools with more automation in their operation. The introduction of electric motors also greatly increased flexibility in machine shop work, and, as in the foundry, mechanization came to include new cranes and overhead tracks to lighten and speed up handling. "In general," an historian of the industry has suggested, "the trend of machine tool development was toward reducing the amount of physical effort and skill required to control tools while at the same time making it possible to rapidly produce work of high quality."[41]

In the closing years of the last century the industry was presented with an opportunity for yet another technological leap which would revolutionize machine shop practice. In 1880 a young mechanical engineer, Frederick W. Taylor, began a scientific study to develop a new and stronger form of steel for machine cutting tools. Twenty-six years later he took the annual meeting of the American Society of Mechanical Engineers by storm with his paper, "On the Art of Cutting Metals" (reprinted the next month in *Canadian Machinery*).[42] The use of this so-called "high-speed steel" allowed cutting speeds to be increased enormously, resulting in higher rates of production ranging from 50 to 400 per cent.[43] As a Canadian business journalist explained in 1910, "All the radical changes in machine tool practice in the past few years have been the result of the introduction of high speed steel."[44]

The widespread adoption of the new cutting steel followed from the insistent demand for greater output per machine. It is not surprising, therefore, that at the same time the machine shop should have been a leading industrial laboratory for new managerial experiments to rationalize and intensify the work process. It was no accident that Taylor should have been responsible for both the new technology of high-speed steel and the new school of scientific management; both aimed at increasing the output of labour at a lower cost per product.

The use of unskilled labour was possible on machine tools which incorporated automatic features, but these mechanisms were installed only gradually. A more common practice for reducing labour costs became subdivision of labour, using handymen as specialists on one simple machine that performed part of the work on a product. A 1913 survey of the industry in Canada indicated how far the process had advanced:

Modern methods of manufacturing are responsible for limiting the employment of men to specific operations only, and pursuit of the plan is making it hard to secure all-round machinists. Young men come into the factory and soon acquire the necessary skill to become proficient drill press operators or milling machine operators. They are able to earn fairly good wages in a shorter space of time than if they served the necessary term of apprenticeship to become competent all-round machinists.[45]

World War I accelerated this trend. Almost every metal-working plant in the city reopened and converted all or part of its production to filling large munitions contracts with Allied governments, mostly for shells. Many thus came to be engaged for the first time in the mass production of identical products. In the face of a severe labour shortage, these firms began to subdivide labour more extensively, using workers with no machining experience to operate simple "single-purpose" equipment which made only one of the series of cuts required on the shell. By the end of the war nine-tenths of the country's shell plants were using this specialized machinery.[46] These simplified procedures facilitated the introduction of unskilled women workers into the shell shops, which the Imperial Munitions Board's Labour Department began to encourage toward the end of 1916. A special employment bureau for women was opened in Hamilton in January 1917 in order to funnel more labour into the factories.[47]

Automation and subdivision of labour, of course, did not sweep aside all skill requirements. Much work, especially of the less specialized kind, continued to be done on machinery that required the touch of the craftsman. And, as one writer stressed, "the use of automatically controlled machines increases the need of skilful supervision and of skilled men for their construction and repair." This latter group included the emerging elite of the machinists' trade, the toolmakers, who prepared the jigs and dies for use on machines handled by the less skilled.[48]

If some skill was still required, managers wanted to apply it as intensively as possible. One of the earliest tactics was doubling the workload by requiring a machinist to run two machines at once, a course which International Harvester followed in 1904. But the issue of operating two machines seems to have declined in importance for the machine-shop managers once high-speed steel had made its impact.[49] Moreover, across North America the two-machine issue was being eclipsed by the ever more common wage-payment schemes based on piecework, which machine-shop owners and managers were installing from the 1890's onward.[50] Since the speed of work in the shop still depended largely on the speed of the individual machine operator, industrialists turned to payment by the piece as an incentive for each worker to produce more each day in the hopes of higher wages and as a goad to competitiveness between shopmates.

It is difficult to document specifically how extensively Hamilton industrialists adopted these new wage incentives, but in the years before World War I the city's machinists were certainly denouncing such plans. In February 1913 workers in the meter assembly department at Canadian Westinghouse objected to "a change in the method of giving out work and the consequent adjustment in the piece work prices," and simultaneously workers in the punch department denounced time-clocks installed to keep closer track of their work. The spontaneous strikes which resulted in both cases quickly petered out.[51] In his first report as the machinists' business agent in 1913 Richard Riley noted: "Mr. Taylor's system of scientific shop management is in use in some shops here. In one case, two cuts in piecework have taken place recently. A great many of the men don't know what they are getting until they get their pay envelope."[52] While it seems unlikely that pure and simple Taylorism was introduced in the city, at least some parts of the new management ideas were finding their way into the plants.

Opportunities quickly opened up during the war, under the pressure of munitions orders and labour shortages, for more managerial experimentation to speed up and rationalize production. A Hamilton employer of over 1,000 munitions workers claimed in 1916 that "There is no industrial system which brings out individual value so well as the piece system;" and Richard Riley reported that almost all shell work used the system.[53] In fall 1915 *Canadian Machinery* revealed how one shrapnel shell factory had increased its daily output from 800 to 2,700, largely as a result of "the efforts and ability of the company's executives in providing labor saving devices, improved machining methods, rebuilding machines, developing chute systems and otherwise keeping up every detail of the work to the last notch of efficiency."[54] Speed-up was under way in the machine shops as never before.

New technology and new schemes of management, therefore, set off what contemporaries called a "revolution" in the machine shop, and by the 1920's the machinists' craft had been fundamentally altered. G.L. Sprague, principal of the Hamilton Technical School, noted in 1921 what few opportunities remained for the highly skilled man:

> Modern manufacturing methods have broken down standards in the machinist trades. Only in the tool room and repair departments are found men who could classify as all-round machinists. The rank and file of men operating machines in what is known as the metal trades are merely machine tenders, operators, and specialists, according to the mastery they possess in producing on some particular machine.[55]

Outside of the toolrooms, repair departments, foremen's offices, and the small railway shops in the city, the day of the artisan in the machine shop was gone.

V

The profound changes of these years did not proceed smoothly or without resistance from the craftsmen who were being displaced. Through their craft organizations they voiced an eloquent critique of the major industrial trends of the age. In fact, their all-round knowledge of the work process made them the most informed critics of the period. The editor of the *Iron Molders' Journal* had pointed out as early as 1897 how the benefits of the new metal-working machinery so often did not extend to the workers:

> In a properly constituted society these innovations and improvements would be hailed with pleasure, as according to mankind further immunity from arduous toil in supplying his wants, but under present conditions the worker has learned too well that progress in this direction means further degradation and poverty for him.[56]

The machinists' union was just as unhappy with the new techniques of workshop management; its constitution denounced the "pernicious" piecework system, which it saw as responsible for "cultivating man's selfish nature to the extent of losing sight of the rights of his brother workman." Similarly the IAM's Canadian vice-president, James Somerville, argued:

When we say piece-work and task-work has [*sic*] the tendency to destroy the finer sensibilities in men, we know what we are talking about, and the world will yet give us credit for loftier motives than restriction of output. Touch the mainstring of the human heart and show an enlightened conscience where this accursed competitive system is leading to, and it is beyond you or I to conceive what the result will be.[57]

There was a general fear, here as in other trades, that increased output would result in cuts in piece rates, and widespread concern about speed-up. In 1903 the union made a last desperate attempt to halt the spread of the system by forbidding machinists to work "by the piece, premiums, task, merit or contract systems," under the penalty of expulsion, but much of the membership failed to conform. The union nonetheless continued to resist these innovations, and in 1909 the IAM president reported that at least 50 per cent of the strikes fought during the preceding year grew out of the employers' attempts to introduce piecework: "yet we can not credit ourselves with preventing the growth of this system, because, in my opinion, it is largely on the increase."[58] During a machinists' organizing drive, a front-page article in the Hamilton *Labor News* conveyed the local workers' indignation at how far these new managerial initiatives had gone: "The 'one man two machines,' the 'Taylor,' 'Scientific,' 'Premium,' 'piecework' and other systems introduced in the metal shops, are making of men what men are supposed to make of metals: machines."[59]

Perhaps the craftsmen's most strident critiques of modern industry percolated through their persistent campaign for shorter hours of work. Not only did skilled metal workers raise this issue in virtually every confrontation with their employers, culminating in the post-war demand for an eight-hour day; the question of shorter hours was also one of the few workplace issues injected into politics. Hamilton's Independent Labor Party stalwart in the Ontario legislature, Allan Studholme, repeatedly introduced bills to establish a legal eight-hour day, and the buoyant Ontario ILP which emerged in 1917 entrenched a shorter-hours plank in its platform.[60] In fact, the eight-hour day had become the leading concern of the entire Canadian labour movement by the time of the convening of the National Industrial Conference in Ottawa in September 1919.[61] In an age when employers were straining their imagination for new ways to increase the workload required each hour, in order to speed up production and cheapen labour costs, skilled workers in Hamilton, as elsewhere in Canada, fought to control how long they would have to labour at the new pace. As a union moulder asserted in 1921, "A working man appreciates life just as much as anyone else does and he should not be expected to slave so that others could have comfort."[62]

As an alternative to the rationalizing tendencies of corporate capitalism, these craftsmen asserted the less authoritarian, more decentralized, craft-dominated routines of the immediate past, which company managers were seeking to root out. Their strategy of opposition, therefore, was to attempt to re-establish the control mechanisms of the crafts over the metal-working factories, by compelling employers to adopt their "schedules" setting out the conditions of employment. They clung tenaciously to their craft unionism and made no substantial efforts to broaden their membership base and draw in their less skilled workmates.

The moulders, of all the metal trades workers, probably had most to lose, since their union and its traditions were so well entrenched in Hamilton at the turn of the century. In the fifteen years after 1905, the stove moulders fought one major strike, which has already been described, and the machinery and jobbing moulders five more. In prosperous periods their value to employers in the booming local economy won for them verbal agreements for wage increases and tacit acceptance of the craftsmen's shop practices; but in each period employers promptly fought back against these union incursions. In May 1919, with unemployment in the foundries mounting steadily, the foundrymen, in Hamilton and other Canadian cities, dug in their heels to resist the union's new demand for an eight-hour day and another wage hike. The Hamilton Employers' Association, formed in 1916, joined hands with Toronto employers to fight the metal trades unions. Once again their refusal to budge kept their shops "open" until depression, which settled in again in 1920, eroded the moulders' bargaining strength.[63] This time, however, the defeat seems to have been permanent; only two of the machinery firms gave in early in 1920, and one of these, the Hamilton Foundry Company, drove out the union in 1925.[64] Moreover, in 1920 the employers consolidated their strength in a large new open-shop organization, the Canadian Founders' Association (renamed the Canadian Founders' and Metal Trades'

Association a few months later), whose commissioner, C.W. Burgess, kept up a belligerent anti-union campaign well into the 1920's.[65] A *Canadian Foundryman* editorial caught the tone of the employers' attempts to roll back the advances workers had made during the war: "What is more important . . . than the readjustment of wage rates is that the workmen agree to remove the restrictions upon output which have been a crying evil in the period now drawing to a close."[66]

Before World War I the machinists' organizations in Hamilton had considerably less success than the moulders in stemming the tide of change in their working lives. In 1917 Hamilton business agent Richard Riley had to admit that "for the past fifteen years in the majority of shops in this city the machinists have not dared to admit they belonged to the IA of M, and employers did as they pleased with them."[67] This record of failure was not always the result of inertia. A province-wide organizing campaign begun early in 1912 generated a spurt of local activity, including weekly mass meetings and home visitations. A new schedule was drafted to be presented to the city's employers, demanding a nine-hour day, higher wages, and a re-establishment of craft controls. In the first article of their new schedule the machinists insisted that "Helpers or handy men shall not be allowed to perform any work designated as machinists' work," and that a four-year apprenticeship system should be reintroduced, with no more than one apprentice for every five machinists employed in any one shop.[68] By summer 1913, as some of Hamilton's largest firms began laying off staff in the first wave of the mass unemployment that was to ensue, Riley indicated how little headway the campaign to re-establish craft hegemony in the industry had made:

> The average machinist who works ten hours per day, which is the rule in this district, and who during that ten hours has a speeder standing over him, or the man who has to work all day at top speed to make $3.25, has not energy enough left to drag his weary limbs to an open meeting or to discuss trades unionism if you call upon them [*sic*].[69]

The wartime boom in Hamilton's machine shops, however, shifted the advantage to the machinists. By April 1915 Riley could report that all IAM members in the city were back at work, and indeed before long a severe shortage of qualified machinists was attracting more craftsmen to the city.[70] The machinists' value to the industrial life of the city, and of the country, reached new heights. So too, however, did their discontent with their working conditions. For the craftsmen working in these munitions plants the wartime labour process was clearly an intensification of pre-war patterns. Initially they found that the new burst of productive activity had made little difference to the long-standing policy of low wages and long hours. "Some of the firms are taking advantage of the unorganized state of the machinists," Riley reported in 1915, "by paying them starvation wages and working them overtime and on Sundays for straight time," and justifying their actions with appeals to patriotism. One Hamilton machinist railed against this situation:

> The workers are by no means less loyal than the manufacturers, and if the capitalist were to contribute his industry and raw material absolutely free or at cost, the worker would be the first to follow, but since they are making fat profits out of the dire needs of the government, we workers should at least receive our share, a living wage.[71]

As more unskilled machine-tenders were hired, the wage question took on a new twist for the skilled machinist and toolmaker. Thanks to long hours at piecework and the accelerated rate of production, many of these new workers were soon taking home enormous pay packets.[72] Many of the skilled men, often working at straight hourly rates, resented the erosion of the wage differential that had always symbolized their value to industry. When asked why he was dissatisfied with his working conditions, one Hamilton machinist told a Royal Commission in spring 1916: "Because, sir, there are other men on single operations who make a lot more than I do." Another complained: "Many men are running machines now who were farm laborers some time ago . . . and they make as much money as I do." The editor of *Canadian Machinery* reported that these newcomers to the machine shop "after a few days of preliminary training were receiving three, four and even five times what they earned before, while the mechanics and toolmakers about the shop who told these men what to do and set the machines in order that they could serve, were forced to work at less than half the wage."[73]

The local IAM lodge and ASE branch lost no time in organizing regular mass meetings to sign up hundreds of disgruntled ma-

chinists,[74] and on 1 April 1916 the IAM circulated to all the city's
metal shops a new schedule of wages, hours, and working conditions for machinists. This new document, like its 1912
predecessor, was a blueprint for reimposing rigid union policing
of working procedures and reasserting the hegemony of the
craftsman over the city's machine shops. An appeal to artisanal
pride had been a keynote of the union's organizing campaign; in
a speech to Hamilton machinists, organizer McCallum said:

> it was not to the credit of skilled machinists who had to spend
> years of apprenticeship and large sums of money for proper
> tools, to be working almost for laborers' wages and long
> hours. He declared that if printers, masons and bricklayers,
> and other building trades worked but eight hours a day,
> machinists at least should work no more.[75]

Hamilton's metal trades employers were soon alarmed at this
resurrection of craft unionism in their midst. Individual skir-
mishes with union organizers gave way to a united front after the
local branch of the Canadian Manufacturers' Association struck
a special committee to co-ordinate a response.[76] As employer
hostility stiffened and a showdown seemed imminent, the federal government intervened promptly by appointing a three-man
Royal Commission to investigate munitions workers' grievances
in Hamilton and Toronto. The Commission's hearings held in
early May gave the machinists the public forum they wanted to
carry on their arguments with their bosses. Riley ushered in a
parade of worker witnesses and was allowed to cross-examine
company officials.[77] The sessions often turned into extended
debates over the nature of work in the city's machine shops, including conflicting views on a worker's productivity in a nine-
hour day. All the resentment against the previous decades'
changes in their workplace experience bubbled up in the munitions workers' testimony.

It quickly became clear that, while most workers wanted
higher wages to meet the rising cost of living, the union demand
for a nine-hour day focused on the crux of their discontent. A
Herald report on the hearings highlighted this concern:

> The evidence of the employees was to the effect that the men
> are dissatisfied mainly because the hours of work are ten to
> the day; that the machines are run at a higher speed than they

were in times of peace, and that the consequent strain on their constitutions was too great to permit them to work ten hours a day. Although the average machinist receives about 37½ cents per hour, a considerable advance compared with some years ago, still the men contend that owing to the strain of production with machines speeded up to the limit, a man's life as a machinist or munition worker contains few attractions aside from the weekly or monthly pay envelope. [78]

The employers nonetheless continued their resistance to a shorter working day, correctly fearing a precedent for post-war industry, and rejected the Commission's final recommendation in favour of the nine-hour principle. [79] Early in June, thirty-eight of the city's leading firms gave birth to the Employers' Association of Hamilton, which announced in a series of strident newspaper advertisements that its purpose was "to see that there shall be no improper restriction of output, and that no conditions shall arise to prevent any workman from earning a wage proportionate to his productive capacity." After several weeks of frantic lobbying by federal and municipal officials to head off the inevitable confrontation, some 1,500 machinists and unskilled munitions workers walked out on June 12, demanding implementation of the Royal Commission's recommendations. According to the *Spectator* the strike was "a contest of the open shop against the one operated under union regulations . . . each is fighting for what it regards as principle." [80] The strike, however, had floundered by the end of the summer, in the face of government censorship and renewed rivalry between the IAM and ASE. [81]

Summer 1916 was thus an historic moment in the evolution of the machinists' craft in Hamilton. War conditions had given both the pressing need and the collective strength to protest changes in their working lives which, while more intense under war production, were simply the culmination of two decades of industrial practice. These artisans of the machine shop were attempting to reassert their old craft control over the work process in which they were involved and in so doing met the combined resistance of Hamilton's manufacturers, who could not countenance such a rupture in the new work routines they had been developing. Never again were the Hamilton machinists able to mount such a challenge. While several firms in the city eventually did concede the shorter working day before the end of the war, it was in each case a gesture meant to pacify their workers without conceding any power to the craftsmen's union.[82] And when industrial unrest in Canada was reaching a peak in spring 1919, Hamilton's machinists were in no position to join the general strikes of metal trades workers in several other centres.[83]

The depression of the early 1920's left little chance for a quick recovery of union strength. But for the first time since the 1890's the return of prosperity in the late 1920's saw no revival of unionism in the machine shops in Hamilton, as elsewhere in Canada. Only in the railway shops was the IAM able to hold on to any significant membership. In 1927 IAM Canadian vice-president James Somerville indicated that organizing efforts had not yet "developed anything to create excitement or to write home about," and a year later he declaimed: "The average wage paid machinists in Canada off the railways is a disgrace."[84] The failure of the machinists to rise phoenix-like from the depression did not simply indicate inertia or apathy. The craft had now been so thoroughly altered that there was no longer a basis on which to build a viable craft union movement in Hamilton's metal-working factories.

The moulders and machinists showed little inclination to re-orient their defensive strategies by uniting with other skilled metal workers or with their less skilled workmates. Within the ranks of the moulders, the men in the stove shops and those in the machinery and jobbing shops went their separate ways, with no hint of a sympathetic strike. In 1913 Hamilton's moulders made their first and only attempt to organize machine-tenders in the foundry and to set a fixed rate for their work – in effect, to extend the union's extensive work regulations to cover moulding-machinery work. But the 1913 strike ended in defeat for the moulders, and they undertook no further efforts to organize the less skilled.[85] Similarly the wartime experience of skill dilution did little to alter the traditional craft pride of Hamilton's machinists. By the 1916 strike the union had begun to include specialists in its membership but not the less skilled shell workers. The local business agent heaved a sigh of relief when the munitions industry shut down: "We say good-bye with great pleasure to the shell operators and hope they will never have another opportunity or excuse for being caught in a machine shop." And rather than turning to a new organizing strategy with a wider membership base, the union took up the cause of a new category of craftsmen outside the factories, the auto mechanics.[86]

There were some halting attempts towards metal trades solidarity, usually spearheaded by the machinists (whose international union after 1912 was committed to socialism and to some form of craft amalgamation as a step toward industrial unionism[87]); but in Hamilton none of these efforts ever effectively broke the bounds of craft exclusiveness. A Metal Trades Council formed in 1910 perished in the pre-war depression, only to be revived again for a year in 1919-20. In each period of its existence the council seems to have been little more than a forum for the exchange of information and the clarification of jurisdictions, although in 1920 a joint organizing drive was undertaken under the council's sponsorship.[88] In 1913 the moulders' representatives in the AFL Metal Trades Department squelched an effort to use these local councils as general strike committees against one or more employers.[89] True to form, the moulders' union in Hamilton refused to join the revived council in 1919.[90] A more overt effort at collective action among the city's metal workers began in spring 1918 when the IAM and ASE formed an Amalgamation Committee. The committee's leading propagandist, Fred Flatman, campaigned vigorously among the other metal-working crafts to generate interest in the fusion idea, winning at least a lukewarm reception, but this initiative collapsed when Flatman and several other militants opted for the short-lived Metal Workers' Unit of the One Big Union.[91] In spring 1919 *Labor News* editor Walter Rollo reminded his readers that there were "thousands of handy men, specialists, grinders, helpers and laborers working in the big East End plants with no organization at all."[92] Perhaps the only significant departure from narrow craft lines was the insistent demand for shorter hours, which arguably would benefit all workers in an industry.

This reluctance of the craftsmen to embrace the unskilled was fed from two directions. The most evident was the nativist bias of the predominantly Anglo-Saxon skilled workers against the thousands of European immigrants who were swelling the ranks of the unskilled in Hamilton's factories in this period. In 1913, for example, a "foreigner" hired by Westinghouse to work in the coremaking department of this foundry was beaten up at quitting time by two English-speaking coremakers, and, when the pair was fired for the assault, their fellow-workers marched out in sympathy.[93] Ethnicity was certainly one of the most effective divisive factors in the Hamilton working class. The other source was a subtler strand in artisanal culture. Craftsmen placed a high value on the self-reliant, independent man of principle who stood by his craft organization. Appeals to non-unionists were usually exhortations to individual conscience and a sense of "manhood." In 1914 the local *Labor News* described "a sort of unwritten law in the Hamilton Trades and Labor Council not to waste much time in giving any aid to any class of wage earners who were persistent in refusing to aid themselves . . . who will not recognize the principle of self help and unite and maintain an organization."[94] The artisans' moral criteria for the independent, self-disciplined character of a good worker apparently blinded them to the concrete difficulties faced by the unskilled in organizing on the job.

The limitations of craft culture, however, do not seem to have been the only obstacle to class solidarity among these skilled men. By the early twentieth century the unions' older notion of "brotherhood" in the workshop was competing with an increasingly potent alternative view of quick economic gain among the rank and file. Several factors intensified this more self-centred, instrumental approach to work. During these years great hordes of workers, especially young men, were setting out from Britain, the United States, or some Canadian town or city in search of work and high wages, always moving in a restless spirit of adventure. The machinists recognized a whole category of such craftsmen known as "boomers," who pursued new jobs and high pay across the continent. The 1916 Royal Commission heard several of these men; one from Buffalo hit the road from Hamilton "just for a change" and another arrived from Detroit "just to see Hamilton."[95] Many of them were keen union activists who carried their union principles through many shop doors. But many, especially those recently off the boat from Britain, were far more interested in the comparatively higher wages they could suddenly earn.[96]

Of course, none of this behaviour was entirely new in the early twentieth century; a great migration of workers around the North American continent was a familiar pattern in the nineteenth century. But two factors combined to make the pattern more compelling after 1900. Both the soaring cost of living and the boom-and-bust cycles of the Canadian economy in this period, with three severe depressions over thirty years, no doubt contributed to a mentality of making hay while the sun shone. Many metal workers probably welcomed the opportunity to swell their pay packets through the new wage-incentive plans. A contributor to the machinists' *Bulletin* in 1916 surveyed with

quiet consternation the boost that wartime production practices
had given to this more materialistic view of work:

> The lust for gain has defeated all reason, and with little or no
> obstruction in the path of the producer it develops into the
> survival of the fittest. To excuse the situation on the ground
> that the times are exceptional and everybody should do his ut-
> termost during the crisis may be acceptable, but the fact re-
> mains that the contract or piece work system has received an
> impetus that a hundred years of oration on its evils will not
> eliminate.
>   . . . [A]s long as it is possible for men to increase their daily
> earnings by the adoption of any system whatsoever that
> system is likely to remain.[97]

Feeling the double pinch of inflation and uncertain employment,
and offered the chance to earn more money, the proud artisan
with workplace traditions to defend could all too easily become
the hustler in search of a fast buck. There is, of course, no way
to gauge how widespread such an attitude became, but craft
unionists certainly recognized it as a crippling factor in defending their principles.

VI

> Twenty years ago a molder was at home with his slick and
> trowel, but place the good mechanic of those years in the
> modern foundry and he would feel like a "fish out of
> water."[98]

In 1928 most observers would have agreed with this Canadian
business journalist that the heyday of the craft worker in
Canada's metal-working industries had passed. A new, rationalized, more highly mechanized mode of work had emerged to
confine the skilled metal worker to small, unspecialized shops on
the periphery of modern industry or to a sharply limited role in
the process of mass production. On the one hand, in the case of
both the moulders and the machinists, the craftsmen found large
areas of their traditional work mechanized and divided up
among less skilled labourers. On the other, a few "well-rounded
mechanics" survived inside large-scale industry, but these crafts-

men found their work narrowed, circumscribed, and intensified. In this new role in production there was increased pressure on the skilled men to apply themselves strictly to work that required their technical know-how. The old artisanal sense of working a product through all or most of its stages of production to completion was lost. And the pace of work, formerly so carefully regulated by custom and entrenched in union regulations, was now set by corporate administrators.[99] The skilled metal workers who hung on in the context of mass production became simply a part of a complex continuum of industrial workers under the detailed supervision of efficiency-conscious managers. The artisan of the 1890's gave way to the skilled production worker whose overall status in the workplace had undoubtedly declined.

The pattern of defeat was slightly different in each of the two crafts discussed above. The mechanization of the moulder's craft came late and was still incomplete by the 1920's; the all-round craftsman was never as thoroughly eliminated from the foundry as elsewhere in the metal-working factory. On the other hand, from the mid-nineteenth century onward the machinist used power-driven tools, which by the early 1900's were becoming sophisticated enough to reduce much more completely the manual skill requirements of machine-shop work. The machinists' craft was also more fundamentally affected by World War I munitions production, which did not incorporate moulding work. On the whole, however, the *predominant* response of Hamilton's metal-working craftsmen to this prolonged crisis threatening their shop-floor power and prestige was craft exclusiveness, that is, a strategy of defending those parts of their trades with continuing high skill content and attempting to re-impose craft control over wider industrial territory in times of full employment. There was no evidence of a transformation of their consciousness towards a broader solidarity with the less skilled.

Artisanal culture was thus highly ambivalent. It was often a reservoir of creative criticism of modernizing industrial practices, but its structure was still fundamentally a defence of craft privilege – "the clinging dross of exclusivism," to use James Hinton's apt phrase.[100] Yet, at the same time, it would be too easy to embrace a theory of an aristocracy of labour in the Hamilton working class. An examination of workplace behaviour alone would be insufficient to confirm such a theory; for as the most sensitive British studies have emphasized,[101] we would need a fuller portrait of artisanal culture that took into account social and political associations outside the workplace. Many of these same men, for example, were prominent in the leadership of the city's working class political organization, the Independent Labor Party, which promoted class unity at the polls. The evidence presented here, in any case, should certainly raise doubts about any suggestion that these skilled workers were enjoying any special favours from capital; they were, in fact, being persistently harassed by belligerent employers.

Clearly specific responses of Canadian workers to the great industrial transformations of the age must be studied in local settings, in order to capture the unevenness and the variety of experience. But more detailed research into the history of skilled workers in other Canadian communities may well reveal that the ambivalence of artisanal culture in the workplace that characterized Hamilton's metal workers was more common than historians of the Canadian working class have so far suggested. The failure to transcend that world view probably meant that the sweeping changes in the work process that accompanied the rise of monopoly capitalism in Canada prompted a highly fragmented response from the working class.

NOTES

1. *Herald* (Hamilton), 4 May 1916.
2. *Hamilton: The Birmingham of Canada* (Hamilton, 1892), n.p.
3. John Sadlier, "The Problem of the Molder," *Iron Age*, 6 June 1902, 26b.
4. Benjamin Brooks, "The Molders," reprinted from *Scribner's* in *Iron Molders' Journal* (hereafter *IMJ*), XLII, 11 (November, 1906), 801-8; Margaret Loomis Stecker, "The Founders, the Molders, and the Molding Machine," in J.R. Commons, ed., *Trade Unionism and Labor Problems* (2nd ed., Boston, 1921), 343-5.
5. *Canadian Foundryman* (hereafter *CF*), XIX, 5 (May, 1928), 39.
6. *Herald*, 8 October 1910; Ontario, Factory Inspectors, *Report, 1908* (Toronto, 1909), 34. *IMJ*, XLV, 5 (May, 1909), 302-4.
7. Canada, Royal Commission on the Relations of Labour and Capital, *Report: Evidence – Ontario* (Ottawa, 1889), 826.
8. L.T.C. Rolt, *Tools for the Job: A Short History of Machine Tools* (London, 1965), 122-91; James B. Jefferys, *The Story of the Engineers, 1800-1945* (London, 1945), 9-14. These craftsmen were known as engineers in Britain and machinists in North America.
9. Royal Commission on Labour and Capital, 827-8.

10. Raphael Samuel, "Workshop of the World: Steam Power and Hand Technology in Mid-Victorian Britain," *History Workshop Journal*, 3 (1977), 6-72.

11. Royal Commission on Labour and Capital, 881.

12. *Herald*, 23 March 1912.

13. Robert H. Babcock, *Gompers in Canada: A Study in American Continentalism Before the First World War* (Toronto, 1974), 38-54.

14. Robert H. Storey, "Industrialization in Canada: The Emergence of the Hamilton Working Class, 1850-1870s" (M.A. thesis, Dalhousie University, 1975), 123; Frank T. Stockton, *International Molders' Union of North America* (Baltimore, 1921), 20.

15. *Labour Gazette* (hereafter *LG*), II, 4 (October, 1901), 250; Mark Perlman, *The Machinists: A New Study in American Trade Unionism* (Cambridge, Mass., 1961), 7; Palmer, "Most Uncommon Common Men: Craft, Culture, and Conflict in a Canadian Community, 1860-1914" (Ph.D. thesis, State University of New York at Binghamton, 1977), 435-6; *Machinists' Monthly Journal* (hereafter *MMJ*), XIV, 11 (November, 1902), 739.

16. Hamilton Public Library, Hamilton Collection, International Harvester Scrapbook, 1.

17. *Pittsburgh Dispatch*, 3 May 1903 (clipping in Westinghouse Canada Archives, P.J. Myler Scrapbook).

18. See Craig Heron and Bryan D. Palmer. "Through the Prism of the Strike: Industrial Conflict in Southern Ontario, 1901-14," *CHR*, LVIII (1977), 446-56.

19. Public Archives of Ontario, RG 7, XV-4, vol. 3; *LG*, IX, 4 (October, 1908), 378; 7 (January, 1909), 744-5; XIV, 2 (August, 1913), 117; *Herald*, 30 January, 22 November 1912; 10 February 1913; *Canadian Machinery* (hereafter *CM*), IX, 7 (6 March 1913), 239; XI, 5 (29 January 1914), 76.

20. The model for this centralized bargaining was the Stove Founders' Defense Association in the United States, which had originally been a militantly anti-union organization but which began annual national conferences with the IMU in 1893. John P. Frey and John R. Commons, "Conciliation in the Stove Industry," United States, Bureau of Labor, Bulletin, XII, no. 1 (January, 1906); Stockton, *International Molders' Union*, 120-5; F.W. Hilbert, "Trade Union Agreements in the Iron Molders' Union," in Jacob H. Hollander and George E. Barnett, eds., *Studies in American Trade Unionism* (New York, 1907), 229-32. On the Canadian experience, see *IMJ*, XXXVI, 3 (March, 1900), 143; 8 (August, 1900), 534; XXXVIII, 6 (June, 1902), 385; XLII, 3 (March, 1906), 148; XLIV, 5 (May, 1908), 351; *Spectator*, 16 February 1909; *CF*, I, 5 (October, 1910), 18.

21. The negotiations and the ensuing strike can be traced in PAC, RG 27, vol. 296, f. 1909-3124; *LG*, IX, 9 (March, 1909), 936-7; 10

(April, 1909), 1146; and in the daily press early in 1909, especially *Spectator*, 15, 16, 18, 19, 23-26 February, 1, 3, 24, 27 March; and *Herald*, 24, 26 February, 15, 23 March.

22. *IMJ*, LV, 2 (February, 1919), 140; LVI, 2 (February, 1920), 130; LVII, 2 (February, 1921), 99; 3 (March, 1921), 157; LIX, 2 (February, 1923), 96; *LN*, 30 January 1923; *New Democracy* (hereafter *ND*), 5 April 1923; Frey and Commons, "Conciliation in the Stove Industry," 125.

23. On the growing interest in "systematic" business management in the late nineteenth century, see Joseph A. Litterer, "Systematic Management: The Search for Order and Integration," *Business History Review*, 35 (1961), 461-76; Daniel Nelson, *Managers and Workers: Origins of the New Factory System in the United States 1880-1920* (Madison, Wisc., 1975), 48-54.

24. Harry Braverman, *Labor and Monopoly Capital: The Degradation of Work in the Twentieth Century* (New York, 1974), 85-138; Bryan Palmer, "Class, Conception and Conflict: The Thrust for Efficiency, Managerial Views of Labor and the Working Class Rebellion, 1903-22," *Review of Radical Political Economics*, 7 (1975), 31-49; Nelson, *Managers and Workers*, 55-78; Samuel Haber, *Efficiency and Uplift: Scientific Management in the Progressive Era, 1890-1920* (Chicago, 1964), 52-5; Heron and Palmer, "Through the Prism of the Strike," 430-4; Graham S. Lowe, "The Rise of Modern Management in Canada," *Canadian Dimension*, 14 (December, 1979), 32-8.

25. *Industrial Canada* (hereafter *IC*), XIV, 4 (November, 1913), 423.

26. Arthur Smith, "Methods of Solving the Problem of Foundry Help," *CF*, V, 4 (May, 1914), 85.

27. *Spectator*, 20 April 1904; 16, 20 April 1907; Arthur Smith, "Moulding Machine Foundry Practice," *CF*, V, 8 (August, 1914), 143; *Herald*, 8 October 1910.

28. "Moulding Machines: Principles Involved in Their Operation," *CM*, IV, 4 (April, 1908), 53.

29. Victor S. Clark, *History of Manufactures in the United States: III, 1893-1928* (New York, 1929), 85.

30. Ontario, Factory Inspectors, *Report, 1908* (Toronto, 1909), 22; Stecker, "Founders, Molders, and Molding Machines," 438. See also Thomas F. Kennedy, "Banishing Skill from the Foundry," *International Socialist Review*, XI, 8 (February, 1911), 469-73; and "A Molderless Foundry," *ibid.*, 10 (April, 1911), 610-12.

31. "Stripping Plate Machine: Inception and Development," *CF*, IX, 6 (June, 1918), 123; Robert Ozanne, *A Century of Labor-Management Relations at McCormick and International Harvester* (Madison, Wisc., 1967), 20-8; Cyrus McCormick, *The Century of the Reaper: An Account of Cyrus Hall McCormick, the Inventor of the Reaper: of the McCormick Harvesting Machine Company,*

the Business He Created; and of the International Harvester Company, his Heir and Chief Memorial (Boston, 1931), 131-250; *Iron Age*, 1 September 1904, 3. This must have been one of the first installations of moulding equipment in Canada.

32. *CM*, II, 4 (April, 1906), 145-6.

33. *Ibid.*; *LG*, V, 9 (April, 1905), 1047; *CE*, XIII, 8 (August, 1906), 303.

34. *CM*, IV, 2 (February, 1908), 58; 12 (December, 1908), 32; IX, 1 (2 January 1913), 23, 52, 59; X, 2 (10 July 1913), 41; *CF*, II, 9 (September, 1911), 18.

35. Abraham C. Mott, "Molding Machines for Stove Plates," *IMJ*, XXXV, 9 (September, 1899), 456-8; Frey and Commons, "Conciliation in the Stove Industry," 129-30.

36. "Foundry Machinery – Molding Machines, Flasks, Mills, Etc.," *CM*, V, 1 (January, 1909), 63-4; 2 (February, 1909), 59-60. The cities which the committee visited in its investigations included Toronto.

37. *Spectator*, 23 February 1909; PAC, RG 27, vol. 296, f. 3148.

38. Stecker, "Founders, Molders, and Molding Machine," 435; *CF*, X, 3 (March, 1919), 58-9; XI, 4 (April, 1920), 115; XIV, 10 (October, 1923), 30; XVIII, 5 (May, 1927), 6-9; 7 (July, 1927), 6; 10 (October, 1927), 8-10; XIX, 5 (May, 1928), 17-18, 39.

39. *Ibid.*, XVI, 8 (August, 1925), 9; XVII, 7 (July, 1927), 6; XIV, 5 (May 1923), 33-7, 40; 7 (July, 1923), 17: Stecker, "Founders, Molders, and Molding Machine," 455; *Census of Canada, 1911*, VI, 310; *1921*, IV, 402; *1931*, VII, 184.

40. *IMJ*, XLV, 9 (September, 1909), 647.

41. Harless D. Wagoner, *The U.S. Machine Tool Industry from 1900 to 1950* (Cambridge, Mass., 1968), 18. See also Roderick Floud, *The British Machine Tool Industry, 1850-1914* (London, 1976); Rolt, *Tools for the Job*; Nathan Rosenberg, "Technological Change in the Machine Tool Industry, 1840-1910," *Journal of Economic History*, 23 (1963), 414-43; *CE*, VII (April, 1900), 321; *CM*, I, 2 (February, 1905), 53; *Canadian Manufacturer*, XXX, 1 (28 January 1910), 84.

42. Rolt, *Tools for the Job*, 197-201; *CM*, III, 1 (January, 1907), 18-21; 2 (February, 1907), 50-1; E.R. Norris, "Machine Shop Equipment, Methods and Processes," *ibid.*, XVI, 15 (12 October 1916), 393-5.

43. *Canadian Manufacturer*, XXX, 1 (28 January 1910), 84.

44. *Ibid.* See also G.S. Keith, "Five Years' Development of Machine Tools in Canada," *CM*, VI, 1 (January, 1910), 27-32.

45. "Developments in Machine Shop Practice During a Decade," *CM*, IX, 10 (20 March 1913), 282.

46. "A Post-War Problem of Labor," *ibid.*, XVII, 15 (12 April 1917), 381; J.H. Rodgers, "Evolution and Revolution in Machine Shop

Practice," *ibid.*, 26 (28 June 1917), 677-82; "Tendency in Machine Tool Development," *ibid.*, XVIII, 23 (6 December 1917), 630; J.H. Rodgers, "There Should Be No Post-War Slump in Machine Tools," *ibid.*, XX, 7 (22 August 1918), 240-1; Rodgers, "More Efficient Methods Follow War Work," *ibid.*, 26 (26 December 1918), 750-3.

47. Mark H. Irish, " 'Dilution' of Labor in Canadian Munition Plants," *CM*, XVI, 26 (28 December 1916), 717-19; *LN*, 12, 19 January, 23, 26 February 1917; *LG*, XVII, 2 (February, 1917), 97; *Herald*, 30 November 1916.

48. L.D. Burlingame, "Lathe and Screw Machine Automatic Control," *CM*, XV, 8 (24 February 1916), 171-5; "The Pre-eminence of the Toolmaker's Craft," *ibid.*, XVIII, 15 (11 October 1917), 422.

49. "Multi-Machine Operation," *CM*, XIX, 2 (10 January 1918), 64.

50. The IAM president claimed in 1895 that "it has become an established system in nearly every section under the jurisdiction of our order. . . ." IAM, *Proceedings* (1895).

51. *Herald*, 19-20 February 1913; PAC, RG 27, vol. 301, f. 13(11); f. 13(15).

52. *MMJ*, XXV, 6 (June, 1913), 588.

53. *MMJ*, XXVII, 9 (September, 1915), 840; *Spectator*, 4 May 1916.

54. *CM*, XIV, 17 (21 October 1915), 384; D.A. Hampson, "Machine Shop Adaptation to Labor Shortage," *ibid.*, XVI, 9 (31 August 1916), 225-6; Rodgers, "Evolution and Revolution," 679.

55. G.L. Sprague, "Interest in Your Work and Absolute Necessity," *CM*, XXV, 2 (13 January 1921), 39. See also T. Daley, "Machinists Should Be Given a Variety of Work," *CM*, XXIV, 19 (4 November 1920), 427. Daley was works engineer at International Harvester.

56. *IMJ*, XXXIII, 5 (May, 1897), 222.

57. *MMJ*, IX, 3 (March, 1897), 218; XX, 9 (September, 1908), 808. The Winnipeg machinists' *Bulletin* lamented that "Overtime and piece work are twin devices by which individual greed is used to degrade the mass." IV, 2 (February, 1915), 1.

58. Perlman, *Machinists*, 29; *MMJ*, XXI, 9 (September, 1909), 928.

59. *Labor News* (hereafter *LN*), 1 March 1912.

60. *Herald*, 18 March 1910; Canada, Department of Labour, *Labour Organization in Canada, 1919* (Ottawa, 1920), 57.

61. See Canada, National Industrial Conference . . ., *Official Report of Proceedings and Discussions. . . .* (Ottawa, 1919).

62. *CF*, XII, 3 (March, 1921), 41.

63. PAC, RG 27, vol. 312, f. 19(104); *LN*, 9, 16 May, 20 June, 8 August, 12 September, 7 November, 25 December 1919; 13 February, 7 May, 5 June 1920; 29 July 1921; *ND*, 14 January 1920; *CF*, XI, 1 (January, 1920), 28; *Herald*, 29-30 April, 1-3, 6-8, 12 May 1919: 17-18 February 1920; *Spectator*, 28 May 1919; PAC, MG 28, I, 230, vol. 17, f. 1918-19, 11 April 1919.

64. PAC, RG 27, vol. 334, f. 25(10).
65. Canada, Department of Labour, *Report on Organization in Industry, Commerce, and the Professions in Canada* (Ottawa, 1923). For Burgess's attacks, see, for example, *CF*, XIV, 6 (June, 1923), 32-4; *MMJ*, XXXVII, 1 (January, 1925), 25; *Canadian Congress Journal*, III, 12 (December, 1924), 37.
66. *CF*, XII, 1 (January, 1921), 37.
67. *MMJ*, XXII, 3 (March, 1910), 244; 5 (May, 1910), 441; XXIII, 3 (March, 1911), 230; XXIX, 2 (February, 1917), 158; *Industrial Banner* (hereafter *IB*), April, 1911.
68. *Ibid.*; *MMJ*, XXIV, 2 (February, 1912), 140, 150; 3 (March, 1912), 225, 247; 4 (April, 1912), 324, 256; 5 (May, 1912), 442, 449; 6 (June, 1912), 518; 7 (July, 1912), 634; 8 (August, 1912), 730; 12 (December, 1912), 1125; XXV, 3 (March, 1913), 254; *LN*, 2, 9 February, 8 March, 19 April 1912; *Herald*, 23 March 1912.
69. *MMJ*, XXV, 6 (June, 1913), 588; 9 (September, 1913), 910.
70. *CM*, XIII, 13 (18 March 1915), 227; Hamilton *Times*, 18 March, 28 June 1915; *MMJ*, XXVII, 5 (May, 1915), 448; 11 (November, 1915), 1021.
71. *MMJ*, XXVII, 5 (May, 1915), 448; 9 (September, 1915), 840; *LN*, 26 March 1915.
72. *MMJ*, XXVII, 9 (September, 1915), 840.
73. *Herald*, 3, 4 May 1916; Rodgers, "Evolution and Revolution," 680; see also "Manpower Demands and the Supply," *CM*, XIX, 17 (25 April 1918), 436. *Spectator*, 22 May 1916; *CM*, XXIV, 19 (4 November 1920), 427.
74. Nationally the machinists' leaders worked with the Executive of the Trades and Labor Congress of Canada to pressure the Borden government into guaranteeing a fair wage clause in munitions contracts. See D.J. Bercuson, "Organized Labour and the Imperial Munitions Board," *Relations industrielles*, 28 (1973), 602-16; Peter Edward Rider, "The Imperial Munitions Board and its Relationship to Government, Business, and Labour" (Ph.D. thesis, University of Toronto, 1974), Chapter 9; Myer Siemiatycki, "Munitions and Labour Militancy: The 1916 Hamilton Machinists' Strike," *L/LT*, 3 (1978), 134-7.
75. *LN*, 7 April 1916; 28 January 1916.
76. PAC, MG 28, I, 230, vol. 17, f. 1915-16, 5 April 1916.
77. *Spectator*, 2, 4-5 May 1916; *Herald*, 3-5 May 1916.
78. *Ibid.*, 5 May 1916.
79. PAC, MG 30, A, Ib, vol. 2, f. 11 (Department of Labour, 1916). The report was printed in *LG*, XVI, 12 (June, 1916), 1295-7.
80. *Times*, 10 June 1916; *Spectator*, 9, 12 June 1916.
81. For a thorough discussion of the evolution of the strike and its demise, see Siemiatycki, "Munitions and Labour Militancy," 137-51. A similar, though less dramatic strike was waged that spring against the Toronto, Hamilton, and Buffalo Railway by the

machinists, boilermakers, blacksmiths, and carmen in a short-lived system federation. It was equally unsuccessful and destroyed the federation. See PAC, RG 27, vol. 557, f. 1916-49B.

82. *LN*, 11 May 1917; 27 March 1918; *MMJ*, XXIX, 4 (April, 1917), 438.

83. *Herald*, 30 April 1919; *LN*, 23 May 1919; Canada, Royal Commission on Industrial Relations, "Evidence" (typescript at Department of Labour Library), III, 2267. A new schedule from the local machinists' union submitted to Hamilton employers in the spring of 1919 was completely ignored. *Ibid.*, 2265.

84. *MMJ*, XXXIX, 3 (March, 1927), 169; XL, 5 (May, 1928), 301.

85. PAC, RG 27, vol. 301, f. 13(27). This dispute involved only thirty-eight machine tenders out of 276 strikers. The union was attempting to establish a minimum wage of $2.50 per day for these workers, compared with $3.25 for skilled moulders. Westinghouse Canada Archives, F.A. Merrick, "Report on Plant and Operation Year 1912" (typescript), 9-10.

86. Royal Commission on Industrial Relations, "Evidence," 2278; *MMJ*, XXXI, 1 (January, 1919), 58; *ibid.*, 12 (December, 1919), 1127.

87. Perlman, *Machinists*, 39-56; John H.M. Laslett, *Labor and the Left: A Study of Socialist and Radical Influences in the American Labor Movement, 1881-1924* (New York, 1970), 144-79.

88. *Herald*, 16 April 1910; Canada, Department of Labour, *Labour Organizations in Canada*, 1911-14, 1919-20; *ND*, 14, 28 January, 5 February 1920; *LN*, 22 January, 13 February, 5 March, 20 August 1920.

89. Albert Theodore Helbing, *The Departments of the American Federation of Labor* (Baltimore, 1931), 48-51; Stockton, *International Molders' Union*, 112-13; Bruno Ramirez, "Collective Bargaining and the Politics of Industrial Relations, 1896-1916" (Ph.D. thesis, University of Toronto, 1975), 197-9.

90. *LN*, 2 May 1919.

91. *Ibid.*, 1 March, 12, 19 April, 5 July 1918; *Labour Organizations in Canada*, 1919, 35. The amalgamation idea was revived under left-wing sponsorship again in 1923. *LN*, 28 August 1923.

92. *Ibid.*, 23 May 1919.

93. PAC, RG 27, vol. 301, f. 13(15); *Herald*, 26 February 1913.

94. *LN*, 25 September 1914.

95. *Herald*, 4 May 1916.

96. *IMJ*, XLVIII, 9 (September, 1912), 733-4; *MMJ*, XXV, 6 (June, 1913), 588; XXXII, 11 (November, 1920), 1014. One writer in the business press compared the cost of living and wages in Hamilton and Birmingham, England, and concluded that Hamilton workers were much better off. W.A. Craik, "British and Canadian Workmen," *IC*, XII, 9 (April, 1912), 1054-5.

97. (IAM) *Bulletin*, V, 1 (January, 1916), 2.

98. *CF*, XIX, 5 (May, 1928), 39.

99. Of course, while formal trade union controls disappeared, we should not ignore informal techniques that workers used to regulate the pace of work in North American industry for years to come. See Stanley B. Mathewson, *Restriction of Output Among Unorganized Workers* (New York, 1931); Donald Roy, "Quota Restriction and Goldbricking in a Machine Shop," *American Journal of Sociology*, 57 (March, 1952), 427-42; Bill Watson, "Counter-Planning on the Shop Floor," *Radical America*, 5 (May-June, 1971), 77-85.

100. Hinton, *First Shop Stewards' Movement*, 337. The evidence presented in this paper, therefore, suggests that a wholesale application of David Montgomery's influential conceptualization of American working-class history in this period would be unwise, at least in the southern Ontario context. While his emphasis on struggles for control in the workplace is crucial for an understanding of craftsmen's activity, his suggestion that the workplace struggles of the skilled and unskilled tended to fuse during and after World War I is not sustained by the behaviour of Hamilton workers during these years. See David Montgomery, "The 'New Unionism' and the Transformation of Workers' Consciousness in America, 1902-22," *Journal of Social History*, VII (1973), 519-20.

101. R.Q. Gray, "Styles of Life, the 'Labour Aristocracy,' and Class Relations in Later Nineteenth Century Edinburgh," *International Review of Social History*, 17 (1973), 428-52; Geoffrey Crossick, "The Labour Aristocracy and Its Values: A Study of Mid-Victorian Kentish London," *Victorian Studies*, 19 (1976), 301-28. For a discussion of a labour aristocracy theory in a Canadian context, see Ian McKay, "Capital and Labour in the Halifax Baking and Confectionary Industry During the Last Half of the Nineteenth Century," *L/LT*, 3 (1978), 63-108.

IV
Violence and Protest

The years between 1896 and 1929 witnessed considerable violence in Canada. The state itself often resorted to force either to coerce by threat or sometimes to repress physically Canadians engaging in strikes or protest activities. The Winnipeg General Strike and the events of Bloody Saturday represent the best known of such events, but the two decades preceding 1919 saw many other such efforts. Two of the lengthier and uglier of these incidents involved the military suppression of strikes of Springhill, Nova Scotia, coal miners from 1909 to 1911 and of their brother coal miners on Vancouver Island from 1912 to 1914. Thus, while the events of 1919 to 1925 in Cape Breton should not be seen as the normal disposition of strikes in Canadian history, equally they cannot be ignored or simply dismissed as exceptional. Clearly, the use of the military to break a strike was not anyone's first choice; indeed, considerable effort had been extended before World War I by Mackenzie King and similar liberal intellectuals and policy-makers to devise alternative methods of regulating class conflict in Canadian society. Yet when these more sophisticated forms of state intervention failed, the troops could be used.

Working-class protest and subsequent violence represented but one type of collective behaviour. Many other groups in Canadian society – farmers, women, nativists, racists – engaged in militant demonstrations which on occasion led to bloodshed. Perhaps among the least attractive elements of Canadian society in this period were the xenophobic excesses which led to anti-

Oriental riots in Vancouver in 1907, to a general anti-immigrant atmosphere which often spilled over into nativist violence, and to an ever-increasing intolerance and bigotry towards French Canadians and Catholics.

Throughout the period an increased consciousness of the need for social order was evident, which led to an expansion of police forces. The Royal North West Mounted Police grew rapidly and in the "Red Scare" which followed World War I was transformed into the Royal Canadian Mounted Police and given a significant new mandate in the area of security and intelligence work.

FURTHER READING:
On military aid to the civil power, see Desmond Morton, "Aid to the Civil Power: The Canadian Militia in Support of Social Order, 1867-1914," *CHR*, LI (1970), 407-25; and R.H. Roy, "The Seaforths and the Strikers: Nanaimo, August 1913," *BC Studies*, 43 (1979), 81-93. On the British Columbia coal strike, see John Norris, "The Vancouver Coal Miners' Strike, 1912-1914," *BC Studies*, 45 (1980), 56-72. Thomas Thorner surveys "The Incidence of Crime in Southern Alberta" in David Bercuson and Louis Knafla, eds., *Law and Society in Canada in Historical Perspective* (Calgary, 1979), 53-88. One interesting account is J.W. Murray, *Memoirs of a Great Canadian Detective* (Toronto, 1907). The growth of the RNWMP is detailed in Rod McLeod's *The NWMP and Law Enforcement 1873-1905* (Toronto, 1970); the creation of the RCMP is described by S.W. Horral, "The Royal North-West Mounted Police and Labour Unrest in Western Canada, 1919," *CHR*, LXI (1980), 169-90.

Don Macgillivray is an historian at the College of Cape Breton who has published on the local history of Cape Breton workers.

Military Aid to the Civil Power: The Cape Breton Experience in the 1920's

by Don Macgillivray

From 1867 to 1933 the military came to the aid of the civil power in Canada on at least 133 occasions.[1] Throughout the period the threat or apprehended threat of domestic disorder was the primary justification for both retention and expansion of military forces. It was the impetus behind the militia increases in the early 1880's,[2] and two decades later Sir Wilfrid Laurier cautioned Lord Dundonald: "You must not take the militia seriously, for though it is useful for suppressing internal disturbances, it will not be required for the defence of the country, as the Monroe doctrine protects us from enemy aggression."[3] In 1909 Sir Frederick Borden, the Minister of Militia, declared: "The reason for the existence of the militia in this country is well understood. The principal object is perhaps the upholding of the Civil power in the different parts of the Dominion."[4]

Interestingly, this significant role has received little attention from military historians. Col. C.F. Hamilton and Lieut. Col. D.J. Goodspeed completely ignored the theme,[5] while G.F.G. Stanley mentioned it only to demonstrate that in peacetime the militia "was not a waste of time or money."[6] The few articles that have concentrated on the subject usually leave the impression that the practice, while disliked by the military, was performed with patience and tact and was quite successful in restoring or preserving law and order.[7] Desmond Morton, for example, in a recent study of the period prior to 1914, argued

From *Acadiensis*, III, 2 (Spring, 1974), 45-64. Reprinted with permission.

that, generally, the "arrival of uniformed, armed troops seems to have been sufficient to restore civil authority or to calm the apprehensions of timid magistrates. In many cases the militia only appeared when trouble had run its course."[8] More recently, Major J.J.B. Pariseau observed that the practice had a salutary effect.[9] Such generous assessments call out for qualification. In labour disputes, which accounted for almost half of the incidents in which military forces were used, the presence of troops may not have been viewed as a neutral, stabilizing force by other participants. If this was the case a reassessment would seem appropriate. With this consideration in mind, this paper will deal with three such incidents, all of which occurred in industrial Cape Breton in the 1920's. While they involved relatively large troop movements and were instrumental in effecting amendments to the Militia Act, they are not unrepresentative of labour disputes during the country's industrial development.

The year 1919, the year of the "Red Scare," witnessed a great deal of tension and unrest in Canada. Early in the summer Maj.-Gen. S.C. Mewburn, the Minister of Militia, piloted an amendment to the Militia Act through Parliament which doubled the authorized ceiling of the permanent force to 10,000. Mewburn used the traditional argument to bolster his case: the increase might become necessary because "circumstances have arisen throughout the whole country which seem to indicate an absolute necessity that Canada should have some force available for the preservation of law and order in this country."[10] In spite of an evident post-war reaction against military spending, Mewburn's amendment was successful.[11] Meanwhile, some high-ranking military figures were eager to implement compulsory military training throughout the country. Brig.-Gen. J.H. Mac-Brien envisaged a comprehensive plan whereby, among other features, boys would commence training at six years of age and continue through various levels well into adulthood.[12] Maj.-Gen. A.G.L. McNaughton, who shared this desire for military training, argued that such a scheme would not only provide the men needed to quash any insurrection but would assist in removing those very dangers by reaching "that element in the country which was most in need of education in responsibility and in citizenship."[13] Others were more realistic. Maj.-Gen. Sir Eugene Fiset thought the plan but a dream,[14] and Sir Arthur Currie explained to MacBrien that both Parliament and the public "were overwhelming[ly] against universal training at this time. There requires a great deal of educational work to be carried out before any such a thing can become a reality. I think it wise not to attempt to force the issue at the present time."[15] Currie soon moved on to McGill University and Fiset, after serving as Deputy Minister of Militia and Defence, retired in the early 1920's, but MacBrien became Chief of the General Staff and McNaughton remained a close associate. Perhaps in part because their desire for universal military training had come to naught, MacBrien and McNaughton considered the possibility of the domestic overthrow of law and order not only real, but the most pressing threat to the country.[16]

This mentality was reflected in the proposed reorganization of the military forces. As early as August 1920, Currie had suggested to Arthur Meighen that the Department of Militia and Defence and the Naval Service be amalgamated into one administrative department. The idea received further support when it was learned that the United States was considering a similar move.[17] Then only a few days after the Liberal electoral victory in December 1921, Maj.-Gen. Fiset recommended to Mackenzie King the amalgamation not only of the Naval, Air and Militia departments, but of the RCMP as well. Such an arrangement, Fiset argued, would decrease overhead charges to a minimum "and the fact that the Royal North West Mounted Police will be administered by the same ministerial head would enable a reduction in the Permanent Force by an equal number, and enable the Government to deal with 'Aid to Civil Powers in Time of Emergency' with a complete force under one control."[18] A few days later Fiset passed on to King a memorandum by C.G.S. MacBrien along similar lines; in this version the RCMP was envisaged as mobile squadrons closely aligned with the cavalry.[19] Mackenzie King was receptive. When his first cabinet was formed, George P. Graham, whom King had not wanted,[20] received the portfolios of Militia and Defence, and Naval Services, and early in April 1922, in the first session of Parliament, Graham introduced a bill to create the Department of National Defence which would include the RCMP. Indeed, according to Graham, the RCMP had already been shifted from the Justice Department and for the last few months had been administered by the Department of Militia and Defence.[21]

Few politicians disagreed with the reorganization of the military forces from the viewpoint of efficiency and economy, but strong opposition arose to the inclusion of the RCMP within the proposed Defence Department. Arthur Meighen maintained that, if the Mounted Police lost its civilian status, it would lose much of its public regard. He envisaged the RCMP, which he thought better suited than the militia for preserving law and order, as a "mobile police reserve" which could be strategically located in a few points in the country, with its services at the disposal of local authorities when required.[22] General Mewburn, speaking for the Conservatives, also argued that the Mounted Police should be left alone. He then added the interesting observation that "We have had troubles in past strikes and that sort of thing, and although under the present Militia Act it is within the power of a municipality to call upon the militia to turn out for the preservation of law and order, that is the very last resort that should be adopted in this country. . . ."[23]

Mewburn was followed in the debate by Mackenzie King, who brought out that only recently the Mounted Police had been requested by municipal authorities in Nova Scotia, but that "the government took the position that if we wished to create an industrial disturbance of very serious proportions, possibly the best way we could go about it would be to order the Mounted Police into those areas." He had, at that time, informed the local authorities that "if they were unable to maintain law and order themselves, as they were supposed to do," they could call in the militia, but he assured them that they would be responsible for expenses incurred. King felt that "if you once open the door to having the Mounted Police called in to aid civil authorities on any occasion when there may be alarm on account of industrial disputes, you will in a very short time have the federal government discharging a function in the matter of keeping law and order which it was never contemplated it should discharge."[24] J.S. Woodsworth agreed that the RCMP was hardly an instrument of peace during industrial disputes and suggested they be confined to the unorganized territories of the country. John A. Clark, a West Coast Conservative who had spent twenty years in the military and had participated in forces in aid of the civil power, spoke out against the troops in civil cases because it merely antagonized the working class, a prime recruiting area for the military. For him, echoing Mewburn, the Mounted Police was the appropriate force, but it should not be associated with the Department of National Defence.[25]

Graham attempted to defend his position by reading statements from the provincial authorities. Nova Scotia's reply should be noted. Aware of the accessibility of troops under the provisions of the Militia Act, and possibly thinking that inclusion of the RCMP under the Defence Department would also mean their availability under the Militia Act, the Nova Scotia government stated "that some advantage might be gained if it were able to call upon a federal police at any time."[26] Eventually, however, the strong opposition from Conservatives and Progressives alike was successful and the RCMP was excluded from the new Department of National Defence. One thing was clear – industrial disturbances were expected. Much of the debate had simply been a discussion as to which force could most effectively deal with them.

These disturbances were not long in coming. Industrial unrest was not a new phenomenon in Cape Breton; in 1876, 1882, 1904, and 1909 military forces had been sent to Cape Breton from the mainland. But since the war two new protagonists had appeared on the scene. One was District 26, United Mine Workers of America, representing 12,000 miners in Nova Scotia and New Brunswick and quickly coming under the control of a number of fiery, articulate activists, many of whom were or who became publicly avowed Communists and members of the Workers Party of Canada. The other was the British Empire Steel Corporation (Besco), the largest industrial consortium in Canada at the time. Late in 1920 a yearly contract had been signed between these two bodies. Employees received significant increases, the highest wages the men would receive for more than twenty years. Then, in January 1922, Besco announced a reduction of 35 per cent. Throughout the spring and summer of 1922 the industrial situation deteriorated. With a strike in the offing, King sent an urgent request to D.D. McKenzie, Solicitor-General and Cape Breton MP, for information on the calling out of the Militia and the Mounted Police in aid of the civil power. In reply, McKenzie included the appropriate sections of the Militia Act and warned King that the federal government "should not be a party to bringing out either the Police Force or the Military Force until sufficient pressure to that effect is brought to bear, not only by the industrial corporations concerned, but by the civil authorities as well."[27] He need not have worried; King was quite content to maintain a passive role.

On the morning of 14 August, Besco president Roy Wolvin requested immediate military protection from the federal authorities on the grounds that the walk-out – scheduled to commence the following day – was to include maintenance men, a situation which would lead to deterioration of the mines. King replied that invoking military forces in such a situation was not a responsibility of the federal government and enclosed the copy of McKenzie's recent memorandum on the procedures to be followed.[28] The strike began as planned on 15 August. Concurrent with the strike was an overwhelming victory for the radicals in the District 26 executive elections. Later that day D.W. Morrison, Glace Bay mayor and Labour MLA, issued the following statement:

> I have been today twice requested to sign a requisition for troops and have refused. I have refused because I felt that there is no need for troops in here. There is absolutely no disorder, much less violence. To bring armed men into the district under these circumstances is, in my opinion, unfortunate and ill-advised and totally unnecessary.
> Today I had the Chief of Police make a careful investigation of the situation and he has reported to me that there is not the slightest necessity for outside interference; he states that there is not even need for special police from outside.[29]

Others obviously disagreed with Morrison's assessment. That same day County Court Judge Duncan Finlayson requisitioned troops under the Militia Act and the District Officer Commanding, Maj.-Gen. H.C. Thacker, immediately forwarded more than 200 Royal Canadian Artillery soldiers from Halifax and a 250-man contingent from the Royal 22nd in Quebec.[30] The first troop train arrived from Halifax on 16 August and was met at the Sydney terminal by rock-wielding strikers and sympathizers. Undeterred, the RCA pressed on to Glace Bay, accompanied by Lewis gun detachments and five eighteen-pound field guns.[31]

Two arguments were used to justify the military presence and to plead for more troops. With maintenance men included among the strikers the mines gradually began to accumulate water and since the mines, as the provincial government frequently pointed out, were owned by the public, they had to be protected.[32] There was also an irrational fear of the dynamic, outspoken, radical union executive, led by J.B. McLachlan and "Red Dan" Livingstone. Cape Breton MP George Kyte wired to Mackenzie King: "People in terror of revolution which radical element threaten. Rush more soldiers with all speed."[33] Besco president Roy Wolvin maintained that 500 troops were totally inadequate and that a minimum of 2,000 more was required immediately. Wolvin added "that if any naval forces are available they should be sent to Sydney harbour immediately."[34] Similar views were expressed by Premier George Murray, Mines Commissioner E.H. Armstrong, and W.S. Fielding.[35]

Other less influential individuals disagreed with this assessment. The mayor of Glace Bay continued to oppose the dispatch of troops and on 17 August forwarded the following message to Mackenzie King: "Do not consider militia necessary in Glace Bay. No disturbances of any kind. Not one arrest. Local authorities are able to cope with conditions. Town will repudiate payment of expenses incurred by Militia. Urge that you order withdrawal of troops as their presence here is aggravating the situation."[36] In a series of mass meetings in Cape Breton over 1,500 "returned men" opposed the military presence. Great War Veterans' Associations in Sydney Mines and Glace Bay maintained that the appearance of troops "only tends to aggravate the situation" and a group of Acadian miners in the area objected specifically to the presence of the Royal 22nd for the same reason. Local union officials and some mainland unionists argued that the troops would be used to break the strike and that the procedure was productive only of harm, while Trades and Labor Congress president Tom Moore regarded it as a "case of intimidation."[37] A few days later the Trades and Labor Congress reiterated its president's position,[38] and a Methodist minister in one of the mining communities informed King of the serious complications which resulted from the new situation, an aspect which generals Thacker and McNaughton both recognized and feared.[39] Mackenzie King attempted to placate those opposed to the military presence by denying that the federal government had any responsibility,[40] and he quickly persuaded Graham to issue a public statement explaining that the government had nothing to do with sending the troops.

On the same day as he made this declaration, however, Graham informed Thacker that his request for an additional 500 troops was being acted upon.[41] Furthermore, not content with almost 1,000 troops on or en route to the island, the Lieutenant-Governor-in-Council proclaimed Cape Breton County a police district and approved the raising of 1,000 special police for duty in the strike area.[42] Since there were no trained and experienced men to act as the nucleus of the force, the provincial Mines

Commissioner, E.H. Armstrong, requested the assistance of the federal government and arrangements, during which both King and Sir Lomer Gouin, federal Minister of Justice, were consulted, were soon completed.[43] Within three days of the initial request ten NCOs from the RCMP were making fast for the East in their new roles as special advisers.[44]

Meanwhile, the miners exhibited a high degree of discipline and determination. When a train carrying the Royal 22nd contingent began its short ride over coal company tracks from Sydney to the mining town of Dominion, it pushed before it an armed gondola which, with its three-foot-thick protection of sandbags, could apparently withstand a barrage of eighteen-pounders. Situated on the front corners were Lewis gun crews while the perimeter was occupied by dozens of armed soldiers. Undaunted, the strikers twice halted this military procession before it reached its destination while a group of miners quietly and efficiently searched the train for "scabs."[45]

In spite of the continued lack of violence, on 19 August the District Officer Commanding suggested the addition of a large contingent of Mounted Police and the use of British battleships then in Newfoundland waters, requesting that they be authorized to land in a support role if necessary.[46] Not since 1884, when a British warship overawed the Indians on the Skeena, had British military forces intervened in a domestic dispute.[47] Nor was the General finished for the day. Through the Senior Naval Officer at Halifax, Canada's two destroyers, the *Patriot* and the *Patrician*, received orders to proceed to Sydney to render assistance.[48] Upon hearing of this latest development, military headquarters cancelled the order directing the destroyers to the area and informed General Thacker that naval forces were not to be used "under existing conditions." General McNaughton, Acting Chief of General Staff while MacBrien was on vacation, directed Thacker to begin preparations to call out the non-permanent militia to meet any future requirements.[49]

The same day that General Thacker attempted to create his amphibious force, Premier Murray met with the District 26 executive. An agreement was reached whereby maintenance men would return to the pits and, Murray informed King, the situation appeared "well in hand."[50] King in turn told McNaughton that "It would be a great mistake in view of this statement from the Premier of the Province to take the extreme kind of action suggested by the Group Officer Commanding without first having it endorsed by Premier Murray himself."[51] The Prime Minister then sent Solicitor-General McKenzie to the area as a "special adviser" and Thacker was informed by McNaughton that if any large number of additional troops were required McKenzie and Murray were to be consulted and their endorsement obtained "if possible." McNaughton then suggested that the military be brought into reserve as soon as the newly created provincial police force was available in sufficient numbers. He went on to offer some questionable advice to Thacker on the use of the Canadian Navy:

> I am informed that such cannot be done except by authority of the Governor-General-in-Council, which if exercised will involve the assembly of Parliament. My own opinion is, that if the situation requires it, they can be used on requisition of the Civil authority in the same way as the military forces. Their entry on the scene at the present moment would, however, be difficult to justify, and their presence would probably be held to be an undue menace, and in consequence illegal.[52]

The following day, General Thacker stated that 1,000 additional troops might become necessary and attempted once again to acquire British ships. It is also likely that he enticed a few sea planes from Dartmouth because the Air Board soon sent a directive forbidding such flights without authorization.[53] Thacker was unperturbed and a few hours later made an unsuccessful attempt to have an airplane squadron dispatched to Cape Breton.[54] The General's attempts to solicit both air and naval support are interesting not only because almost all the reports – including many of his own – mention that the situation remained quiet throughout, but because neither force was included under the terms of the Militia Act.[55]

But the Militia Act was a curious document and many of the people involved were not entirely sure how it operated. While the forces being used were federal forces, the federal government really had little authority in the matter once the "aid to the civil power" clause was invoked. The maintenance of law and order was a local concern. County Court Judge Finlayson was the only one who could cancel the requisition and General Thacker was the only one who could reduce, but not completely withdraw, the troops. And so while Thacker was ordered on 23

August to bring his forces into reserve as soon as possible, more Royal Canadian Dragoons arrived in Cape Breton by special train, with full equipment and additional horses, on the following day.[56]

By this time King was being criticized by the Trades and Labor Congress, which was holding its annual convention and saw little reason for the presence of the military in Cape Breton. King made it known he would like the troops withdrawn.[57] On 26 August, General Thacker passed on King's message to Judge Finlayson, but Thacker refused to press Finlayson to cancel the requisition and declined to reduce significantly the number of troops involved.[58] On the same day, an industrial settlement was reached, but it was hardly suggestive of a lasting peace. The union president later commented:

> The wage schedule was accepted by miners under the muzzle of rifles, machine guns and gleaming bayonets with further threatened invasion of troops and marines, with warships standing to. The miners, facing hunger, their Dominion and Provincial governments lined up with Besco . . . were forced to accept the proposals.[59]

Nonetheless, a settlement it was. The provincial force, which never did manage to send a significant number over to the island, disbanded on 28 August. Three days later the RCMP advisers left the area.[60] On 1 September requisitions were cancelled and the troops began their homeward trek. According to the military authorities, the episode had served only to drain their already meagre resources and interrupt their summer training.[61]

It is difficult to state definitely that the miners would have remained as peaceful as they did had the military not been conspicuously present. Yet, many people felt that the proximity of the military heightened rather than alleviated tensions. That there were no arrests throughout the period of occupation was essentially due to the miners themselves. Organized since 1879, and with activist, strongly supported leadership, the Cape Breton miners had a solidarity among Canadian unionists second to none. Military intrusions were not new to these communities. Throughout the strike they had massive but orderly parades and they suppressed the accessibility of liquor to their members during the dispute.[62] Perhaps this very cohesiveness was a partial explanation of General Thacker's reactions. Thacker's background was very much a military one and there is nothing in it to suggest that he was able to acquire a significant understanding of mining communities in general or Cape Breton miners in particular.[63] What was obvious was that Thacker was quite prepared to give industrial Cape Breton an appearance not unlike – in the bitter phrase of one Cape Breton veteran in a note to King – "an occupied region of Germany during the last war."[64]

When a number of politicians, led by J.S. Woodsworth and Arthur Meighen, later questioned the necessity for troops in the Cape Breton dispute, the federal government simply repeated that, once properly requested, there was no alternative but to forward military forces. Nor did the government wish to alter the procedure; when Meighen further inquired if they were considering amendments to the Militia Act, he received a negative answer.[65] The Liberal administration would soon regret its lack of concern. On 28 June 1923, after a prolonged period of discussion and the adamant refusal of Besco to consider a wage increase, a decrease of hours, or union recognition, the Sydney steel workers went on strike.[66] Within hours Judge Finlayson again requisitioned the military "in anticipation of disorders that may arise."[67] Thacker complied immediately.

Unlike the miners, the steel workers had only a weak organization. The first evening of the strike a confrontation between strikers and corporation representatives occurred at one of the plant gates. The pattern was repeated the following evening. One local paper observed: "The crowd seemed to be aware that soldiers were on their way to Sydney and seemed determined to make as much trouble as possible in the few hours left before the troops would arrive."[68] Early in the morning of 30 June, the rumble of a troop train was again heard in the vicinity of Sydney. Once again the armoured gondola, piled high with sand bags and bristling with machine guns, appeared.[69] These forces were the first of more than 1,150 troops to be sent to the island by General Thacker. A few hours later provincial police were requested. That evening, the pattern of conflict continued. The troops, stationed just outside the plant gate, fired over the heads of the angry crowd as they retreated out of range of the rocks being hurled by the protesters.[70] This action was met by shouts of defiance and the crowd apparently did not disperse until a machine gun was placed in position and preparation was made to fire.[71] The following morning the provincial force, now known as "Armstrong's Army," arrived.[72] Before the day was complete this force had made a major contribution to Cape Breton's "Bloody Sunday." According to one reporter, "Mounted police charges on the mob, police raids, and steel-hatted soldiers advancing with fixed bayonets, lent a war-like and spectacular touch to the strenuous scenes [until] . . . the soldiers and police called it a day and retired behind their stockades."[73] This report neglected to mention that some of the recipients of the police charge were returning from evening church services and included women and children.[74] But as the Liberal *Record* observed: "Stamping out lawless violence is not apt to be a gentle process."[75]

After this display of authority, confrontations were rare. The main reason was the determination of the provincial police, supported by the military, to prevent any gatherings, including picketing. Meetings by militant unionists were regarded as unlawful assemblies and subject to visitations by both provincial and military forces.[76] As in 1922, military outfits with a high percentage of mounted troops, such as the Royal Canadian Horse Artillery and the Royal Canadian Dragoons, were very much in evidence.[77] Unlike 1922, however, there is no evidence of requests for naval or air forces.

The entire issue was soon hurled into the middle of the national political arena. The Cape Breton miners, 8,500 strong, walked out in protest against the authorities' measures on 3 July. This prompted the *Record* to declare the whole affair a "miniature rebellion."[78] Sympathetic strikes soon broke out in Pictou, Nova Scotia, and in the coal fields of Alberta; throughout the country opposition to the use of the military became intense. The Prime Minister was worried by "this very serious aspect of the situation" as both he and Labour Minister James Murdock were bombarded with telegrams of protest and warnings that they would be held responsible.[79] Organized labour was completely unimpressed with the federal government's explanation that the military presence in Cape Breton was not a responsibility of the federal authorities.[80] King then turned to his Acting Minister of National Defence, E.M. Macdonald,[81] and to Premier Armstrong, and declared that the workmen were "held in subject by the presence of armed forces" which "seems to have exceeded all bounds of necessity or prudence." While requesting them to convey his feelings on the matter to Judge Finlayson, Mackenzie King also suggested that Armstrong might be able to substitute a special provincial force for the militia units.[82] Duncan Finlayson proved adamant. The judge stated that the troops would remain until he decided otherwise and that such a time had not yet arrived.[83] This prompted the federal authorities to seek a way around the impasse. It proved unfruitful; Finlayson was correct, although the Departments of Justice and Defence were not in agreement in their interpretations of the Militia Act.[84] The troops remained.

Then, on 11 July, Mackenzie King admitted for the first time that the Militia Act needed amending. The tone of the statement, included in a reply to a protest by TLC president Tom Moore, is suggestive:

> The presence of troops in Cape Breton to the numbers there at the present time, and under circumstances which appear to render it most doubtful that the expense incidental thereto will be borne, as the law clearly contemplates, by the municipalities concerned, render it apparent that there is need for revision of the statute respecting the calling out of the militia in aid of the civil power.[85]

Meanwhile, although E.M. Macdonald had assured King and James Murdock on 8 July that military forces from western Canada would not be sent to Cape Breton, an assurance which the Labour Minister eagerly utilized in an attempt to placate Canadian labour leaders, troops continued to arrive from Cape Hughes, Manitoba, as late as 12 July.[86] This prompted a bitter note from Labour Minister Murdock to Acting Defence Minister Macdonald and a public statement by the former suggesting that the leading provincial Liberals "make an effort to find out more about the human side of the situation."[87] But Murdock's methods proved far more effective in creating antagonism within the Liberal Party than in returning the troops to their camps. Eventually, on 17 July, UMW International president John L. Lewis intervened, deposed the radical district executive, and, unconstitutionally,[88] appointed a provisional executive. By 24 July the miners decided to return to work. The steel workers, with no chance of success, gamely limped on to 31 July. Troops began departing by 28 July and all were back on the mainland by 15 August.

Once again, it is difficult to assess just how effective the military presence was as a stabilizing force. Throughout the country organized labour was antagonized and a few sympathetic strikes developed. For various reasons the Cape Breton situation was more volatile than that of the previous year. There had been confusion and disagreement between the Departments of Justice and National Defence regarding the Militia Act.[89] Similar, if more intense, feelings existed within the federal government. Unlike the miners, the steel workers had no effective union organization and their discipline was weak. Nonetheless, one report did suggest that the knowledge that troops had been requisitioned had actually increased the violence. After the first few days there were violent outbursts but they were generally initiated by the provincial police force. The miners did not enter the fray until the provincial and military forces had entered the area. Indeed, the presence and actions of these forces had prompted the walk-out by the miners. When the dust had settled ten people were convicted of rioting or unlawful assembly – a small percentage of 10,000 strikers.[90]

It was time for a Royal Commission to investigate industrial unrest in Cape Breton. The chairman, appointed by the federal government, was Dr. J.W. Robertson, president of the Canadian Red Cross Society. Prior to the commencement of the Commission work the Prime Minister wrote a "strictly confidential" letter to Robertson suggesting some aspects he could investigate carefully:

> I have come to feel that the law as it stands governing the calling out of the troops in aid of the civil power at times of industrial unrest needs to be amended so as to prevent corporations from taking advantage of the powers which can be exercised, through any Judge to whom appeal may be made, where civil authorities themselves are unwilling to take the initiative required. . . .
>
> From what I saw last year of the telegrams . . . the effort then made not only to call out the militia, but to bring into play the naval service and the air forces as well – has led me to see how dangerous it is to the whole national situation that a power of this kind should be given to a few men without due restraints in the way of a control from a responsible source.[91]

A few months later General MacBrien, faced with another decrease in financial allocations to the military and apparently unaware of the highly variable winds by which Mackenzie King tacked through political seas, pointed out that aid to the civil power was one of the three main functions of the permanent force. Oblivious to the furor of the previous summer, MacBrien argued that:

> One of the most serious threats to the reduction of the Permanent Force is that the Department of Defence will be unable to supply troops for aid to the Civil Power in the same measure as has been done in the past. Thus the government will be left without any force with which to maintain law and order in strike areas or in the event of any other national emergency arising.
>
> When it is remembered that during the recent strike in Cape Breton last summer, practically all the combatant troops were collected at Sidney [*sic*] and brought from points as distant as Winnipeg, and even then an adequate number was not available, very serious consideration should be given before reducing the already limited numbers available.[92]

The argument proved unconvincing and actual troop strength continued to decrease.[93]

Early in 1924 the Robertson Commission completed its study on Cape Breton unrest. While not a particularly perceptive document, it did, as King had suggested, recommend changes in the Militia Act.[94] After considering them for four months, the government, in early June, prepared to introduce what were essentially the Commission's recommendations. Henceforth, the provincial Attorney General would, upon receiving notification from a superior or district County Court judge and satisfied that such a force was required, sign a requisition. The District Officer Commanding would then be required to call out the permanent troops or such portion as the DOC considered necessary. The Attorney General would be required to initiate an inquiry within seven days, with the report to be forwarded to the Secretary of State. The province would be responsible for the costs and, if necessary, the federal government would be able to retain any unpaid balance from the annual grant to the appropriate province. The Attorney General would be responsible for recalling the troops.[95] The only differences between the Commission recommendations and the proposed legislation were the explicit statement of provincial financial responsibility and the method by which the federal authorities could, if necessary, acquire the money.

The proposed legislation brought a strong reaction from Nova Scotia Liberals in both Halifax and Ottawa. All but one of the Nova Scotia Liberals in Parliament opposed the legislation; the exception was E.M. Macdonald who, as Minister of National Defence, introduced the legislation. The provincial administration was equally adamant, with Premier Armstrong tersely arguing that the maintenance of peace, order, and good government was a "peculiar obligation" of the federal government and Provincial Secretary Cameron contending that, because the doctrines proclaimed by the radicals threatened the "constitution," the costs should be absorbed by the nation.[96] Their concern for the nation's continued existence was doubtless intensified by their awareness of their new financial responsibilities.

In the federal House of Commons, E.M. Macdonald defended the changes and set the theme for much of the debate which ensued by referring to pecuniary considerations. He noted that on the fifty-nine occasions in the last fifty years on which troops were invoked in aid of the civil power, only $40,291 of the $556,291 spent had been collected by the federal government. The two recent episodes had cost $162,916 – not including pay and allowances – and the municipalities, true to their word, had refused to pay.[97] The use of the military was becoming expensive. But there were numerous objections to the amendments. Liberal whip and Cape Breton MP George Kyte echoed the provincial Liberals and argued that, as most of the disputes were in the coal fields and thus of national concern, the province should not be held responsible for the costs. William Irvine, the Labour MP from Calgary, had other criticisms. He maintained that judges were rather ignorant of industrial conditions and should be the last persons invested with the authority to call out the troops. He was also dissatisfied with the government for not including any additional regulations on the amount of military force which could be invoked. In the light of King's earlier comments to J.W. Robertson, this omission was curious and was immediately subjected to the penetrating glance of Arthur Meighen. The Conservative leader strongly objected to the vast discretionary power wielded by the District Officer Commanding. Relying less on the Robertson Report than on the realities of 1923, Meighen asked what would happen if the Cape Breton experience occurred again and, with the majority of Canadian troops in the area, the Saskatchewan farmers became aroused or the Winnipeg situation was repeated? Such a concentration of military forces, he maintained, "would leave the rest of the country utterly stripped, and the government would stand stark and helpless, unable to do anything." For Meighen it was a "preposterous condition of affairs."[98]

Meighen hammered constantly on this theme and eventually his argument had some effect. Before final reading, Macdonald offered another change whereby the DOC would be required to contact the Adjutant-General before going beyond his military district for additional forces and the Adjutant-General, in turn, would decide from which locations these forces would come. Unsatisfied, Meighen persisted, and finally Macdonald included a provision giving the Adjutant-General full discretionary powers concerning the use of troops from outside any military district.[99] In effect, this meant that if General Thacker, or any other District Officer Commanding, wished to bring in forces from outside his own military district the Adjutant-General would make the decision.

Aside from the financial alterations, the only changes in the Militia Act originally proposed by the King government were to abandon the initial role of the mayor or warden and to insert the Attorney General between the judge and the military.[100] Macdonald was rather vague about the reasons for the deletion of the local, elected representatives from the procedure.[101] That municipalities were to be no longer held responsible for expenses was doubtless a factor, but it should be remembered that in the recent incidents some local elected authorities had declined to call out the troops and this was a period of intense labour involvement in local political activity with labour councilmen and mayors quite evident in the Cape Breton industrial towns. Whatever the reasons behind the alterations, the amendments, as King privately assured Premier Armstrong, were not very significant,[102] although they were satisfactory to the TLC delegation, who in their annual pilgrimage to Parliament in January 1925 deleted their previously expressed desire for Militia Act amendments.[103]

The autumn and winter of 1924-25 were sluggish for the island's steel and coal industry, with direct and dire consequences for the workers and their families. Employment in the mines was sparse and those who were working were managing one or two shifts a week. By mid-February a Glace Bay health officer reported that 2,000 idle miners and their families were "on the verge of starvation."[104] The situation became more desperate when Besco abruptly terminated all credit at its company stores in early March. Faced with little work and less food, the miners reluctantly went on strike a few days later. By April many families were dependent on donations from across the country merely to remain alive.[105] In spite of frequent prodding by J.S. Woodsworth, Agnes Macphail, Arthur Meighen, and others, the federal government refused to intervene. Assistance of this type was not a federal responsibility and Mackenzie King maintained he would only intervene upon the request of the Armstrong government.[106] Armstrong, however, declined to seek relief assistance.[107] One prominent Halifax Conservative privately declared: "It looks as if governments are trying to create such a situation that there will be riots and bloodshed with the result that troops will be rushed in and men forced to return to pits."[108]

Finally, on 11 June 1925, a clash between miners and Besco policemen at New Waterford resulted in the shooting death of one miner and the serious wounding of another. Five others were hospitalized, as were thirty policemen. The provincial police force, which had been secretly organizing for a week,[109] was immediately sent from Halifax to Cape Breton. Again Judge Finlayson was ready and quickly sent a request for troops to the Attorney General, W.J. O'Hearn.[110] The latter contacted General Thacker and, for the third time in four years, military forces began pouring into the area. The feelings of many were expressed by one western trades council in a bitter note to Mackenzie King: "It is our earnest hope that they will take sufficient feed with them as they will find little or none on their arrival. It would be a national catastrophe if troops on arrival suffered any hardships through insufficient nourishment."[111] Soon there were an estimated 2,000 troops on their way to Cape Breton.[112] General Thacker quickly used up all available district troops but a message to the Adjutant-General, which included the unconfirmed report that the workers were in possession of a machine gun and that while there was no ammunition for it a man had apparently left Sydney to obtain some, soon made short shrift of the previous year's amendment prompted by Meighen's criticisms.[113] In Parliament, Defence Minister Macdonald simply explained that "Under the law . . . once the Attorney-general of a province requests the military forces . . .

they are bound to be sent there. No discretion is left." [114] It was a familiar response.

There was a great deal of violence. What is interesting is not that it occurred but that it continued, in spite of the military presence. The first fire occurred on 11 June, several hours after the first troops had been requested. Raiding, looting, and burning continued throughout the month of June. [115] The destruction was not wanton. Most of the company stores were looted and several were burned to the ground. Similar fate befell Besco warehouses, a coal bankhead, and two antiquated wash houses of which the miners had complained for years. In all, there were twenty-two fires, the last occurring on 30 June. Damages were between $500,000 and $1 million. [116] Eventually, quiet returned and the troops departed on 15 August. Only one person was ever charged as a result of the excesses of June 1925: the Besco policeman accused of killing William Davis, the deceased miner. He was acquitted.

The role of the military in the Cape Breton industrial disputes of the 1920's does not easily fit into the pattern detected by previous historians. The absence of violence in 1922 was probably attributable more to the organization and solidarity of the miners than it was to the military presence. Spokesmen for the miners repeatedly stated that they viewed the dispatch of troops as a method of intimidation which intensified feelings, an interpretation shared, or recognized, by other individuals, not all of whom were labour sympathizers. With the forceful appearance of the provincial police the situation was altered somewhat the following year. It can be argued that the military presence in this instance did prevent even worse confrontations between the provincial force and the workers. But the roles of the federal and provincial contingents cannot easily be separated.

The miners went on strike, significantly broadening the dispute, because of the presence of both forces. The striking steel workers and miners viewed the military presence as an intimidating one, a sentiment shared by highly vocal elements of organized labour throughout the country. Even Mackenzie King and James Murdock saw the troops as a force for "subjection" and an "unfair and indecent attempt to cow the men into submission." [117] Also, the provincial force was not on a permanent basis but was created to meet a particular situation and then disbanded. This the provincial authorities did at least four times during the period. Thus it was hardly a highly disciplined, stable force and it is at least possible that its members' enthusiasm and willingness to engage in direct, physical confrontations were increased by the knowledge that Canada's permanent troops were always close at hand. This evident facility in invoking the military may be a partial explanation of Besco's non-conciliatory policy, a policy detected in the corporation's contract negotiations throughout the period.[118] The quick and repeated requisitions for the military doubtless increased the bitterness of many workingmen in the area and gave those radicals committed to class warfare an excellent platform. Thus, the very legislation which was relied on so frequently in industrial disputes may have contributed to an increase in both the number of the incidents and the intensity of the conflict. When the violence did arrive on a large scale, as it assuredly did in June 1925, a military force twice as large as the earlier contingents did not halt the miners from expressing their anger and despair. The apparent willingness of both the federal and provincial governments to ignore the acute distress, coupled with the recurring appearance of federal troops, doubtless contributed to these feelings.

Throughout the period neither the provincial nor the federal government exhibited a strong desire to alleviate the immediate or the fundamental causes for the frequent use of the military in aid of the civil power. The provincial administration, while hardly opposed to the use of troops, was strongly, and unsuccessfully, opposed to acquiring legal or financial responsibility. The federal government, under Mackenzie King, maintained a constitutional aloofness. Their concern, it became apparent, was less with limiting a power of this kind "to a few men without due restraints" than it was with correcting a financial situation which had proved quite costly to the federal government. After an extended controversy, Mackenzie King deducted $133,116.73 from Nova Scotia's subsidy in 1929.[119] It was payment for the cost of the troops in 1925, but that sum was only a small fraction of the total costs resulting from the disputes. The effects of the disruption of production and the bitterness, deprivation, and despair which accompanied these disputes were deep, lasting, and incalculable. The steel workers acquired a company union after their defeat in 1923 and did not become more effectively organized until the late 1930's, while the miners did not regain the elusive wage scale of 1920 until World War II. Major-

General H.C. Thacker was less unfortunate; he became Chief of the General Staff in 1927.

NOTES

1. Major J.J.B. Pariseau, *Disorders, Strikes and Disasters: Military Aid to the Civil Power in Canada, 1867-1933* (Ottawa, 1973). Pariseau's list of 132 incidents is the most comprehensive to date. One minor episode not mentioned centred on a racial riot in Glace Bay, Cape Breton, on 2 September 1918.
2. W.S. MacNutt, *Days of Lorne* (Fredericton, 1955), 177-8.
3. G.F.G. Stanley, *Canada's Soldiers: The Military History of an Unmilitary People* (Toronto, 1960), 294.
4. *Canadian Annual Review of Public Affairs*, 1909 (Toronto, 1910), 277-8.
5. Col. C.F. Hamilton, "The Canadian Militia," a series of articles in *Canadian Defence Quarterly*, 1928-32; Lt.-Col. D.J. Goodspeed, *The Armed Forces of Canada, 1867-1967* (Ottawa, 1967).
6. Stanley, *Canada's Soldiers*, 291.
7. Major T.V. Scudamore wrote that the practice was "the most unpopular duty that the militia can be called upon to perform." "Aid to the Civil Power," *Canadian Defence Quarterly* (1932), 253. See also U. McFadden, "A Civilian's View of the Military," *Canadian Defence Quarterly* (1935), 221-4; R.H. Roy, ". . . in Aid of a Civil Power, 1877," *Canadian Army Journal* (1953), 61-9.
8. D. Morton, "Aid to the Civil Power: The Canadian Militia in Support of Social Order, 1867-1914," *CHR*, LI (1970), 414.
9. Pariseau, *Disorders*, 20, 38, 48, 50.
10. Canada, House of Commons, *Debates,* 1919, 3967-8.
11. *Ibid.,* 3966-82.
12. PAC, Sir Arthur Currie Papers, J.H. MacBrien, "Memorandum on a Future Military Force for Canada," 1919.
13. J. Swettenham, *McNaughton* (Toronto, 1968), I, 183.
14. J. Eayrs, *In Defence of Canada* (Toronto, 1964), I, 69.
15. PAC, Currie Papers, A. Currie to J.H. MacBrien, 12 April 1920.
16. Swettenham, *McNaughton,* I, 182.
17. Eayrs, *In Defence,* I, 224-5.
18. PAC, W.L.M. King Papers, E. Fiset to King, 15 December 1921.
19. *Ibid.*, E. Fiset to King, 19 December 1921.
20. R.M. Dawson, *William Lyon Mackenzie King, 1874-1923* (Toronto, 1958), 372.
21. *Debates*, 1922, 734.
22. *Ibid.*, 665-75.

23. *Ibid.*, 666.
24. *Ibid.*, 667.
25. *Ibid.*, 670-3.
26. *Ibid.*
27. King Papers, W.H. Measures to D.D. McKenzie, 10 August 1922; D.D. McKenzie to King, 10 August 1922.
28. *Ibid.*, R. Wolvin to King, 14 August 1922; King to Wolvin, 15 August 1922.
29. Halifax *Herald*, 16 August 1922.
30. Canada was divided into military districts. District 6, with headquarters at Halifax, encompassed Nova Scotia and Prince Edward Island. A County Court judge since 1908, Finlayson had requisitioned the military during the bitter strike of 1909-10. PAC, Department of National Defence Records, HQ 363-15, vol. 8, D. Finlayson to DOC, 17 July 1909.
31. Sydney *Post*, 17 August 1922.
32. Toronto *Globe*, 16 August 1922.
33. King Papers, G.W. Kyte to King, 18 August 1922.
34. *Ibid.*, Wolvin to King, 16 August 1922.
35. *Ibid.*, E.H. Armstrong to W.S. Fielding, 16 August 1922; Fielding to King, 17 August 1922.
36. *Ibid.*, D.W. Morrison to King, 17 August 1922.
37. *Debates*, 6 March 1923, 867; King Papers, H. Spracklin, Wm. McDonald to J. Murdock, 16 August 1922; J. Guest to King, 18 August 1922; D.J. Aucoin *et al.* to King, 17 August 1922.
38. *Ibid.*, A.P. Walker to King, 18 August 1922; T. Moore to King, 18 August 1922. *Labour Gazette* (September, 1922), 968-9.
39. King Papers, C.A. Munro to King, 17 August 1922; PAC, A.G.L. McNaughton Papers, Thacker to Ottawa, 19 August 1922; McNaughton to Thacker, 23 August 1922.
40. King Papers, King to H. Spracklin, 17 August 1922.
41. *Ibid.*, King to Beaudry, 17 August 1922; Halifax *Herald*, 18 August 1922.
42. *Canadian Annual Review*, 1922 (Toronto, 1923), 731.
43. King Papers, E.H. Armstrong to L. Gouin, 19 August 1922; J.E. Tremblay "Memorandum," 20 August 1922; J.C. Tremblay to E.H. Armstrong, 20 August 1922; Armstrong to Tremblay, 21 August 1922.
44. *Ibid.*, J.E. Tremblay, "Memorandum," 22 August 1922.
45. Montreal *Star*, 19 August 1922.
46. McNaughton Papers, G.O. 6 to Militia Council, 19 August 1922.
47. Morton, "Aid to the Civil Power, 1867-1914," 419, note 19.
48. McNaughton Papers, Senior Naval Officer to Ottawa, 19 August 1922.
49. *Ibid.*, C.G.S. to O.C. 6, 19 August 1922; Naval Headquarters to Halifax, 19 August 1922.

50. King Papers, G.H. Murray to King, 19 August 1922; C.B. Wade, "The History of District 26, United Mineworkers of America" (unpub. ms., n.d., Public Archives of Nova Scotia).

51. McNaughton Papers, King to McNaughton, 20 August 1922.

52. *Ibid.*, McNaughton to H.C. Thacker, 20 August 1922.

53. *Ibid.*, Air Board to Air Station Superintendent, Dartmouth, 21 August 1922.

54. *Ibid.*, General "Six" to Militia Council, 21 August 1922.

55. *Ibid.*, Lt.-Col. R.J. Odre to C.G.S., "Employment of Naval and Air Forces in Aid of the Civil Power," 7 September 1922.

56. King Papers, McNaughton to Thacker, 23 August 1922; McNaughton to King, 23 August 1922.

57. *Ibid.*, T.L.C. to King, 22 August 1922; King to T. Moore, 23 August 1922.

58. *Ibid.*, G.O. 6 to Militia Council, 26 August 1922.

59. Glace Bay *Maritime Labour Herald*, 23 June 1923.

60. "Report of the R.C.M.P.," Canada, House of Commons, *Sessional Paper* 21, LIX, 5 (1923), 14.

61. "Report of the Department of National Defence (Militia Service)," Canada, House of Commons, *Sessional Paper* 17, LX, 4 (1924), 12.

62. King Papers, J. Moffatt to F.A. Acland, 17 August 1922; C.A. Munro to King, 28 August 1922.

63. Thacker, the son of a Major-General in the British Army, was born in India. His father retired to Canada and Thacker was educated at Upper Canada College, Royal Military College, and a variety of theatres of war. Editorial, *Canadian Defence Quarterly* (1927), 379.

64. King Papers, H. Spracklin to King, 19 August 1922.

65. *Debates,* 1923, 863-99.

66. Sydney steel workers had a seven-day week, with day shifts of eleven hours and thirteen-hour night shifts. With a changeover every two weeks they were required to work a twenty-four-hour shift. The Amalgamated Association of Iron, Steel and Tin Workers of America had experienced difficulty in getting established since its first appearance in 1917. At the time of the strike approximately one-quarter of the steel workers were members, a reflection both of the union leadership and the anti-union policies of the employers. Canada, *Report of Royal Commission to Inquire into the Industrial Unrest Among the Steelworkers at Sydney, N.S.* (Ottawa, 1924), 17-21 [hereinafter cited as *Robertson Report*].

67. Sydney *Post*, 30 June 1923.

68. Sydney *Record*, 30 June 1923.

69. Sydney *Post*, 30 June 1923.

70. *Robertson Report*, 14; *Labour Gazette* (August, 1923), 869.

71. Halifax *Chronicle*, 2 July 1923; Halifax *Herald*, 2 July 1923.

72. E.H. Armstrong succeeded G.H. Murray as provincial Premier when the latter retired in January, 1923.

73. Halifax *Herald*, 2 July 1923.

74. Sydney *Post*, 5 July 1923; *Labour Organizations in Canada* (1923), 186; D. Fraser, *Narrative Verse and Comments* (Glace Bay, 1944), 269; King Papers, RCMP Report 183, 12 July 1923.

75. Sydney *Record*, 3 July 1923.

76. T. O'Shea, correspondence with writer, October, 1970.

77. "Report of Minister of National Defence (Militia Service)," Canada, House of Commons, *Sessional Paper* 17, LXI, 4 (1925), 67.

78. Sydney *Record*, 5 July 1923.

79. King Papers, King to E.M. Macdonald, 7 July 1923.

80. *Ibid.*, Primary Correspondence Files, July-August, 1923.

81. Macdonald, whom King had also apparently desired to keep out of his cabinet, was Acting Minister from 30 April to 6 September.

82. Dawson, *Mackenzie King*, 373; King Papers, King to E.M. Macdonald, 7 July 1923; King to E.H. Armstrong, 7 July 1923.

83. *Ibid.*, Macdonald to King, 8 July 1923.

84. *Ibid.*, W.S. Edwards to E.M. Macdonald, 8 July 1923; G.S. Desbarats to D.W. Morrison, 11 July 1923.

85. *Ibid.*, King to Moore, 11 July 1923.

86. *Ibid.*, E.M. Macdonald to King, 8 July 1923; J. Murdock to W.A. Sherman, 8 July 1923.

87. *Ibid.*, J. Murdock to E.M. Macdonald, 12 July 1923; PAC, Arthur Meighen Papers, Canadian Press Clipping, 12 July 1923.

88. *Labour Organizations in Canada* (1923), 24.

89. King Papers, Desbarats to Morrison, 11 July 1923; Edwards to Macdonald, 8 July, 10 July 1923.

90. Sydney *Post*, 13 November 1923.

91. King Papers, King to J.W. Robertson, 21 September 1923.

92. McNaughton Papers, J.H. MacBrien to Minister, 16 February 1924.

93. "Report of Minister of National Defence (Militia Service)." Canada, House of Commons, *Sessional Paper* 17, XLI, 4 (1925), 54; "Report of the Department of National Defence (Militia and Air Services)," *Annual Departmental Reports*, 1925-26 (Ottawa, 1926), II, 58.

94. *Robertson Report*, 24.

95. *Debates*, 1924, 2862.

96. King Papers, Armstrong to King, 4 June 1924; D.A. Cameron to King, 6 June 1924.

97. *Debates*, 1924, 2862-72.

98. *Debates*, 1924, 2872-8.

99. *Ibid.*, 4621-8.

100. Although it had not been discussed during the debates, the final form of the amended act included a provision whereby the Attorney General could also initiate a requisition. 14 and 15 George V, c. 57, s. 81.
101. *Debates*, 1924, 2871, 4623.
102. King Papers, King to Armstrong, 11 June 1924.
103. *Ibid.*, TLC delegation, 31 January 1925.
104. *Ibid.*, Armstrong to King, 19 February 1925 (enclosure).
105. Meighen Papers, Rev(s) M.A. MacAdam, A.M. MacLeod to Meighen, 2 April 1925; W.H. Dennis to Meighen, 2 April 1925.
106. *Debates*, 1925, 1059, 1291, 1339, 1530, 3516-17.
107. A few days after the Roman Catholic Bishop of Antigonish issued a pastoral letter describing conditions of the "direst want" and urging contributions, the provincial government gave $20,000 to the Canadian Red Cross to assist in maintaining health standards in the area. It was a relatively insignificant contribution and was not repeated. Ottawa *Citizen*, 21 April 1925.
108. Meighen Papers, W.H. Dennis to Meighen, 2 April 1925.
109. *Ibid.*, Dennis to Meighen, 11 June 1925.
110. *Labour Gazette* (July, 1925), 662.
111. King Papers, J. Dealtry to King, 12 June 1925.
112. *Labour Gazette* (July, 1925), 663.
113. *Debates*, 1925, 4243.
114. *Ibid.*, 4245.
115. On June 25 the reorganized and rejuvenated Conservative Party under the leadership of E.N. Rhodes ended the forty-three-year Liberal rule in the province, winning forty of forty-three seats.
116. E. Forsey, *Economic and Social Aspects of the Nova Scotia Coal Industry* (Toronto, 1926), 78; Sydney *Record*, 30 June 1925.
117. King Papers, King to E.M. Macdonald, 7 July 1923: Murdock to Macdonald, 12 July 1923; "Canadian Press," Ottawa, 12 July 1923, clipping in Meighen Papers.
118. Miners' perceptions of this attitude are expressed throughout the *Evidence Presented Before the Royal Commission Respecting the Coal Mines of the Province of Nova Scotia* (Nova Scotia, 1925); see also Forsey, *Nova Scotia Coal Industry, passim*.
119. Public Archives of Nova Scotia, Rhodes Papers, E.N. Rhodes to King, 12 February 1929.

V
Social Control

The arrival of immigrants in massive numbers, the concomitant urban growth, and above all the rising perception of poverty and of class conflict had effects which went beyond the realm of labour relations. The new, aggressive business ideal, which we have already encountered in its workplace guises as scientific management and welfare capitalism, also had its urban government counterparts. As the most directly accessible level of government to the new, much-worried-about masses, the city became a significant place of experiment for the emerging corporate do-gooders and their newly arrived middle-class professional helpers. The rise of these professions, many of which were closely associated with the re-emergence of women in the public sphere, created new careers in what had formerly been the charitable realm. The rapid expansion of the state into all aspects of life, which had commenced with public education and the various asylums of nineteenth-century capitalism, proceeded with a new rapidity in the early twentieth century. The urban reform movement, described here by John Weaver, was only one arm of a growing army of "helping" professionals who were laying the foundation in this period of what has recently been termed the therapeutic state. These "social engineers" represented as new and scientific innovations in the area of social reform the same notions of efficiency and education which were being promulgated in industry. The professional engineer had his counterpart in the emergent social worker. Both were prophets of the new efficiency so highly valued by monopoly capital.

FURTHER READING:
The religious underpinnings of much social reform are explored in Richard Allen, *The Social Passion* (Toronto, 1971). For a study of one earlier urban reformer, see Desmond Morton, *Mayor Howland* (Toronto, 1973). For a sampling of urban reform in the experts' own words, see Paul Rutherford, ed., *Saving the Canadian City, 1880-1920* (Toronto, 1974), and his "Tomorrow's Metropolis: The Urban Reform Movement in Canada," *Historical Papers* (1971), 203-24. On the impact of social reform on children, see Neil Sutherland, *Children in English-Canadian Society* (Toronto, 1976). For a contemporary sardonic view, see Stephen Leacock, *Arcadian Adventures Among the Idle Rich* (Toronto, 1914). H.V. Nelles and C. Armstrong caution against too-easy acceptance of Weaver's argument in "The Great Fight for Clean Government," *Urban History Review*, 2 (1976), 50-66. See also their *The Revenge of the Methodist Company: Sunday Streetcars and Municipal Reform in Toronto* (Toronto, 1977). A brilliant treatment of the rise of the engineer in the United States is David Noble's *America by Design* (New York, 1977). On educational reform in Ontario in this period, see Robert M. Stamp, *The Schools of Ontario, 1876-1976* (Toronto, 1982).

John C. Weaver is an historian at McMaster University and has published broadly in the field of urban history.

Elitism and the Corporate Ideal: Businessmen and Boosters in Canadian Civic Reform, 1890-1920

by John C. Weaver

> The People of Toronto are nothing more or less, from a business point of view, than a joint stock company. As a member of several such companies when I go to the annual meeting whom do I support for directors but those who are successful in their own business, have a reputation for being honest and capable. . . . This looks reasonable, and if we would only manage our business as private corporations manage theirs we certainly would not have such a queer lot of directors – aldermen we call them – or make presidents – mayors as we call them – out of men who have never proven themselves as good businessmen in their own personal matters. (*Saturday Night*, quoted in the *Toronto Star*, 22 December 1899.)

Directly or indirectly, many studies – by discussing struggles against corruption and vested interests or analysing the treatises of early civic specialists – have touched on municipal reform in Canadian cities during the late nineteenth and early twentieth centuries. For the most part, they have singled out the efforts of the few outstanding publicists and politicians.[1] Overall these works have primed an interest in an aspect of urban history, but the term "reform" may have contributed to an unwarranted impression of progress, of men alarmed by corrupt and careless

From A.R. McCormack and Ian Macpherson, eds., *Cities in the West*, National Museum of Man Mercury Series, History Division, Paper No. 10 (Ottawa, 1975), 48-73.

practices acting altruistically to fashion plans for better cities.[2] No doubt sincere individuals did step forward in accord with a concern for the well-being of the general public. Nonetheless, several farsighted spokesmen and a handful of exceptional civic politicians did not embody the thrust of "good government" reform. One swallow does not make a spring.

A related problem has been to recognize that expression of fine ideals and adoption of the label "reform" are quite often distinct from actual practice. In fact, reform promises of working toward administration in the public interest masked some very contrary activities. Therefore, to realize a more complete knowledge of the municipal reform movement and its implications for the city requires a close analysis of the actual practices and achievements of the economic and political groups engaged in campaigns for better civic government across Canada. To attain this understanding a set of questions should be considered: What classes or interests did the many citizens' reform committees in Canadian cities represent? To what values did they adhere? From whence did they derive their reform schemes? What were their accomplishments? Did they, for example, seek to extend popular participation in the processes of urban government? Finally, in what ways did their actions influence subsequent developments in the urban setting?

I

Before moving directly onto these paths of inquiry, it is useful, for the sake of balance and perspective, to consider how the system of local government operated both in statute and in practice. At the advent of the reform era, in the 1890's, the general shape of local government had been cast along lines similar to those of the Baldwin Act of 1849. In its philosophy and in its application, this municipal legislation functioned as a model across Canada. It established the notion that municipal government should "teach the people to conduct their own affairs."[3] The reform movement demoted this ideal to accent another by maintaining that "the modern city is a corporation or a huge business with many branches, most of which call for special aptitude and training."[4]

In practice, Canadian towns and cities, before the onset of reform, were divided into wards with one or more aldermen elected from each. At the first meeting of Council after what was usually an annual election, the aldermen formed the committees that were to function as the executive. Real power rested with these committees rather than with the mayor or Council as a whole. The politically ambitious coveted positions on certain of these committees. Water, light, streets, works, and transportation, because of their frequent negotiations with private corporations concerning contracts and franchises, offered rewards for the unscrupulous. Contractors, utility corporations, and streetcar companies found it advantageous to buy members on these committees or to assist the campaigns of friendly aldermen. In Regina, an enterprising contractor tried to reach an agreement with the city by offering $1,000 to the mayor and a team of horses to an alderman.[5] Occasionally a brash alderman might solicit bribes, adding unanticipated expenses to a business. The parks, fire, police, and works committees, because of ample payrolls particularly in larger communities, also furnished important fields of opportunity. One could provide appointments for his lodge brothers and ward backers: in Toronto by 1905, the deputy fire chief, the heads of the Parks Department and Streets Department, the city engineer, city clerk, medical health officer, city treasurer, and assessment commissioner had, in all probability, received appointment for delivering the Orange vote.[6]

In Montreal, the cash nexus accompanied patronage. Applicants for civic employment paid aldermen for smooth processing of their requests.[7] Moreover, there were reports that the Police Committee operated a protection racket; brothels and gambling dens provided payments and only token raids were executed on establishments warned in advance. Members of Council accepted bribes to ignore Health Department recommendations regarding dairies, a fact that may help to account for the severity of typhoid.[8] Less sensational were "innocent" acts of negligence or examples of incompetence such as those leading to leakages in the new Calgary water mains in 1905 and to that city's precarious financial state. Similarly, to take an East Coast illustration, Saint John endured serious breaks in its water mains and because of wharf construction and books "juggled in the most flagrant manner" it stood "face to face with a money stringency."[9] From city to city, proponents of change had an extensive list of abuses and crises at hand when they set out to criticize civic government, ranging all the way from the outrageous activities debasing Montreal to the petty favours of low assessments and minimal light bills granted to several members of the Regina Council.[10] Reformers promised to sweep out both the "cobwebs and dirt." In kind, though not in degree, Canadian cities clearly harboured practices that had evoked Lord Bryce's famous condemnation of urban government in the Republic.

The rumours and exposés of corruption in Canadian cities are manifold and colourful, but more important than narrative is a theory of causation. This becomes an essential consideration since reformers proffered their own explanation for the sordid mess that had settled upon the Dominion's city halls. They held the structure of government responsible: the ward, as the basis for municipal government, made for an inordinate degree of aldermanic fence-mending; tedious Council meetings drove talented men from civic politics and into more rewarding careers; the committees brought politics and personality into the executive realm where they did not belong. Unfortunately, these tidy theories betray biases and, contrary to the expectations of reformers who stressed structural explanations, the remodelling of civic machinery alone would prove incapable of banishing error and corruption. Unprecedented urban growth and a pervasive get-rich-quick mentality provide more basic explanations for political ills, but as we shall see from the social profile of reformers, as businessmen and boosters, they scarcely could have indicated their very ethos as the source of the problem.

Regarding the reform of municipal government in the United States, Samuel P. Hays has stated that "available evidence indicates that the source of support . . . did not come from the lower or middle classes, but from the upper class. The leading business groups in each city and professional men closely allied with them initiated and dominated municipal movements."[11] The Canadian situation fell into a congruent pattern. Toronto in the early 1890's had a solid coterie of municipal reformers, perhaps a score of men, drawn from business and the professions. They sparked a movement supported by at least 100 of the city's elite.[12] Labour leaders and representatives from the city's ethnic ward three did not appear on the rosters of the self-styled citizens' committee. Members of the early Toronto Italian and Jewish communities, in a quest for mobility and acceptance, found more congenial surroundings in the Conservative machine of boss Beattie Nesbitt.[13] As for the Trades and Labor Council, its interest in municipal reform remained minimal and its essential concerns were economic – a municipal coal yard to break the combine in the city, and court action to force Consumers' Gas Company to lower rates.[14] Subsequent forays into municipal reform, between 1895 and 1914, came once again from the Toronto establishment, one of whom, Morley Wickett, stood out as a leading Canadian publicist of reform. An admirer of German bureaucracy, a businessman, and a holder of executive offices in the Canadian Manufacturers' Association, Wickett joined several acquaintances in 1914 to establish the Bureau of Municipal Research. The co-founders included a box manufacturer, who sat on the Council of the Board of Trade, an accountant, and a well-to-do merchant. They received financial support from corporations and wealthy individuals.[15]

Meanwhile, Montreal's great bursts of reform zeal came in 1909 and the list of those citizens who supplied the sinews of war and carried forward the campaign consisted almost entirely of the city's great men of commerce and industry. To conduct a plebiscite campaign favouring structural reforms in September 1909, Sir Hugh Graham and Sir Edward Clouston each contributed $1,000. Sir George Drummond, Henry Birks and Sons, Sir Thomas Shaughnessy, and G.W. Stephens brought $500 each. Greenshields Limited, Lake of the Woods Milling Company, and Thomas Robertson and Company each provided $250. The Hon. L.J. Forget, organizer of the Montreal Light, Heat and Power Company and president of the Street Railway Company, gave $200.[16] To secure sufficient names on petitions demanding a Royal Commission investigation into civic affairs, some of the city's large employers circulated forms for signature among employees. Indeed, from its inception in January 1909, the Montreal reform campaign bore the stamp of the business community. Four groups had initiated a reform committee that steered the movement, namely, the Board of Trade, the Chambre de Commerce, l'Association Immobilière de Montréal, and the Montreal Business Men's League. When a Royal Commission prompted into existence by their efforts did commence an investigation, these groups provided counsel to represent what they deemed the public interest. At the same time, several "merchants" and an individual who described himself as a "gentleman" organized l'Association de Citoyens de Montréal, Limitée, to investigate and improve municipal conditions in the district of Montreal.[17]

Blatant vice and its cosy relationship with civic corruption perhaps jarred the veneer of decency in the business community, but there may have been another motive for the involvement of a few in seeking change. Bribes were becoming a business burden. For example, Mr. W. McLea Walbank, managing director of the Montreal Light, Heat and Power Company, heartily endorsed municipal reform. His company dealt regularly with the city. The very survival of the utility firm depended on franchises and limited civic regulation. Thus, given the practices of the day, one would expect that Walbank had every reason not to see leeway for bribery and influence peddling constricted. In fact, his corporation, according to Alderman Clearihue, had attempted to bribe members of Council in 1907 during contract negotiations between the city and the company. Nonetheless, one finds Walbank among the ranks of the reformers in 1909; immediately suspicion mounts. In public he was denouncing the "unwieldy" nature of Council, which in the argot of his business probably meant that he could no longer extract concessions at a favourable price. His testimony to the Royal Commission suggests that this was the case. During the municipal elections of 1908, he admitted that an alderman had demanded $10,000 for expenses to guarantee the re-election of company friends. Structurally reformed machinery permitting domination by men of his own class, though having certain risks, just might have beckoned as a less costly tactic for ensuring cordial relations with the Hôtel de Ville.[18] The outright blackmailing tactics of greedy politicians could only be tolerated to a certain point.

The character of the Montreal movement can be ascertained further by considering that organized labour vigorously attacked the proposed reform changes. Claiming to speak on behalf of 25,000 members of labour unions in Montreal, Monsieur Rodier resisted reform proposals at every legislative step. When the draft measures went before the Private Bills Committee of the Legislative Assembly and discussion turned to a proposed reduction of aldermen, Rodier and Monsieur Francq, president of the Trades and Labor Congress, noted that if this were designed for better government then, logically, the Assembly should invoke the principle with respect to itself. On an earlier occasion, Rodier claimed that bad administration was not due to the number of aldermen, "but because some of them are in the hands of the trusts." He also spoke "energetically . . . about class divisions and the fact that changes were only proposed by large organization." In a circular issued by the Montreal Trades and Labor Council asking working men to vote against the alleged reforms, a counter set of reforms was presented: abolition of property qualifications for holding office and municipal ownership of all public utilities.[19]

The business leadership of reform that struck Rodier seemed to permeate all Canadian communities, the great and the small. Even the town of Carleton Place boasted a "Municipal Protective Association . . . composed of some of the best business men of Carleton Place and intended to watch closely the business transactions of the council, to advise its members when necessary and to lend its influence to the election of the best men to the council board."[20] Advocates of reform in western towns and cities shared characteristics with those active in the East. One of Winnipeg's most persistent champions of administrative modification, George F. Carruthers, a graduate of Upper Canada College, a prosperous insurance executive, and president of the Canada Brick Company, had served as secretary of the Citizens' Committee on Civic Government in 1896. Almost ten years later, in 1905, as secretary of the Municipal Committee of the Board of Trade, he joined other representatives of "the principal organizations of business men in the city" in meeting with Mayor Thomas Sharpe to discuss the city's "constitution."[21] Sharpe, a wealthy contractor who specialized in sidewalks and an exponent of a municipally owned quarry and asphalt plant, already had initiated a campaign for change with a speech to the Winnipeg Canadian Club in which he asserted that at the top civic government required the talents of businessmen. Moreover, he felt that the city's many foreigners could not comprehend civic issues and hence the role of the wards which gave them a degree of influence should be reduced in any new system. Sharpe thus favoured election at-large.[22] Wealth and municipal reform combined in Regina, too, where the advocate and mayoralty candidate for structural change, Alderman McCarthy, was known as "the Merchant Prince" and claimed he paid $3 out of every $100 received by the city in taxes.[23]

Not just in Winnipeg and Regina but across the Prairies, Boards of Trade worked for new forms of municipal government. There is, for example, the experience of Edmonton. When that city received its charter in 1904, it claimed to have the most modern system of civic government in the Dominion. Drafted by a Toronto lawyer and municipal expert, C.W.R. Biggar, and rushed into operation by the Edmonton establishment, the charter provided for the hiring of commissioners to execute the daily administration of the city. Mayor James Short, who vigorously backed the plan, praised its placing of authority in the hands of men not directly responsible to the public.[24] When expectations were not satisfied, reformers, that is to say the Board of Trade, decided that the city required the services of a "Czar" to manage its affairs. Thus in 1910 the city hired a former utilities commissioner and reform mayoralty aspirant from Seattle. Much to the delight of those who wanted to see the city run like a business, the Commissioner galloped roughshod over Council and Council's appointees in the various departments. Council, supported by much of the public, soon tired of the Commissioner's arrogance and dismissed him. His supporters rushed down to the Board of Trade office and drafted counter-measures. They threatened to run their own candidates at the next election and boasted they would turn the scoundrels out; they also retained legal counsel to resist dismissal through the courts.[25]

In 1911, members of the Edmonton Board of Trade had only threatened to field candidates, but the Calgary Board of Trade actually did so in 1903. Similar direct political action by men of property and standing had been undertaken in Toronto at the turn of the century. At a meeting in the Board of Trade building a number of key businessmen decided to bring out E.B. Osler for mayor, "a man of tried business capacity."[26] After all, if businessmen did not run cities, who would? According to Edmonton's Mayor Short it might be "the hail fellow, well met . . . or it may be that the trades unions' political party may place a man in the council irrespective of his fitness."[27] Undoubtedly, the proponents of "reform" were construing notions of right and wrong, efficiency and inefficiency, along class lines.

Throughout the Dominion, leaders of Boards of Trade and later Chambers of Commerce conceived of their members as the true custodians of civic propriety and order. And, as the above statement by Short implied, there surfaced bitterness when the electorate failed to appreciate their self-proclaimed superiority. Consider the declaration of T.J. Drummond, president of the Montreal Board of Trade, made in 1908:

A Board of Trade should be a power in whatever municipality it is established. It represents generally the people most in-

terested in the Municipality, and should surely be in a position to give good advice on matters affecting public welfare.
Unfortunately, this is not always appreciated by Municipal
Councils, or perhaps I should say Municipal Councillors . . .
the fact still remains that Boards of Trade composed of intelligent men . . . should be able to at least assist and advise
the City Fathers.[28]

It is striking how fully this coincides with an address by J.H.
Laughton of the London Chamber of Commerce delivered at
the annual meeting of the Ontario Municipal Association over a
decade later. Laughton claimed that "until the Chambers of
Commerce, made up as they are of the best representatives and
most intelligent people of every community, take advantage of
its . . . ability in bringing about the co-ordination between itself
and its municipal government, citizens will continue to keep in
charge of your government that type of official who does not
represent that degree of efficiency approved by the good thinking people of your community."[29] A parallel attitude in Saint
John caused one harried alderman to retort: "We are not the in-
competent fossils our zealous members of the Board of Trade
would make us out to be."[30] In truth, city councils embraced a
variety of talents, but they also represented a range of interests.
One wonders whether the state of the former stirred as much
concern as the existence of the latter among members of the
Boards of Trade and Chambers of Commerce. With ambitions
to have certain public works undertaken, business associations
found that in civic politics they were but one of many competing
interests. Unwilling to accept fully the realities of political
pluralism, they worked to scupper the rules of the game. Aldermen were thus considered as fools; labour candidates had no
skills; businessmen were efficient. Above all, the system required radical change to reduce the effectiveness of other interests.

II

For objectives and ideals, groups and individuals who directed
the assaults against established municipal institutions reached
into their day-to-day experience and extracted business or corporate analogies. Dwelling on what they assumed to be parallels

between efficient administration of business and the proper course for city government comprised a regular aspect of their reasoning. It followed that since corporations had shareholders whose powers varied directly with their holdings and who in turn vested authority in executives, so it should be with the copy. Scores of reform speeches proposed that citizens receive multiple votes in relation to their property assessments; many more declarations maintained that property owners, like stockholders, should grant executive authority to a civic officer styled after a corporate general manager. Needless to say, the traditions and meaning of local representation did not occupy a niche in this pattern of constitutional thinking. Emphasis on order and efficiency outweighed ideals of democracy. All of this found concrete expression in measures proposed as well as adopted.

To present in detail the precise course of reform measures applied across Canada would be tedious. Hybrids flourished and, as the fortunes of reform swelled and receded, particular innovations would be altered or revoked. London, for example, adopted a reformed "constitution" one year, only to rescind it the next. Moreover, reformers disputed among themselves, disagreeing as to the most efficacious system of government – board of control, government by commission, or government by a series of special commissions controlling specific areas such as utilities, parks, and planning.[31] Yet an emphasis on variety would be deceptive. Measures can be reduced to general patterns. Many good government schemes, for example, included some device to emasculate local representation by eliminating or amalgamating wards; a few others even reduced the electorate by introducing higher property qualifications. This suggests that reformers sought to oust wrongdoing by shifting the social composition of civic representation heavily toward the middle and upper classes. According to the basic inclination of municipal reformers, the transient labourers, boarding-house dwellers, and recent immigrants should have been excluded from participating in civic affairs. Much attention has been called to the existence of a "floating proletariat" in nineteenth-century industrial cities, and it appears that Canadian reformers sensed the turnover of the working classes when they identified the city's "real interests" with propertied men of community standing.[32] Wickett wrote that the restrictions on the franchise deserved retention since they operated chiefly "against newcomers of various classes and nationalists who have little ground for interest in civic affairs."[33] Mayor Richard Deans Waugh of Winnipeg reflected similar sentiments in an address to the Conference of the Civic Improvement League of Canada.

. . . our democratic system of government does not permit us to vote according to the value of our interest in the municipality, that is to say, according to the value of shares we own in the corporation, our real estate and business interests.

Take our great banking institutions for instance. The President is, as a matter of course, re-elected every year. He is, in many instances, a man who has risen from the ranks and doesn't need to worry about his re-election. But if he had to depend on his customers for re-election he would be in much the same position as the mayor [*sic*] of our cities.[34]

Reformers could not accept the fact that people, many of whom were transient, formed the essence of the city; they preferred, instead, to consider the city as a business enterprise that had yet to shape up to corporate standards.

But, to provide an evaluation of reformers that includes their contributions as well as their flaws, it is worthy of note that both Wickett and Waugh had distinguished public careers. Wickett's lobbying for a provincial body to supervise the conduct of Ontario municipalities contributed to the creation of the Ontario Municipal Board, and, as early as 1913, he had prepared a plan for a Toronto metropolitan government. A one-time president of the Winnipeg Real Estate Exchange, Waugh was a civic booster dedicated to orderly but ever-mounting growth for "the Chicago of the North." To improve Winnipeg's services and hence attract business and residents, he had promoted public ownership of hydroelectric power and worked for the building of the ninety-six-mile-long Shoal Lake Aqueduct. Subsequently, he served as chairman of the Greater Winnipeg Water District Commission from 1915 to 1920. This pioneer effort in Canadian metropolitan government and Waugh's conservative credentials brought him to the attention of Prime Minister Borden, who was searching for some seasoned civic authority to lead the Halifax Relief Commission after the Great Explosion. Waugh rejected the offer, but he later accepted appointment to the League of Nations Commission for the Saar. There he alone opposed the aggressive actions of the French. Though narrow in their conception of the city, both men left works that benefited later generations.[35]

Having suggested who civic reformers were and to which general notions of good government they subscribed, it remains to sketch in more precisely what activities they undertook in several Canadian cities. The wards, because they appeared to business-minded reformers as creating too much of a focus on local problems at the expense of city-wide questions such as water, sewer, transportation, beautification, and civic boosting, provided an immediate target for change. Toronto reformers in 1891 achieved a reduction in the number of wards by amalgamation.[36] Once executive powers in some cities were transferred from Council committees to new organs such as the Board of Control or the Civic Commission, the representative function of the wards slipped since election to these new positions was at-large. Some municipalities, in a flurry of reform enthusiasm, simply abolished wards. Galt, Lindsay, Owen Sound, Peterborough, Belleville, Chatham, Barrie, Guelph, London, St. Catharines, and Hamilton followed this course after Ontario passed general enabling legislation in 1898 and again in 1903. Many, however, soon returned to the ward system.[37] Saint John and Fredericton, as early as 1894, eliminated their wards and elected aldermen by a vote of the whole city.[38]

As a further tether to popular government at the local level, some reformers proposed restrictions on the franchise. Edmonton, very much to the fore with innovation in these years, serves once more to illustrate a point. At first glance, the city charter's provision for a plebiscite on money by-laws appears to represent a broadening of public involvement, but its application had limits of a contrary intent. Two classes of voters were proposed. Electors assessed at $100 could vote only for mayoralty and aldermanic candidates. A second class of voters, burgesses, alone would be entitled to vote in the plebiscites. Further, they were to receive ballots in proportion to their assessment: an individual assessed at $2,000 or more was entitled to four ballots; $1,200 to $2,000 brought three; and $600 to $1,200 two.[39] A few reformers in Montreal and Toronto unsuccessfully advocated extending the franchise, but to companies.[40] Some reform propositions maintained that elected representation was far too unstable a base for the technical and fiscal decision-making that now had to concern city government; they submitted that there should be interest group representation. One London, Ontario, reformer felt that civic bureaus of research, rotary clubs, ratepayers associations, and the Board of Trade should be represented. A reform alderman in Montreal recommended that a five-man executive run the city: the mayor, two members elected by Council, one by the Board of Trade, and one by the Chambre de Commerce.[41] Such corporate or special interest representation, as we shall see, was extremely popular in plans for establishing utility, parks, fire, and planning boards or commissions.

Each of the above represented an assault on the representative base of government. Meanwhile, complementary sets of innovations directed toward the top sought to attenuate the ward from executive decisions by developing and strengthening a central bureaucracy removed from aldermanic "meddling." Extremists, not trusting the slightest infringement of the ballot, demanded provincially appointed commissions to manage the whole city.[42] Though these views did not quite carry the day, the notion that there was to be a separation of the executive and legislative arms was far-reaching.

In a sense, this reflected the general influence of the American municipal reform movement, but there arises a complication since Canadian reformers often claimed that their particular scheme really represented the establishing of a parliamentary cabinet for municipalities. Drawing irrationally from the catchphrases of both the American and British political systems generated a muddled reform rhetoric with only the business analogies suggesting a true purpose. Toronto's Board of Control arrangement established an executive elected at large which could only have its recommendations defeated by a two-thirds vote of Council. However, reformers insisted on drawing a comparison between it and a cabinet.[43]

Though frequently misunderstood, the adherence to British political traditions had a mitigating influence preventing the adoption of extreme American plans. Numerous middle-sized cities in the United States had abolished Councils, replacing them with four- or five-man executive commissions elected at large. Calgary reformers discussed this so-called Galveston plan, but they never considered eliminating Council.[44] In 1911, Vancouver Council likewise considered at length the possibility of establishing a commission form of government. According to Morley Wickett, who opposed this American commission system when it was being considered by some Toronto reformers, it was necessary to retain Council as a civic parliament and as a school for democracy.[45] Only one Canadian city did plunge ahead enthusiastically with wholly American blueprints – Saint John, New Brunswick, introduced the commission form of government with the democratic element provided for by recall, initiative, and referendum. Feeling that it was "abundantly evident under the present cumbersome system . . . that it is impossible to conserve, protect and economically administer the affairs of the city," reformers were attracted to provisions of the "expert hand" claimed for the Galveston and Houston scheme.[46] In summary, the United States provided an ever handy reservoir of ideas to be debated, though the British heritage frequently interceded to prevent swings toward the extreme of a commission without Council. Despite imported rhetoric and labels, Canadian cities established executive branches that were, for the most part, neither model parliamentary cabinets nor pure Galveston-style commissions. Canadian municipal reform in its constitutional details, though not in social direction, varied from that pursued in the United States.

In addition to Board of Control and commission government, there remained another means of reducing the authority of Council and its committees, namely, the specialized board or commission with independent powers in a specified area of city government. Precedents for this were well established in Ontario where the Boards of Health as well as Police and Harbour Commissions long had appeared on the statute books. New to the reform era, however, were the multitude of plans for a variety of commissions; an old institutional device with limited application rapidly came into vogue. Although commissions had indigenous precedents, the enthusiasm for them owed much to the American reform movement. Judge Denton of York County reflected this when he observed that

> in the principal cities of the northern States the fire brigades are governed by a Commissioner or Commissioners. They are appointed in different ways. In some cities there are three commissioners; in others four; in others five, and in some there are six. In some places they are appointed by the Mayor, the term of office being three to six years, one or more commissioners retiring alternately. In other cities the nominations of the Mayor must be confirmed by the Council. . . .
>
> A commission selected in this manner . . . should produce a more efficient and useful fire brigade than one that is under

the control and governed by a constantly changing body of municipal representatives. . . .[47]

Guelph, Ontario, adopted the specialized commission remedy with a vengeance, and its experience illustrates some of the attendant problems. In 1907, Guelph eliminated its wards. A general vote elected aldermen and the mayor. Council created a series of special commissions in subsequent years, each with its own budget. Two aldermen and the mayor constituted a commission. Thus, executive decisions came to be executed by officials who lacked a local representative dimension and who were not accountable to the whole of Council due to their independent budgets. The scheme proved highly inefficient because of a lack of co-ordination between the quasi-autonomous bodies.[48]

At least the members of Guelph's commissions were all elected officials. In other instances, reformers, suspicious of popular or representative government, advocated appointed membership. Again and again, Toronto reformers prescribed this remedy. The Toronto Civic Guild, a silk-stocking group interested in bringing the American "City Beautiful" movement to Toronto, articulated a plan for a Parks Commission composed of appointees drawn from business and the professions. Support for the concept poured in from the Ontario Association of Architects, the Engineers Club, the Riverdale Business Men's Association, the Board of Trade, and the Island Association.[49] The Riverdale Business Men's Association also endorsed the idea of a Fire Commission consisting of "a member of the Board of Trade, a member of the City Council and a member of the Fire Underwriters' Association."[50] While these plans went unrealized, the city did acquire a Hydro Electric Commission, a Transportation Commission, and a reformed Harbour Commission; all had appointed members and only liaison representation from Council.

Reformers in other cities also took an interest in commissions. During the busy year of 1909 in Montreal, a Civic Improvement League formed and within a few months of its founding had called for a provincial bill permitting appointment of five persons by the Lieutenant Governor-in-Council, to be known as the Metropolitan Park Commission, to draft plans for a system of parks extending over the entire island.[51] Vancouver reformers in 1906 recommended either a Board of Control or a Water Works

Commission with two of its five members appointed by Council. According to Vancouver's Mayor Bethune, a commission could attract the "services of bright, able men who have not the time to serve in the Council."[52] In other words, businessmen and professionals would be more inclined to accept an appointment than to engage in a ward contest and endure the tedious routine of attending to constituents' requests. They wanted their goals of a centralized, efficient, and technical overview to city government accomplished without their having to surrender personal leisure or the private drive to get ahead; elections, the effort to know a constituency, and log-rolling in Council all seemed unnecessary. By contrast, many ward politicians, despite faults, rolled up their sleeves and made an effort to attend to individual and local matters. As Michel Gauvin concluded in his study of reform in Montreal, "the ward politician . . . dealt with the miseries of his constituents."[53]

Though enthusiasm for another reform scheme, the city manager plan, swelled only after 1920, particularly in Quebec, it deserves brief mention here. Guelph, Ontario, once more near the forward edge of reform experimentation, inaugurated the system in January 1919. One of the participants in drafting the measure reflected on its genius. His comments return us, full circle, to the epigraph that introduced this inquiry.

> The organization is now like a joint stock company; the aldermen are the directors, the mayor is the president; they are legislative. The city manager, through his different departments, plans the work, submits same to the council for their approval. When approved, it is up to the city manager to carry it out in a business-like manner, without interference from the aldermen.[54]

That this corporate simile, intrinsic to municipal reform, seemed to penetrate every cranny of the good government movement through the years connotes the infallible image of business that had existed not just among the directors of the great concerns, but in the minds of lesser businessmen as well as professionals.

Yet this raises a question. If influential groups worked for the remodelling of civic government along business lines, why did they not carry their ideals into an equally forceful campaign for altering the provincial or federal government structures?[55] The answer is related to the rapidly changing city in the era under consideration. Bearing the mark of technological revolutions, above, on, and under every street, the cities appeared as special domains quite unlike larger governmental units. Engineering and fiscal questions demanding immediate attention made the city seem more of a technical environment than either the provinces or the nation. The sage of the Grange, Goldwin Smith, in speech after speech from 1890 onward, drew attention precisely to this point. In the past, city government, he alleged, was a proper setting for debates on principles but now "a city is simply a densely peopled district in need of a specially skilled administration."[56] Thus reformers accented the technical and service dimensions of the city while wedding the concept of good government to business models. In sum, because of an urban revolution and their community influence, they successfully narrowed the objectives of urban government and established a foundation for a half-century of bureaucratic expansion.[57]

Aside from seeking to circumscribe the philosophy of good government so that business and technical standards were accepted and public access to decision-making slighted, reformers are open to criticism on additional grounds. Granting that efficiency and economy constituted worthy aims, it can be maintained that the activities of reformers did not necessarily realize them. As had been noted in several studies, the regime of honest men in Montreal met with embarrassing failure.[58] The establishment of new executive offices in other cities frequently led to conflicts or deadlock with Council, internecine struggles between recently created boards or agencies, and excuses for inaction or duplication of effort.[59] As early as 1899 there surfaced some recognition that structural modification did not necessarily eliminate "wasteful" conflict. A *Toronto Star* editorial noted that between Council and Board of Control there had developed "a game of shuttlecock and battledore."[60] And illusions of smooth government by an appointed commission did not square with performance. During a Toronto civic investigation in 1927, a Harbour Commissioner testified that there arose "lots" of serious conflicts.

Q. And strong language?
A. Everyone fighting for his hand, arguing and that sort of thing. By Judge Denton.
Q. No profanity of course?
A. Yes, lots of it.[61]

Of course, waste and corruption were not banished. In fact, businessmen or professionals in appointed or at-large offices could be as prone to self-interest and favouritism as the very ward-heelers whom they had castigated. The activities of several of Toronto's Harbour and Transportation Commissioners testify to these shortcomings.[62] One might also question whether the $5,000 car, sporting "a special paint and a special siren horn," purchased by Calgary's Commissioners for their use in 1913 represented an act in the public interest.[63]

Though it is easy to accept the proposition that partisan or lodge politics accompanied by graft and patronage under ward bosses could not have provided an adequate foundation for urban leadership in a period of extreme stress, it must be acknowledged that municipal reformers also merit a share of critical appraisal. Their misplaced indignation, their narrow values, and their excessive faith in structural change, all magnified by a compliant press that in most communities shared a high regard for business objectives, did nothing to alleviate the social and economic distress that accompanied Canada's urban revolution from 1890 to 1920. The proponents of the social gospel, labour leaders, and health officials who did direct some efforts in these areas could muster neither material resources nor political influence as readily as the municipal reformers. Indeed, the business community pursuing self-interest did much to determine tempo in a number of urban reform categories. Thus, aside from structural change, the other aspect of reform accorded some measure of success was municipal ownership or regulation of utilities where business support figured as an essential consideration. However, while businessmen of every rank and activity – manufacturers, financiers, and merchants – could work for the conservative ends of municipal reform, those with a local focus promoted public ownership. Opponents of regulatory measures or ownership naturally included utility executives, but also financiers and entrepreneurs of national scope. The first resisted for obvious reasons; the latter two did so because they did not have the pragmatic local interest in municipal ownership that attracted businessmen whose profits depended on the expense and quality of water, gas, electric, and transportation services.[64]

Though cleavages and diversity existed, particularly beyond campaigns for good government which raised little substantive controversy, Canadian businessmen and their organizations secured prominence in urban "progressive" movements ensuring that crises and demands for change would result in new conditions, but, nonetheless, ones which remained closely identified with their biases, needs, and ambitions.[65] Precisely how this relationship worked in each city can suggest much about its physical, administrative, and even social make-up until the advent of new pressures arising after the Second World War.[66]

NOTES

1. For published works, see Carl Berger, *The Sense of Power, Studies in the Ideas of Canadian Imperialism, 1867-1914* (Toronto, 1970), 189-91; Joseph Levitt, *Henri Bourassa and the Golden Calf, the Social Program of the Nationalists of Quebec, 1900-1914* (Ottawa, 1969), 47-56; Desmond Morton, *Mayor Howland, The Citizens' Candidate* (Toronto, 1973); Paul Rutherford, "Tomorrow's Metropolis: The Urban Reform Movement in Canada, 1880-1920," Canadian Historical Association, *Historical Papers* (1971). Several theses are worthy of attention: Dennis Carter-Edwards, "Toronto in the 1890's: A Decade of Challenge and Response" (M.A. thesis, University of British Columbia, 1973); Daniel J. Russell, "H.B. Ames as Municipal Reformer" (M.A. thesis, McGill University, 1971); Michel Gauvin, "The Municipal Reform Movement in Montreal, 1886-1914" (M.A. thesis, University of Ottawa, 1972). The latter two have made excellent use of American scholarship and have noted the conservative nature of municipal reform.
2. For a generous interpretation of reformers, see Rutherford, "Tomorrow's Metropolis," 217.
3. *Municipal World*, II (10 February 1892), 14; J.M.S. Careless, *The Union of the Canadas: The Growth of Canadian Institutions, 1841-1857* (Toronto, 1967), 123.
4. "Mayors' Salaries," *Municipal World*, XV (April, 1905), 88; also see "Treat Municipal Government as Business," *Municipal World*, XV (November, 1905), 283.
5. *Montreal Daily Star*, 30 January 1909, 1.
6. Accounts of patronage and corruption in Toronto can be found in the newspapers, but typescript copies of inquiries and printed conclusions in the appendices to Council minutes are most useful: *In the Matter of the Investigation before His Honour Judge McDougall . . . Evidence* (5 vols., typescript, 1894); *Investigation into Toronto Water Works at the Main Pumping Station, 1899* (typescript); *Fire Brigade Investigation* (typescript); *Investigation into Civic Elections, 1904* (typescript); "In the Matter of Investiga-

tion of the Assessment Rolls of the City of Toronto," *Minutes of the Council of the City of Toronto . . . 1904*, Appendix C; *Parks Investigation Report, April 11, 1908* (typescript); *Works Department Investigation*, 1911 (typescript); *Toronto Fire Department Investigation, 1915* (typescript).

7. See the summary of 1899 Montreal Police inquiry in the *Toronto Star*, 15 September 1899, 2.

8. Newspaper accounts of the Commission are detailed; see especially the *Montreal Star*, 18 September 1909. However, the depositions, anonymous letters, and testimony are most useful and are located in the Provincial Archives, Quebec City (C-9).

9. *Calgary Evening Journal*, 14 July 1904, 4; *Weekly Herald*, 24 November 1904, 6; 5 January 1905, 12; 12 January 1905, 3; *Regina Standard*, 28 June 1905, 4; *Saint John Daily Sun,* 12 November 1907, 6; 10 December 1907, 1.

10. *Regina Standard*, 16 May 1906, 9.

11. Samuel P. Hays, "The Politics of Reform in Municipal Government in the Progressive Era," *Pacific Northwest Quarterly*, LV (October, 1964). Rutherford refers to the "middle-class" impetus for reform, but cites businessmen and newspaper executives as prominent reformers.

12. John C. Weaver, "The Meaning of Municipal Reform: Toronto, 1895," *Ontario History*, LXVI (June, 1974). Long lists of reform supporters appeared in the press and quantitative techniques could establish a profile of those with an interest in reform. However, since most meetings were held on weekdays in mid-afternoon it seems most unlikely that the working class could attend.

13. From the press and various manuscript collections I have been attempting to reconstruct the career of Dr. Nesbitt, the ward organizer who was "boss" between 1890 and 1907. Some interesting letters on patronage, immigrants, and bosses are found in the Sir John A. Macdonald collection. See, for example, PAC, Macdonald Papers, Hebrew Society of Toronto to Alderman Piper, May, 1886; D. Davis to Piper, 27 November 1886; Piper to Macdonald, 7 December 1886.

14. *Evening Star*, 7 December 1895, 3.

15. Toronto Bureau of Municipal Research, *Minute Book,* April 13-September 14, 1914; *Toronto Star*, 10 January 1911, 7. The three were John Firstbrook, John Sutcliffe, and John Macdonald.

16. *Montreal Star*, 23 September 1909, 6.

17. *Montreal Star*, 23 January 1909, 8; 2 February 1909, 4; *Gazette*, 3 February 1909, 4; 15 April 1909, 1; *Montreal Star*, 21 September 1909, 6. Also Provincial Archives, Quebec City, C-9-1, Henry Miles, President, Montreal Business Men's League, to Judge Cannon, 27 April 1909.

18. *Montreal Star*, 26 February 1909, 1; Provincial Archives, C-9-12, *Rapport du Commission* (typescript, 1909), 130. For Clearihue's

statement and his vindication in a libel action, see *Saint John Daily Sun*, 7 March 1910, 3.

19. *Montreal Star*, 14 April 1909, 6; *Gazette*, 15 April 1909, 1; *Montreal Star*, 15 May 1909, 27; 18 September 1909, 13.

20. *Municipal World*, xi (2 July 1901), 102.

21. William Douglas, "Winnipeg Parks," *Historical and Scientific Society of Manitoba*, Series iii, 61-3; Alan Artibise, "The Urban Development of Winnipeg, 1874-1914" (Ph.D. thesis, University of British Columbia, 1971), 457-65; *Manitoba Free Press*, 10 November 1905, 4; 13 November 1905, 1; *Winnipeg Free Press*, obituary file.

22. *Manitoba Free Press*, 11 January 1905, 8; *Free Press*, obituary file.

23. *Regina Leader*, 7 December 1904, 1; *Regina Standard*, 7 December 1904, 1.

24. City of Edmonton, microfilmed Council and Committee Minutes and Reports, Reel 180-R, *Council Minutes, 1900-1914*, 14 February 1903, 119; 29 April 1904, 90; *Evening Journal*, 21 July 1904, 10. In Regina, the Board of Trade applauded commission government and was consulted by the mayor when the city considered a new charter. *Regina Standard*, 16 May 1906, 9; 6 June 1905, 5.

25. *Daily Edmonton Bulletin*, 31 December 1909, 8; 6 January 1910, 1; 7 April 1910, 4; A.W. Cashman, *The Edmonton Story, The Life and Times of Edmonton, Alberta* (Edmonton, 1960); J.G. MacGregor, *Edmonton, A History* (Edmonton, 1967), 185; for the most colourful accounts, see the *Daily Edmonton Bulletin* and the *Edmonton Capital*, January-August, 1911.

26. *Calgary Albertan*, 27 November 1903, 4; Goldwin Smith quoted in the *Globe*, 23 December 1902, 8.

27. Mayor Short, Edmonton, "Municipal Government by Commission," *Canadian Municipal Journal*, iii (April, 1907), 144.

28. T.J. Drummond, President, Montreal Board of Trade, "The Value of Boards of Trade," *Canadian Municipal Journal*, iv (July, 1908), 275.

29. J.H. Laughton, "Chambers of Commerce and City Government," *Municipal World*, xxix (December, 1919), 176.

30. *Saint John Daily Sun*, 14 December 1908, 8.

31. For brief surveys of the shifting attitudes, see G.H. Baker, City Clerk, London, "Ontario Municipal Government," *Municipal World*, xxv (October, 1915), 209; "Municipal Government Reform," *Municipal World*, xxvii (October, 1917), 154. Also see the debate held by the Literary and Scientific Society at the University of Toronto, *Globe*, 16 November 1912, 8; Province of Saskatchewan, *Annual Report of the Department of Municipal Affairs, 1910-11* (Regina, 1911), 10; *Calgary Weekly Herald* for 1904-1908.

32. See, for example, Stephan Thernstrom, "Urbanization, Migra-

tion, and Social Mobility in Late Nineteenth-Century America," in Barton J. Bernstein, ed., *Towards a New Past* (New York, 1969); Michael Katz, "The People of a Canadian City: 1851-2," *CHR*, LIII (December, 1972), 406.

33. Morley Wickett, "Municipal Government of Toronto," *University of Toronto Studies, History and Economics*, II (1902), 55.

34. Mayor Waugh, "Systems and Personnel in Civic Government," *Municipal World*, XXVI (April, 1916), 73.

35. Public Archives of Ontario, Whitney Papers, S. Morley Wickett to Premier Whitney, 19 September 1906; Wickett, *Memorandum re Metropolitan Area* (Toronto, 1913); *Canadian Annual Review* (1913), 350; *Winnipeg Free Press* file on Waugh.

36. For details on this and several other aspects of reform in the 1890's, see Carter-Edwards, "Toronto in the 1890's."

37. *Municipal World*, VIII (October, 1898), 156; IX (December, 1899), 196; XI (June, 1901), 86; XVII (November, 1907), 250; XIX (January, 1909), 2, 13; *Canadian Municipal Journal*, IV (October, 1908), 449.

38. *Municipal World*, IV (November, 1894), 164.

39. *Calgary Weekly Herald*, 13 October 1904, 11; also see Alderman Gariepy, "A Daring Experiment in City Government," *Municipal World*, XX (November, 1910), 289.

40. *Municipal World*, XIX (February, 1909), 26; *Gazette*, 15 April 1909, 1; S. Morley Wickett, "Present Conditions," *University of Toronto Studies, History and Economics*, IV (1907), 170.

41. *Montreal Star*, 2 March 1909, 15. For similar viewpoints, see *Montreal Star*, 18 September 1909, 13; *Gazette*, 3 February 1909, 4.

42. *Globe*, 12 November 1895, 6; *Gazette*, 14 April 1909, 4.

43. Weaver, "The Meaning of Municipal Reform," 98.

44. *Calgary Weekly Herald,* 8 November 1906, 2; Norbert MacDonald, "A Critical Growth Cycle for Vancouver, 1900-1914," *B.C. Studies* (Spring, 1973), 37-8.

45. Wickett, *City Government by Commission, An Address before the Canadian City of Hamilton, delivered in November, 1912* (n.p., n.d.), 5, 11; W.J. Bell of Guelph favoured retaining Council "as an advisory board and a school in which to try out desirable commissioners." *Municipal World*, IX (November, 1909), 273.

46. T.J. Moore, City Clerk, Guelph, "City Government," *Municipal World*, XXVII (October, 1917), 157; *Saint John Daily Sun*, 3 December 1907, 4.

47. Toronto City Archives, *Toronto Fire Department Investigation, Report of His Honour Judge Denton* (typescript, 1915), 70-3.

48. Moore, "City Government," 156.

49. *Toronto World*, 27 November 1907, 9; Toronto City Archives, Guild of Civic Art, *Report on a Comprehensive Plan for*

Systematic Civic Improvements in Toronto (Toronto, 1909), 5; Rosalyn Berger, *History of Planning Organization in Toronto* (typescript, City of Toronto Planning Board, 1958); Civic Improvement Committee, *Report of Civic Improvement Committee for the City of Toronto, 1911* (Toronto, n.d.); *Minutes . . . of the Council of the City of Toronto . . . 1908*, 174-5, 194.

50. *Minutes . . . of the Council of the City of Toronto . . . 1915*, 55.
51. *Montreal Star*, 21 April 1909, 11; 23 December 1909, 10.
52. *Daily News-Advertiser*, 9 January 1906, 2; 4 January 1907, 2; *Daily Province*, 24 December 1907, 2. In 1914, Vancouver Council again discussed the Board of Control plan. MacDonald, "A Critical Growth Cycle for Vancouver," 37-8.
53. Michel Gauvin, "The Municipal Reform Movement in Montreal," 152.
54. T.J. Moore, City Clerk, Guelph, "Guelph's City Government," *Municipal World*, xxx (November, 1920), 195.
55. A brief for bureaucratic government and the abolition of the Provincial Assembly actually did appear in British Columbia in 1938 and was supported by the Vancouver Board of Trade and the Associated Boards of Trade of Eastern British Columbia. Martin Robin, *Pillars of Profit, The Company Province, 1934-1972* (Toronto, 1973), 317.
56. Toronto City Archives, City Clerk's Office, Scrap Book for 1859-1899, *Mail*, 10 November 1890; also see Smith quoted in the *Toronto Star*, 22 December 1902, 4.
57. See the excellent study of Toronto, Bureau of Municipal Research (Toronto), "The 101 Governments of Metro Toronto," *Civic Affairs* (October, 1968).
58. John Irwin Cooper, *Montreal, A Brief History* (Montreal, 1969), 134-5; Terry Copp, *The Anatomy of Poverty* (Toronto, 1970), 147.
59. See Thomas J. Plunkett, *Urban Canada and Its Government: A Study of Municipal Organization* (Toronto, 1968), 69-73.
60. *Toronto Star*, 23 September 1899, 4.
61. Toronto City Archives, *Toronto Harbour Board Enquiry, Evidence Taken Before His Honour Judge Denton, Commissioner*, 4 vols. (typescript, 1927), iii, 2405.
62. Toronto City Archives, *Toronto Harbour Board Enquiry, Evidence Taken Before His Honour Judge Denton, Commissioner; Toronto Transportation Commission Judicial Investigation, Report of His Honour Judge Denton* (typescript, 1929); Belinda Sugarman, "Too Many Chefs Spoil the Broth" (unpublished paper on deposit at the Toronto Archives), 26-7.
63. City of Calgary, microfilmed Council and Committee Minutes and Reports, Reel D.209, *Council Minutes, 1913*: 3 March 1913, 90.
64. This is implied in Charles W. Humphries, "The Sources of On-

tario 'Progressive' Conservatism, 1900-1914," Canadian Historical Association, *Historical Papers* (1967), 122. Many prairie Boards of Trade supported ownership, seeing it as a means of providing immediate services and stimulating expansion, hence enhancing business and speculative prospects.

65. See, for example, the discussion of the aims and achievements of housing reformers in Toronto in Shirley Spragge, "Providing Workingmen's Housing in Toronto, 1905-1920: Examples of Private Enterprise and Public Policy" (M.A. thesis, Queen's University, 1974).

66. This study has profited from discussions with my former colleagues at the Institute of Local Government, Queen's University, especially Tom Plunkett, Chris Leo, and Bill Hooson. C.M. Johnston of McMaster University rendered criticism that prevented errors in the final draft and Norbert MacDonald of the University of British Columbia called attention to the Vancouver experience.

VI
Women

The early twentieth century was the highpoint of the women's suffrage movement, and with the coming of World War I women finally gained the vote. As part of the late Victorian wave of feminism associated with the suffrage campaign, many women in this period entered the professions or actively created new professions such as social work, library science, and domestic science. In the 1920's, a decline set in and that decade provides a useful vantage point from which to assess the gains of early feminism. As Veronica Strong-Boag suggests, an evaluation from the point of view of working-class women leads to rather dismal conclusions.

Yet, equally, the trends which have transformed women's role in contemporary Canadian society were already apparent. The rising participation rate of single women and the slow but steady increase of married women in the labour force were harbingers of the future, as was the rapid increase of women in clerical work in both the private and public sectors. The increasing bureaucratization of business and government which accompanied the rise of monopoly capital created a whole new range of jobs for which women came to be seen as the natural employees. The extent to which ideology, not biology, dictated these choices is particularly apparent in office and bank work, which the Victorian world viewed as men's work but which was transformed in the early twentieth century into women's jobs.

FURTHER READING:
Collections of essays which include useful material on women's history in this period are: Janice Acton *et al.*, eds., *Women at Work* (Toronto, 1974); Susan Trofimenkoff and Alison Prentice, eds., *The Neglected Majority* (Toronto, 1977); and Linda Kealey, ed., *A Not Unreasonable Claim: Women and Social Reform in Canada* (Toronto, 1979). On early twentieth-century feminism, see Veronica Strong-Boag, *The Parliament of Women: The National Council of Women in Canada 1893-1929* (Ottawa, 1976). The fight for women's suffrage is described by Catherine Cleverdon, *The Women's Suffrage Movement in Canada* (Toronto, 1950). On working women, see Wayne Roberts, *Honest Womanhood: Feminism, Femininity, and Class Consciousness Among Toronto Working Women 1893-1914* (Toronto, 1976); Star Rosenthal, "Union Maids: Organizing Women Workers in Vancouver, 1900-1915," *BC Studies*, 41 (1979), 36-55; and Joan Sangster, "The 1907 Bell Telephone Strike," *L/LT*, 3 (1978), 109-30. Documentary collections with useful material on women are Irving Abella and David Millar, eds., *The Canadian Worker in the Twentieth Century* (Toronto, 1978); and Ramsay Cook and Wendy Mitchinson, eds., *The Proper Sphere: Women's Place in Canadian Society* (Toronto, 1976). On women, children, and the family, see Joy Parr, ed., *Childhood and Family in Canadian History* (Toronto, 1982). A useful discussion of women and clerical work is Graham Lowe, "Women, work and the office: the feminization of clerical occupations in Canada, 1901-1931," *Canadian Journal of Sociology*, 5 (1980), 361-81.

Veronica Strong-Boag teaches in the History Department and Women's Studies Program at Simon Fraser University and is one of Canada's leading historians of women.

The Girl of the New Day: Canadian Working Women in the 1920's

by Veronica Strong-Boag

Canadians recovering from World War I hoped that the 1920's would at last usher in the century that was to be theirs. The modern world's new technologies and new methods of bureaucratic organization might be harnessed to guarantee a better life for all citizens. Liberal feminists also anticipated that much progress towards the liberation of women would come about directly through the invigorated pace of modernization during the decade. Nowhere was their faith in progress greater than in the world of work. A modernized capitalism that stressed employment and promotion based on merit would replace traditions which dictated occupations allocated on the basis of the ascribed and inferior status of women. Working women were thus to be beneficiaries of a reorganized and updated capitalist order. Yet, as recent literature on the 1920's suggests,[1] the decade finally offered little to those who hoped for general liberalization. For women, inequality in the workplace did not disappear, it merely modernized its forms.

The failure to make great gains has sometimes been obscured by a fascination with women doctors, lawyers, and other professionals.[2] Yet at best such individuals constituted a small, atypical minority. The fate of most working women lay in non-professional employment. This study is an exploratory survey of the situation facing that majority. It begins with a brief characterization of the work force followed by a lengthier evaluation of

From *Labour/Le Travailleur*, 4 (1979), 131-164. Reprinted with permission.

some of the influences which determined job selection. As we shall see, "career" choices were basically of two types. The first, familiar blue-collar occupations, was found in personal service and manufacturing. The second, in large measure white collar, originated at the heart of the modern industrial state in the transportation and communication, commerce and finance, and clerical fields which had only relatively recently welcomed significant numbers of women. Neither choice offered women the equality which feminists hoped for. The study then investigates women's collective and individual reactions to a discriminatory work situation. More exploited than their white-collar sisters, blue-collar workers, notably those in manufacturing, exhibited higher, more visible levels of unrest. The concluding section reviews the minimum wage legislation which, ironically enough, confirmed how little had really changed despite all the hopes of the early 1920's.

I

The 1920's – the first decade in which the majority of Canadians were urban-dwellers – continued long-established trends favouring a disproportionately large female population in the cities and increased female participation in the labour force. The predominance of women in urban areas was especially noticeable in the fifteen to twenty-four and twenty-four to thirty-four age groups, when women were most likely to be seeking both paid work and marital prospects. Not unexpectedly, as Table 1 indicates, the proportion of women between sixteen and thirty-four years old who were gainfully employed was considerably larger than the figures reported for all women in 1921 and 1931. For age groups beyond the mid-thirties employment among women dropped dramatically. Not yet was there that massive return to the labour force of older wives which later characterized the female work force.[3]

Unchanged from the nineteenth century was the fact that the majority of these young working women were single. Once women won husbands, they generally withdrew from paid labour. Nevertheless, steadily increasing numbers of married women entered wage employment: 35,202 or 7.19 per cent of the female labour force in 1921 and 66,798 or 10.03 per cent in 1931.

Divorced or widowed women were also relatively common: 51,202 or 10.4 per cent of female wage-earners in 1921 and 61,335 or 9 per cent in 1931. The size of these groups fluctuated considerably from season to season or even month to month. It was generally observed, for instance, that whenever there arose a "scarcity of work for men, the number of married women applying for casual employment was greater than under ordinary conditions."[4] This pattern added flexibility to the family's earning power just as it strained women assuming a double burden of responsibility.[5] Nor were wives the only female workers with additional obligations. Commentators on female employment regularly concluded that the "single girl often has the financial responsibility of the support of a relative."[6] The absence of any widespread pension system cast many older men and women upon either charity or their families for support. Adult children were expected and, in some provinces, required to support their dependent parents. Others assumed the care of needy brothers and sisters.

TABLE 1
Labour Force Participation Rate of Female Population,
10 Years and Over by Age Group, 1921 and 1931

	1921	1931
Total	15.27%	17.04%
10-15 years	2.84	1.37
16-19	32.16	30.33
20-24	35.06	42.36
25-34	17.23	21.73
35-64	10.68	11.99
65 plus	6.22	6.17

SOURCE: *Census of Canada,* 1931.

These female wage-earners found the necessary jobs in various ways. In most cases personal contact was probably essential. Family and friends provided information about opportunities, conditions, salaries, and bosses.[7] The textile industry was typical among the older manufacturing processes in being recognized as a "'family' industry in that often the children and sometimes the wife, in addition to the family head, find employment in one mill."[8] In this way first jobs could be discovered near home and in familiar company. In the 1920's vocational advice from schools, magazines, and employment bureaus increasingly augmented older informal networks. This formalization of the job selection process reflected the rapid modernization of the Canadian economy during this period.[9] Ever more powerful pressure from the expanding state and corporate bureaucracies was employed to ensure that citizens enlisted in jobs which met the needs of the social and sexual status quo.

Girls in contact with such influences discovered generally cheerful forecasts in the early 1920's. Although most "guidance" advisers presumed that girls would eventually opt for marriage, they were also cautiously optimistic about employment.[10] Subscribers to a whig view of history, they congratulated themselves that there was in modern Canada a wide range of jobs *suitable* for girls. Among these they included stenography, nursing, bee-keeping, millinery, retailing, clerking, and telegraph operating. According to them modern opportunities made it unnecessary for respectable young women to seek employment in "masculine" fields such as carpentry, electrical work, automobiles, iron and steel, and the like. Counsellors liked to believe that the expansion in woman's "own" sphere supplied opportunities enough and, in addition, offered benefits more precious than money. The manual authorized for use in Ontario schools in the 1920's, for example, anticipated that "The increasing opportunities of girls, both in home-making and paid employment, are likely to become a contributing factor in the humanizing of every form of industry."[11] For those with more practical concerns, some commentators even predicted new upward mobility. In 1919 the principal of Toronto's elite girls' school, Havergal College, was generally confident, for all her admission of preliminary hardships: ". . . remember, the road will be long and tiresome. There will be plenty of room at the top, but there is no elevator to swing you swiftly aloft; your only access will be steep and stony stairs."[12] Prospective job-seekers who culled advice from *Saturday Night* and *Maclean's*, both leading magazines of the decade, would have been similarly reassured about the satisfying posts awaiting eager young women.[13] Even occupations with unhappy records did not escape favourable reassessment. Ontario's vocational brochures on the garment trade, for instance, promised that "For those with executive gifts the opportunities are good."[14]

Hopeful forecasts sprang in part from the high expectations

born of suffrage and wartime victories. Nothing, however, could fully exclude cold realism. Principal Knox, for instance, acknowledged the special shortcomings of banks:

> It is no fun working night after night for a missing three cents; no fun training juniors and, if these juniors are boys, seeing them shoot ahead at higher salary; no fun working on and on without the ghost of a chance of being general manager; no fun working at top speed and seeing the man beside you, who is working at what you call ten dollar speed, for the sake of increased salary quickening to fifteen or twenty dollar speed, and never turning a hair over it.[15]

Similarly, Ontario's essentially optimistic vocational bulletins on the textile and furniture industries could not entirely ignore the prevailing low wages.[16]

The thrust of such guidance was finally discriminatory, envisioning that, in large measure, men and women were suited to different types of employment. It also took as operating assumptions that women would neither have to support a family nor seek power and status. Instead they would be well satisfied with pleasant surroundings, congenial workmates, and, above all, male bosses. The rapid growth in white-collar employments was widely regarded as proof positive of improvement by those who guided girls to critical job decisions. Indeed, these were regularly made glamorous, unlike the older manual jobs whose records sternly resisted all efforts at reclamation.

Governments did nothing to broaden girls' chances or outlook. The application of the 1919 Technical Education Act maintained official interest in promoting domestic service for poorer female students and domestic careers for all. Programs under this plan, together with the more successful Écoles ménagères in Quebec, were part of the earlier discriminatory pattern of female education.[17] To be sure, newer trends found acknowledgement in typing and stenography courses. These proved so attractive that Ontario's Assistant Director of Technical Education had to admit that "it is almost impossible to induce our adolescent girls to take up this specialized training [domestic science]."[18] Governments did their best to offset "unsatisfactory" career choices. Ontario, for example, planned to have boys in all programs study "Fundamentals of Business" and "Sociology" and enrol all girls for "Child Welfare" and

"Elements of Nursing."[19] The other major vocational initiative by governments in the 1920's was still more discriminatory. Ontario's 1928 Apprenticeship Act made no provision at all for girls. It applied solely to boys entering nine building trades.

Governments channelled job-seeking women into suitable jobs in other ways as well. The Free Employment Bureaus established in provinces in the 1920's with the assistance of Ottawa, for example, concentrated on placing female domestics.[20] Middle-class householders soon became accustomed to using the services of these public agencies in much the same way as they relied on the efforts of immigration officials to discover foreign-born domestics when none could be found at home.[21]

The restricted options presented to female job-seekers at every turn reflected two facts of Canadian life. First, the great majority of citizens supported and employed socialization practices which consigned each sex to different duties.[22] Guidance in job selection was no different. Women had careers in motherhood; at best, they had jobs in the marketplace. Second, the range of employment was tailored in the first instance to the "needs" of poorer Canadians. Since it was generally believed that few women with adequate family resources would seek work, serious advice, particularly from governments, was pre-eminently designed to place working-class girls in "suitable" posts, particularly domestic service. In this way the class and sexual hierarchy in the workplace, as elsewhere, would be maintained. This narrow, class-conscious vision expanded slightly in the 1920's, but its influence acted in concert with sexual stereotyping to eliminate effectively better, "male" occupations from serious consideration for girls.

II

The continuing conservatism of attitudes to female employment ensured that modern women, like their grandmothers, would be ghettoized into relatively few occupations. While men were widely dispersed over a broad range of industrial groups, non-professional women were concentrated in five – personal service, manufacturing, transportation and communication, commerce and finance, and clerical – which contained 73.61 per cent of all female labourers in 1921 and 78.36 per cent in 1931. Jobs in these blue- and white-collar categories were characterized most often by low wages, irregular work, and dull, dead-end tasks. Considerable job mobility was the inevitable outcome. It was not uncommon, for instance, for women to shift from factory work to waitressing or from millinery to fruitpicking within a single year.[23] Naturally skill, age, marital status, and education restrained interchange between jobs, but transiency was a feature of many women's employment history.[24] This mobility was ever-present, inevitably blurring the boundaries between the six occupations which, for clarity's sake, are examined separately below.

As in every previous decade of Canada's history, more women were registered in personal service than any other single occupational category. Here workers confronted traditionally small work units, low productivity, non-standardized conditions, and unregulated authority. Since occupations such as domestic service and waitressing stressed health and stamina, workers by and large had little need of formal schooling. Not only did such jobs attract the poorly educated, they also enlisted both the youngest and oldest of paid workers – those presumably whose skills and attractiveness were least and whose need and vulnerability greatest.[25] Here, too, were grouped the largest number of immigrants as well as an increasing number of non-Anglo-Saxons. New job opportunities opened during World War I had confirmed an earlier trend away from domestic service by the native-born.[26] Contemporaries believed that new skills together with "the possession of fairly substantial bank accounts as a result of war work, the great increase in the number of marriages subsequent to the return of the troops" added to "the disinclination to turn to an occupation whose social standing is erroneously rated below that of factory work."[27] By 1931, 64.44 per cent of all gainfully employed central European women and 70.43 per cent of all gainfully employed eastern European women toiled as domestics. Their contribution was increasingly important because one traditional source of recruitment continued to dry up after the war. Quebecers were not alone in lamenting that "our young country girls, who formerly used to engage with families, now prefer going into factories, where wages are higher."[28] Its heavy non-native-born makeup helped lower this occupation's prestige within the working woman's world.

Between 1921 and 1931 the number of general servants or maids of all work jumped from 78,118 to 134,043. Much of this gain was probably due to the especially severe economic crisis of

1931, although 1921 was also depressed. Whenever there was an economic downswing "Many workers . . . registered for house-work . . . they intended to return to their trades when an opportunity arose."[29] For those with limited resources it offered promise of housing and feeding children. The Employment Bureau of Toronto, for instance, noticed that women regularly sought "positions where they can take a child . . . [even] two or sometimes three children."[30] The persistence of domestic openings, however unsatisfactory, meant that service often operated as the unemployment insurance of the poorer woman. Few with alternatives stayed on. The reaction of twelve White Russian refugee women placed as domestics in Ottawa would have been commonplace, but that five were "aristocrats." Ontario's Employment Service had to report that "Within two months only two remained in domestic service."[31] Notably, none of the "ladies" stayed; all fled to Toronto and a department store.

When they could not escape domestic work, women tried to obtain either day work or employment other than in a private home. In particular the great majority resisted "living-in" with all the control and supervision this entailed. For all the ingenuity of governments in promoting domestic service (an effort they made for no other industry to the same degree), women voiced familiar grievances. Relatively unchanged from the nineteenth century were "the long hours and the lack of freedom." Servants were "the only class of labour who continue to work, not from seven to seven but often from seven to nine or ten o'clock with only every other Sunday afternoon off."[32] Long hours were aggravated by lack of privacy, poor accommodation, and low status – in a word, dependence. Recurring efforts to modernize the occupation through emphasis on professional conduct and sound training were always shipwrecked on the popular evaluation of housework as women's work, therefore, by definition, meriting low pay and prestige.

Restaurant dining had proliferated along with Canadian cities. By the 1920's women were commonplace in this highly competitive field, especially in the more vulnerable smaller establishments. There is also some evidence that women with lower wages were displacing waiters.[33] Like domestic service, hours were almost always long and the pace uneven with precise conditions fluctuating unpredictably from one business to another.[34] Meals, often eaten on the run, were generally provided and gratuities were essential to survival. The variability of this tip income added immeasurably to the instability of the employment. Nevertheless, while posts in this occupation were often at the mercy of relatively minor shifts in supervisors and finances, their skills could be quickly acquired and they offered, as domestic service rarely did, contact with a world of equals as well as role-delimited superiors.[35]

Women did not predominate in manufacturing as they did in personal service. Nonetheless, it too remained a major employer. For example, it included 33.5 per cent of Montreal's female workers in 1921 and 23.4 per cent in 1931.[36] Low-wage, highly competitive industries such as clothing, but also textiles, shoes, and food processing, had hired relatively large numbers of women and girls for many years but higher wage, capital-intensive, often monopolistic firms engaged in the production of such commodities as automobiles, electrical machinery, farm equipment, and liquor had little if any room for them.[37] Wherever they were found, females were generally assigned their own particular "sphere." Custom and unions not only excluded them from entire areas of production but often segregated them into distinct operations within individual industries. In clothing, as elsewhere, for example, women were barred from the more skilled and well-paid work. As a result, female apprenticeship, when this existed, was short. Even when it is difficult to appreciate the difference of expertise or effort involved, as in pocketmaking (male) and buttonhole sewing (female) in the ready-made clothing industry, you could still be sure of a substantial wage difference.[38]

Yet old practices remained subject to change in the 1920's. The continuing introduction of new technologies frequently left precise sex jurisdictions confused. They sometimes offered employers the opportunity to shift from better paid men to cheaper women. Such substitution added to industrial turmoil without granting women any significant improvement in status or wages. The installation of more up-to-date equipment was commonly accompanied by a general speed-up. This was true, for instance, of Edmonton's Great West Garment Company which in 1929 installed "special two needle machines," allowing it both to cut staff and maintain production levels.[39] The result encouraged unrest in the clothing trades throughout the decade.

Closely related to speed-up in manufacturing were bonusing and piecework. The former was "extra" money granted after certain production goals were met. In practice such funds were often essential, not incidental, to a woman's budget. Piecework was the policy of paying by amount rather than time – the quicker, more efficient workers earning the most. Both policies pushed workers, men and women alike, to raise their speed to match the quickest, often resulting in considerable physical and nervous strain. Neither bonusing nor piecework was unheard of earlier but they appear to have been taken up with a vengeance in the 1920's, at least in industries where there were large numbers of women.[40] In many cases as speed increased rates were reduced, thus starting the vicious circle over again.

The regularity of work stoppages owing to the introduction of piecework spoke volumes for labouring women's opposition. More often than not, however, their collective vulnerability compelled women to endure the regime condemned by one Jewish immigrant in a Montreal dress factory:

> You can never do enough for the boss. Every half hour the boss counts the number of dresses on our chairs. I am a finisher, and sometimes I feel like doing something desperate when I see the girls rushing the lives out of themselves, each to do more dresses than the other. The Jewish girls are just the same. I can't keep up with them. . . . We fight all the time at the table because of this. Some of the girls because they thought I was a "green" at the beginning stole some of my dresses and put them on their chairs when I went out of the room for a few minutes.[41]

Nor were such conditions limited to "fly-by-night" or smaller firms. Even the Eatons, who publicized their on-the-job "philanthropy," did not hesitate to take advantage of clothing trades workers.[42]

Factory conditions continued to add to women's difficulties as well. The construction of modern premises and the remodelling of older establishments had improved safety, ventilation, and sanitation somewhat since the abuses uncovered by the 1889 Report of the Royal Commission on the Relations of Labour and Capital, but numerous dangers went uncorrected. In addition, safer conditions sprang ironically from unrelated developments. Two popular fashions of the decade, bobbed hair and short skirts, freed workers in certain industries from being scalped or pulled into machinery.[43] In some factories the introduction of individual motors with their elimination of overhead belting also helped do away with the cause of earlier accidents. Despite these improvements, provincial authorities had to be vigilant. "Modern" advances were not always accepted with alacrity. Too often "employers" objected "to modern safety equipment being placed on their machines, fearing it will retard production."[44]

Industrial hygiene was similarly often lamentable. The 1920 Nova Scotian commission investigating women's working conditions branded firms with a typical indictment.

> The toilets in a great many factories should be condemned. It would appear in many cases, as if the management thought it a waste of room to give up to toilets a greater space than four or five feet square, even for the use of a large number of employees. Frequently they were found to be dirty, ill ventilated, indifferently lighted, and . . . toilets for women, instead of being entirely separate, were found to be entered directly from the factory and separated from the men's toilet by only a thin wooden partition.[45]

The survival of such conditions made a laughing stock of government regulations which, in most jurisdictions, had first been passed in the nineteenth century.

Yet for all the failings of factories, they remained preferable to the home labour which continued so much a feature of clothing manufacture in particular.[46] As is often the case modern practices incorporated the old as much as they eliminated them. Throughout the decade inspectors observed that increasing amounts of work were escaping supervision by being subcontracted either to small middlemen or to the individual homeworker. Of course not all such operations abandoned the factory. The Quebec Minimum Wage Board joined others in identifying the special difficulties presented by a subcontractor using the contractor's premises:

> The sub-contracting workman employs young girls or boys to help him and pays them what he thinks is fair or what he sees fit. As oftenest happens, the wages of this help do not appear in the employers' pay-sheets, the latter claiming that they are not in his employ, although working in his factory.[47]

The majority of subcontracting, however, was removed from the factory altogether into still more unsatisfactory premises. A "family group of foreign origin who baste and hem around the kitchen stove"[48] might recall pre-industrial patterns, but the exploitation was modern. Although sheltered from the critical eye of a strange foreman, such workers also lost whatever protection the law or a union might offer. Sweatshops survived because they were "an ideal arrangement of course from the employers' viewpoint as it is much cheaper labour and at the same time save him [sic] factory space and the purchase of extra sewing machines. . . ."[49]

In view of the hardships of the traditional blue-collar employments, it is little wonder that job applicants, especially the native-born and the better educated, looked increasingly to what newer white-collar employment might offer. Here would lie the real test of the benefits of the modern economy for women. Had equity really been won in the efficiency-conscious, bureaucratically oriented structures of corporate capitalist society?

The introduction of the telephone gave women their first opportunity to enter the field of transportation and communications in significant numbers. The steady increase in telephones from 779,000 in December 1919 to 1,383,000 in December 1929 and the heavy reliance on manual rather than automatic switchboards underlay a relatively strong demand for operators, or traffic employees as they were commonly called.[50] The switchboard, with all the dexterity, quickness, and patience it required, dovetailed with the prevailing female image. Talkative, uncreative females were best equipped, so it seemed, to withstand the tension of close supervision, variable rates of business, and clients' eccentricities. Conditions had improved since the early days of Canadian telephones but the work remained stressful and exhausting.[51]

Young women had replaced early male operators as the mainstay of businesses like the Bell Telephone Company of Canada, the Manitoba Telephone System, and the Maritime Telegraph and Telephone Company. Just as in the United States, Canadian companies "preferred to hire from among the untrained and relatively impressionable young just entering the job market. . . ."[52] Preliminary training for operators took several weeks at company offices where young women were encouraged to identify with the company. In this way "team spirit" could be harnessed to the goal of higher profits. Not coincidentally, it also tended to foster views which isolated telephone employees from other workers.

Although both men and women were expected to give company loyalty top priority, they were rewarded very differently. Qualified male personnel might advance steadily within company ranks but women's ambitions were confined to the position of chief operator.[53] To offset such disadvantages as well as sidestep demands for unions, businesses conferred recreational, health, and welfare plans on their young employees.[54] Such paternalistic experiments were a partial explanation for the poor record of unions in this sector. Company benefits were not, however, sufficient to retain staff. Turnover remained considerable. Few operators continued into their thirties.

Women in search of better white-collar employment turned also to commerce and finance, an industrial group which showed a marked rise of 15.4 per cent in the number of female employees from 1921 to 1931. Many of these women, again often high school graduates, served behind counters in shops and department stores. Salesgirls had been replacing male clerks fairly steadily since the 1880's. The emergence of department stores and, in particular in the 1920's, chain stores with their abundance of menial employments accelerated substitution.[55] Such opportunities were, however, strictly limited. In 1914 a survey of the four Winnipeg department stores reported between 2,432 to 3,200 female employees, yet not one female department head. The assistant buyer was generally the highest position open to women. One store, for instance, ruled that no women could be managers.[56] The journalist Marjory MacMurchy, advising high school students five years later, observed that it was occasionally possible to move to the head of a department "and in somewhat rare cases she may become a buyer."[57] There is no reason to believe matters improved in the later 1920's. The path of advancement, such as it was, in department stores stretched from parcelling through the cash office, clerical work or the stock room to the salesforce, headship of a section, and then, very uncommonly, management.[58]

Opportunities were still fewer in the smaller notion stores where "Though there are from four to five times as many women and girls as men and boys . . . the position of management is seldom open to women."[59] Chances for promotion were best in areas clearly marked as fields of female expertise such as millinery. Here, almost alone, female managers could be found. Self-service grocery chains such as Loblaws of Toronto and Carroll's of Hamilton revealed much the same pattern of discrimination as did drug store chains such as G. Tamblyn Company and Louis K. Liggett of Toronto. Such stores justified failure to give female staff greater responsibility by emphasizing their lack of "independence of thought."[60]

The relative pleasantness and respectability of store work attracted a large pool of applicants.[61] Drawn on as part-timers in busy periods, they threatened wages and hours for all full-time employees. Nonetheless, occasional jobs did offer unique advantages to women whose household responsibilities allowed only brief absences.

The clerical field offered advantages similar to commerce and finance. It, too, welcomed more applicants than it required. In 1920, for instance, the Toronto office of the Employment Service lamented that "The signing of the armistice had its effects upon the clerical . . . situation. The closing of many offices left a great number of stenographers and clerks without positions. . . ."[62] Oversupply continued in the later 1920's when private and public agencies competed in turning out stenographers and typists to fill jobs created by "the bureaucratic and commercial revolution of the twentieth century."[63] Oversupply was all the more permanent a phenomenon because women were bunched at the lowest ranks of business and government. Although MacMurchy advised that, "The girl who is a college grad is not too well equipped to be a stenographer,"[64] even superior qualifications did not guarantee promotion. The inauguration of a degree course in secretarial science at the University of Western Ontario in the mid-1920's was an excellent indication of how bright girls were expected to limit their horizons.[65]

The federal government harboured typical reservations about its female clericals. Women had enlisted in its ranks by the 1870's but World War I brought the great influx of women into the "inside" service in Ottawa. The rapid expansion in the number of female clerks soon sparked controversy. Alarm grew lest they disrupt male recruitment to the higher levels of the service. Traditional stereotypes were then dusted off to justify restrictions on women's "unseemly" progress.[66] The federal government went so far as to institutionalize discrimination when it allowed the Civil Service Commission to restrict competitions on the basis of sex in 1918. Veterans need not worry that there would be no place for them.[67] Ottawa's long-time policy of equal pay for equal work was meaningless because it never offered women equal opportunities. Equality was still further undercut in 1921 by stringent regulations on the hiring of married women. In addition, a married woman might keep her existing post only if a real need for her particular services could be proven, a rather dubious proposition in the recession year, 1921. "Lucky" working wives were rehired as new and temporary appointees. Further penalized, they sacrificed all former seniority and were paid the minimum rate in their classification. Not surprisingly, the number of women in federal and provincial employment in Ottawa dropped 13.2 per cent from 4,296 in 1921 ᴛᴏ 3,729 in 1931. It is unlikely that this decline was due solely to economic stringency since male civil servants jumped from 6,080 in 1921 to 6,466 ten years later, a gain of 6.5 per cent.

As Table 2 shows, the generally gloomy picture was reaffirmed by wage discrimination. Between 1921 and 1931 women earned on average 54 to 60 per cent of male wages. The contrast is all the more striking when individual occupational categories are considered. In 1921 women's wages as a percentage of men's exceeded 50 per cent in only two employments. By the next census this had climbed to a mere four. As usual the largest single employer of women – personal service – was by far the worst in each year. The situation in manufacturing was almost as bad, a fact which helps explain industrial militancy. In contrast, the

TABLE 2
Women's Annual Wages as a Proportion of Men's in
Various Occupational Categories, 1921 and 1931

	1921	*1931*
All Occupations	54%	60%
Manufacturing	43	44
Transportation and		
communication	54	63
Trade	44	40
Finance, insurance	44	52
Service	39	33
Professional	47	43
Personal	40	38
Laundering, cleaning,		
dyeing	—	58
Clerical	63	71

SOURCE: *Census of Canada*, 1921 and 1931.

rather better record of white-collar jobs could be interpreted as progress, of a sort.

The wage situation was not standardized across the Dominion. Employers in eastern cities tended to be rather more discriminatory than those in the West.[68] In 1921, for instance, gainfully employed females in Calgary were considerably better off than their counterparts in Quebec City. As can be seen from Table 3, this pattern also held true ten years later. Why this was so owes something to many factors, including regional and urban variations, the number of low-paid nuns, the range of occupational choice, the character of the industrial structure, and the proportion of women in the local population.

TABLE 3
Women's Annual Wages as a Proportion of Men's in
Selected Cities of Population 30,000 and over, for 1921 and 1931

	1921	1931
Halifax	50%	51%
St. John	52	55
Quebec	39	39
Montreal	54	56
Ottawa	51	55
Toronto	58	59
Hamilton	51	59
London	49	54
Windsor	60	72
Winnipeg	55	56
Regina	58	57
Calgary	59	60
Edmonton	59	58
Vancouver	66	69

SOURCE: *Census of Canada,* 1931.

Women did not in every case receive their devastatingly lower wages because they worked any less time. Their work week, especially in blue-collar jobs, regularly stretched beyond forty or forty-eight hours without overtime. The only consolation was some women's ability to work more steadily. In 1921, for instance, the average female worker was employed just over a week longer a year than the male; in 1931 something like 5.5

weeks longer. Significantly, as Table 4 also demonstrates, there were substantial variations from the average. Women in many employments including manufacturing worked much the same hours as their male co-workers. For them the situation was especially disheartening.

TABLE 4
Average Number of Weeks Worked in 1921 and 1931, by
Sex and Occupational Category

	1921		1931	
	Male	*Female*	*Male*	*Female*
All Occupations	46.45	48.27	41.07	46.59
Manufacturing	45.95	45.31	41.70	42.18
Transportation and communication	47.27	49.00	44.40	48.83
Trade	49.32	48.23	47.34	45.83
Finance, insurance	50.58	49.78	49.15	49.12
Service	49.01	48.90	47.16	47.54
Professional	49.79	49.48	49.01	49.65
Personal	47.84	48.61	44.79	46.70
Laundering, cleaning, dyeing	—	—	41.77	45.53
Clerical	49.53	49.54	48.01	48.20

SOURCE: *Census of Canada*, 1931.

As Table 5 shows, gainfully employed women on average experienced a drop in dollar income between 1921 and 1931. The range between the highest wage sector, finance and insurance, and the lowest, personal service, meant an immense difference in lifestyle and expectation. The former at $18.87 a week in 1921 and $24.54 a week in 1931 was safely above the cost of the bare necessities estimated for a Toronto saleswoman in 1921 at $12.56 a week or $653.25 a year and in 1930 at $12.50 and $653.[69] In contrast, personal service was abysmal at $6.27 weekly in 1921 and $5.69 ten years later. Even the figure for Toronto was meagre. In 1929 the Employed Girls' Council of Regina raised the required minimum to $20 a week by including allowances for loss of time, holidays, other unexpected costs, and savings for unemployment and old age.[70] Nevertheless, if women could maintain their wage levels, some improvement occurred during the decade in terms of real wages. The cost of living index dropped from 132.3 (100 – 1935-39) in December 1921 to 109.9 in December 1931. Nevertheless, even a deflationary trend could not make the lives of most working women approach comfort and security.[71]

TABLE 5

Average Annual Wages for Women in Various
Occupational Categories in 1921 and 1931

	1921	1931
All occupations	$573	$ 559
Manufacturing	504	472
Transportation and communication	675	701
Finance, insurance	981	1,275
Trade	591	561
Service	482	467
Professional	775	853
Personal	326	296
Laundering, cleaning, dyeing	—	448
Clerical	785	832

SOURCE: *Census of Canada,* 1931.

Opportunities and wages were not the only means by which the community reflected its different views of men and women. Since most women were routinely socialized from infancy to accept male leadership, discipline, and assistance, it was hardly surprising that the workplace often echoed the assumption of deference and dependence. The special restraints and expectations women laboured under in both blue- and white-collar employments were also reminiscent, to some degree, of the traditional family economy of the pre-industrial world.[72] This economy encouraged employers to act paternalistically towards all employees. Female workers in particular were to be chaperoned and disciplined by bosses as by fathers.[73] This tradition acted in concert with up-to-date socialization practices to distinguish women's experience of the workplace.

Women's morality occupied a special place in new and traditional attitudes. Domestic service came specially recommended owing to the supposed superiority and safety of domestic life.

The regular imposition of early curfews on domestic servants, for instance, could be defended as pseudo-parental discipline. Louis Guyon, the chief factory inspector for Quebec, reiterated the familiar dreary justification for greater protection for female factory hands by pointing to the "objectionable and constant promiscuous contact with the workmen who [sic] no factory rule can fully control."[74] Among Guyon's colleagues, however, the more modern attitudes of co-workers like Louisa King were slowly gaining ground. She concluded "after many years experience that young girls working in factories are not more exposed in regard to their morals than are those who do other work for a living."[75] Unlike Guyon she felt confident that "modern" training had produced girls who, if not ladies, were at least ladylike. Guyon continued, nevertheless, to find sympathizers among certain employers who were determined to remain stern, if self-serving, guardians. In January 1921, for instance, the Atlantic Underwear Company of Moncton, New Brunswick, opened an "apartment house to accommodate one hundred of their female operatives . . . at a nominal cost."[76] The exact intentions of the firm are obscure but one may well suppose that charity, efficiency, and morality were all to be served.

In Quebec the power of the Roman Catholic Church sometimes resulted in more traditional methods of ensuring an obedient labour force. In a Montreal cigar factory the inculcation of proper attitudes clearly included a conspicuous degree of religious control.

> When you get used to noise and look around a little closer, you notice statues in the corners of the rooms. You wonder if the boss is such a lover of art that he wants to always gaze at beauty. You look again at the statues, you notice they are statues of saints and religious heroes.
>
> For a minute you imagine yourself back in the middle ages when the priesthood were [sic] so powerful that they wanted the mass to constantly gaze and think of holy emblems and figures, to keep them meek and docile. . . . Very often do the priests come down during working hours and speak to the girls. Of course, everybody must stop working, but what does the boss care about that, as it is piece work.[77]

As this remark suggests, submission to male authority (here the Church) always occupied a large part of any proposed morality for women. A further aspect of this same discipline system included the regular docking of pay for petty infringements of regulations, for a few minutes' tardiness or minuscule errors. These punishments appear to have been employed more often with females than males, a reflection both of women's relative weakness and of a persistent difference in bosses' attitudes to female workers.

Blue-collar workers were not alone in meriting special attention as women. Female employees in a variety of occupations seem to have inspired many early experiments in welfare capitalism.[78] Some of these modern initiatives offered real advantages. Telephone companies and larger retail outlets often pioneered in setting up recreational, health, and welfare plans. During their extensive expansion in the decade Eatons' maintained Eatons' Welfare Secretaries, motherly women to supervise the well-being of female help, and in 1927 opened the Christie Street Recreation Area for its Toronto "girls."[79] In addition to assisting badly paid workers, such plans yielded obvious public relations benefits and undercut the appeal of unions. In most cases women had to demonstrate respectability in order to gain "perks." "Some stores," for example, would "not employ any person who paints, powders, chews gum or smokes cigarettes."[80] In keeping with this, guidance manuals stressed the centrality of deferential behaviour and attractive looks for young job-seekers. This is not to suggest that good grooming and an agreeable manner were insignificant for male applicants but that such qualities were not, as with women, emphasized to the near exclusion of competence.

Much of the feminist movement flourished on the expectation of the imminent birth of a technocratic, truly meritocratic society, in which the historical inequality of women would finally give way to genuine equality of opportunity in the workplace. Such hopes and expectations were bolstered by a temporary illusion of progress when the burgeoning corporate and state bureaucracies of the 1920's fleshed out their lower reaches with thousands of female wage labourers. Only years of direct experience of frustrated upward mobility would teach feminists that the entry of women into the ranks of the intermediate status white-collar groups could not of itself transform the sexist discrimination which lay at the heart of the male-controlled capitalist system. The longer and more intimate familiarity of blue-collar women with unequal opportunities and wages brought the lesson home somewhat sooner, for some at least, that paid work is not necessarily liberating.

III

Recognition of injustice drove more and more women to investigate alternatives to continued oppression within the labour market. A number turned to collective action. Unfortunately, the 1920's were not propitious for unions.[81] Hounded by unsympathetic governments, antagonistic employers, and unfavourable economic trends, organized labour was unable to offer much assistance to a group which it had traditionally neglected. Although many unionists worried that "women's physiological handicaps make them more subject than men to the new strain of industry,"[82] they also concluded that women were nearly unorganizable. Not only were women likely to desert the labour force, they did "not seem to possess that spirit of solidarity, characteristic of men in industry."[83] Such assumptions so exaggerated differences between male and female workers that even when women proved loyal recruits, they frequently won little encouragement from male organizers.[84] The views of the newly established Confédération des travailleurs catholiques du Canada that working women deprived deserving family heads of jobs and that women had but a doubtful claim to a voice in its deliberations were somewhat extreme.[85] Skepticism, together with fears of female competitors, however, strengthened secular groups like the Journeymen Barbers International Union of America in rejecting female applicants.

The weakness of women's position was sometimes evident in work contracts. The 1921 agreement between the Merchant Tailors of Sault Ste. Marie and the Journeymen Tailors' Union of America Local 73, which stated that "Women [were] to be paid the scale as men for the same class of work,"[86] was unusual. Much more frequent was explicit provision for unequal rates as with the 1924 contract between "certain local employers" and the International Brotherhood of Bookbinders Local 147 in Victoria which guaranteed journeymen a minimum wage of $42 a week and journeywomen a relatively miserly $21 for the same hours.[87] Whatever their sympathies or awareness of the danger of wage undercutting, unionists in this decade were rarely able to reject discriminatory clauses. Craft unions, in particular, with their traditional interest in skilled workers, were ill-equipped to deal with large numbers in industries like textiles, shoes, and clothing, not to mention newcomers in the white-collar trades. Industrial unions were often the answer but they, too, found organizing women hard going.

Even such radical publications as the *BC Federationist* (Vancouver), *One Big Union Bulletin* (Winnipeg), *The Western Labor News* (Winnipeg), *The Worker* (Toronto), and the *Maritime Labor Herald* (Glace Bay) devoted few pages to female labour. Too often they consoled themselves piously that "Unless we are very much mistaken, class consciousness will spread amongst our female wage slave comrades with startling rapidity."[88] As yet far too little is known about the influence of radical leaders and associations such as Elizabeth Hall Gauld, Annie Buller, Florence Custance, Rebecca Buhay, the Women's Labor League, and the United Women's Educational Federation of Ontario. Although it is impossible to evaluate their impact on working women, their work may well have helped groom women to assume a greater role in organizational activity in the 1930's.[89] In addition, the acceptance of powerful female leaders like Bella Gauld by the Communist Party and others was a visible symbol of women's increasing importance to any who aimed to mobilize the Canadian working class.

Although the union record was generally depressing, industrial unions such as the International Ladies Garment Workers Union of America (ILGWA), the Amalgamated Clothing Workers of America (ACW), and the Industrial Union of Needle Trades made noteworthy efforts to rally women, especially in Toronto, Montreal, and Winnipeg. The strike records of the federal Department of Labour reveal women repeatedly walking out in demands for union shop and better wages and protests against violation of contract and speed-up, piecework, and contract shops.[90] Union problems were tremendous, not least being the need to operate in a variety of languages. Indeed, ethnic loyalties were a constantly divisive force among women as well as men labourers.[91] In addition, organization drives almost invariably roused in their wake the proliferation of "contract," sometimes referred to as "bedroom" or "social," shops. Union leaders recognized bitterly that there was really no front upon which these smaller establishments may be attacked. The active owners, usually skilled men, engage their sisters, brothers, mothers, children, sweethearts and other kin and make the entire scheme a kind of community shop, although it is usually reinforced by outsiders.[92]

Unions were undercut in still other ways. Some entrepreneurs, such as Lippe and Gariepy, a men's clothing firm in Montreal, retaliated by "simply moving our factory to Joliette [a smaller town] because the situation caused by the union is so unbearable that we are compelled to go outside the city if we mean to stay in business. . . ."[93] Not all operators chose to pack up. Scabs and private guards remained popular alternatives. In some cases police joined forces with employers. In 1925, for instance, Mary McNab of the ILGWA addressed the Toronto Trades and Labour Council and "denounced heartily a certain sergeant of police . . . who when she went forth to hold a meeting, threatened to give her a ride as a 'vag' – and had six huge policemen and two plainsclothesmen follow her everywhere she went."[94] Such harassment often led to arrests. The 1926 ACW strike against the Society Brand Clothing Company in Montreal provides one typical example. Four teenagers – Rose Chernoff, eighteen; Dinah Chernoff, seventeen; Annie Saxe, sixteen; and Yetta Demsky, sixteen – were charged with assaulting an arresting constable.[95]

Young female clothing workers were not alone in their use of militant trade union action, yet such tactics remained, as with men, the exclusive preserve of blue-collar, manual workers. Clerical and sales employees suffered from an absence of almost any organizational tradition whatsoever. A large reservoir of potential employees made secretaries and saleswomen naturally reluctant to appear troublesome. At the same time the fact that their work was frequently a clear step above – in terms of safety, cleanliness, and respectability – that previously offered female wage-earners made them still more unlikely activists.

All across the nation, however, female manual workers, alone and in concert with men, withdrew their services in the 1920's. The issues at stake ranged widely, from the demand for a union contract by male and female employees of the City Café in Calgary in 1923 to wage disagreements between telephone operators and the Maritime Telephone Company in Halifax in 1925, to the discharge of a popular foreman in a Hamilton knitting factory in 1928, to the demand that "things . . . be like they were before the efficiency experts came along and changed them" in Hamilton's Canadian Cottons Ltd. in 1929.[96] Although men were most conspicuous in the labour battles of the decade, it was not uncommon to discover newspapers branding women as "the chief offenders."[97] The visibility of the less numerous female strikers was high because they challenged the prevailing image of female normality.

Sabotage and pamphlet distribution were regular tactics, but women's participation took other forms as the following two strikes illustrate. The first occurred in Stratford from August to October of 1921. After two years' effort the United Textile Workers of America felt strong enough to support the female work force in a strike against the Avon Hosiery Company. The issues were higher wages, specifically a minimum wage of $12.50 a week, the elimination of bonusing, and recognition of the union. The employer had attempted to head off the Textile Workers by setting up a company union, but this plan collapsed. After a carefully supervised election, the manager confessed that "When we came to count the ballots we found that so many . . . had either been put in blank or mutilated it was impossible for us to decide who this committee [of workers' representatives] should be. . . ."[98] Admitting that it lacked "the loyalty and cooperation of our present employees,"[99] Avon mounted an attack, giving the girls one minute "to sever affiliation with the Union or get out."[100] At that point the new unionists struck. Matters further deteriorated when fifteen girls were arrested on picket duty. Two were so young that they had to be transferred to Juvenile Court. At the end of September a sympathy meeting at Stratford's Majestic Theatre elicited widespread support from local unionists including the Trades and Labor Council, which was providing financial assistance to the hard-pressed women. As winter approached, however, the situation deteriorated. After the intervention of a federal mediator the strike was settled largely on the company's terms on 20 October. Avon agreed to reinstate all strikers without discriminating against unionists, but it refused to recognize the Textile Workers. The firm, however, later asserted that economic conditions made it unable to rehire everyone and those with least seniority were released. No agreement was reached on wage increases; the strike had failed.

A similar situation occurred three years later in Hull, Quebec. In fall 1924 the E.B. Eddy Match Company issued an ultimatum to women returning after some weeks unpaid "holiday" while the plant underwent repairs. The workers were handed "yellow dog" contracts repudiating unions and informed of the decision to fire forewomen, leaving moral authority and, more importantly perhaps, chances of promotion in the hands of men alone. Rejection was immediate and spontaneous. Under the leadership of forewomen, "Girls gather[ed] near the Eddy Company offices and plant . . . to prevent their former co-workers from signing such forms."[101] Although the girls were affiliated with the Confédération des travailleurs catholiques, the union received no prior warning of the walkout. Upon notification, the conservative confessional syndicate appeared most concerned because foremen meant "morals will not be safeguarded. . . ."[102] Unfortunately, it is difficult to know just how important the women considered this "moral question." Nevertheless this issue provoked more widespread support than would have been the case if solely economic considerations had been involved.

Eddy Match attempted to outflank the women and their allies by shifting operations to its Deseronto plant. Workers gave little sign of intimidation. On the contrary, they took the initiative, grappling with the manager as he crept back into the factory. There

he was seized by several score of his former employees, mostly girls, and was forcibly prevented from doing so. . . . He returned at 9:30, and when he was seen by the girl strikers a shout went up. There was a concentrated rush for the superintendent. He was pushed, pulled and jostled. . . . During the rush he was struck.[103]

The company retaliated by hiring scabs. Not long afterwards, however, a settlement was negotiated. E.B. Eddy gave a verbal promise to rehire forewomen and permit union activity. Once in operation it reneged on both pledges. At the close of a bitter struggle the matchwomen, like the textile workers earlier, had little to show for their efforts.

Such setbacks appear increasingly common as the decade progressed. According to the files of the federal Department of

Labour most strikes were only partially successful at best. Too frequently unions went unrecognized, complaints about rates and machinery unremedied, and scabs undeterred. Although reports were notoriously incomplete, the Labour Department's assessment of the *total* male and female membership of the Boot and Shoe Workers' Union (1,127), the Amalgamated Clothing Workers of America (6,300), the International Fur Workers' Union (600), the United Garment Workers of America (1,218), the International Lady Garment Workers (656), the Hotel and Restaurant International Alliance and Bartenders' International League of America (1,138), the Retail Clerks' International Protective Association (100), the United Textile Workers of America (80), and the Industrial Union of Needle Trades Workers of Canada (1,200) in 1929 did little to exaggerate how bad times were for unions, particularly in employments where there were significant numbers of women.[104] This unpromising situation underlay women's search for more congenial environments.

Women's experience of a discriminatory workplace was shaped, inevitably, by the expectation that they, like the great majority, would marry and subsequently escape the paid work force. In the 1920's this expectation was reinforced by increasingly powerful mass media which celebrated the importance of love and marriage for women.[105] The celebrated goal of marriage did not require that women accept femininity which emphasized passivity and patience.[106] Just as many rejected domestic service in part because the middle-class house isolated them from potential suitors, they were just as capable of taking concrete steps to find a husband. Dancing the Blackbottom and the Charleston the night through, girls might not only forget the frustrations of earning their daily bread but possibly encounter new boyfriends.[107] Warding off the dreariness of factory and shop life, they built private dreams in discussing "dress and boys and movies all day long."[108] At length released, "at night the girls all fix themselves up, the paint and powder is put on thick, and they pretend not to be working girls."[109] Such girls were active participants in the marriage market. For the great majority marriage was the sole possibility they had of offsetting inequality in the workplace. Just as importantly it offered a focus for hopes which dead-end jobs could not satisfy. To be sure, marriage, childbirth, and childcare might be painful and disillusioning but how much better were a woman's chances if she looked to weak, often sexist unions and an unequal place in the paid labour force? We need to examine very closely the argument that "Working-class women as a group never chose to make employment a primary means of identification in their lives."[110] Certainly in Canada in the 1920's the familiar lessons girls learned in the fine art of male seduction were as up-to-date and possibly a good deal more effective in securing the good things in life than any purely job-related skills.

IV

Women's plight in factory, office, and store did not leave contemporaries unmoved. As we have seen some unions battled to improve conditions and female workers found private solutions. Efforts to promote women's welfare also came from governments. The special vulnerability of females had been acknowledged as early as the 1880's with the first factory acts in Quebec and Ontario. When Canada entered World War I, laws regulated hours and conditions of labour in industries and shops across the country. Some legislation responded to feminist criticism, some reflected the fears of progressive capitalists, but perhaps the majority was owed to the prevailing consensus that future mothers needed additional protection.[111] In any case most such legislation acknowledged female inferiority much more than it aimed at its elimination. The series of laws which established minimum wage guidelines for women was in the mainstream of this tradition. The very fact of their implementation acknowledged women's vulnerable and subordinate rule in the marketplace. Nothing occurred in the 1920's to render them superfluous.

By the 1920's minimum wage legislation had a lengthy history beginning in New Zealand in 1894 and entering North America in Massachusetts in 1912. Conscious of the Versailles Peace Treaty's espousal of a "living wage," Canada's Royal Commission on Industrial Relations recommended minimum wage legislation for women and labourers in 1919. The National Industrial Conference held in Ottawa in the same year reaffirmed that recommendation. In 1920 the Nova Scotia Commission on the Hours of Labour, Wages and Working Conditions of Women Employed in Industrial Occupations recognized "that if we are to have a healthy virile race, it is of primary importance to preserve the homes and conserve the health, morals and efficiency of that large class of women dependent on their daily wage for a living."[112] The developing consensus on this issue was reflected in regulations setting minimum wage for women in Alberta in 1917, in Manitoba and B.C. in 1918, in Quebec and Saskatchewan in 1919, and in Nova Scotia and Ontario in 1920.

Feminists like B.C.'s Helen Gregory McGill and Ontario's Lydia M. Parsons joined Minimum Wage Commissions in order to superintend one part of that brave new world their movement hoped to usher in. Ontario's Commission identified not only what spirit it believed lay at the heart of the new legislation but the spirit which all liberal reformers wished to see govern modern economic life: "This principle is the right of the worker to live from her work. It asserts the value and dignity of human life within the industrial sphere."[113]

More than idealism, however, had brought the minimum wage laws into being. Down-to-earth convictions were also crucial. Defending his work, the first chairman of Ontario's Minimum Wage Commission argued forcefully: "Wages here and there are unsociably low, representing a pathological condition in business. The function of minimum wage administration is to correct these unwholesome aberrations from the prevailing standards."[114] The time had come to eliminate "shyster," "indifferent," and "negligent" employers who brought with them "incoherent and inexplicable diversity."[115] Insisting that no general increase of wages was intended, the chairman clearly believed that minimum wage legislation was working with "good" businessmen everywhere to rid the community of the small minority of bad corporate citizens. In this way "minimum wage administration" would guarantee "industrial peace."[116] The Quebec division of the Canadian Manufacturers' Association and others of the same mind were reassured by promises that "nothing would be done under the act which would in any way disturb the industrial activities of the province."[117] The cautious handling of the business community by governments reflected the ambiguity which surrounded the legislation. While its very necessity implicitly indicated prevailing business practices, it at the same time depended for its success on co-operation from the offending class of capitalist employers.

Continuing mistrust on the part of this powerful group helps explain why, although all the provinces except P.E.I. and New Brunswick had minimum wage on their books early in the decade, Nova Scotia did not set up a Board until 1930 and Quebec did not appoint a commission until 1927. Nor were commissions as strong as radical reformers might have preferred. While there was considerable variation in the size, make-up, and authority of provincial minimum wage commissions, all suffered from inadequate staffs and budgets. For all such critical handicaps, they were given an awesomely wide mandate: to set wages for both experienced and inexperienced female workers in most employments with the conspicuous and damning exception in all provinces of domestic servants, farm labourers, and bank employees. Inclusion of the first two was regarded as both political suicide and administrative nightmare. The latter escaped surveillance due to provincial inability to regulate establishments operating under federal banking legislation. Wage orders were based on a hypothetical budget for an average single working woman in the occupation concerned. Separate orders were required for each industry, which often occasioned substantial delays in extending the legislation. All provinces except Quebec eventually assigned commissions the complementary power to dictate the maximum number of working hours. Rates and hours were generally fixed in consultation with representatives from the public, the employers, and the employees.

The acts of the provincial commissions were largely limited to urban areas and occupations. Even then, mandated wages for the same job often differed from city to city and province to province. In addition, the minimum could vary tremendously within a single industry. In Montreal in 1928-29 females in the boot, shoe, and leather trades might receive from $7 to over $12.50 a week depending upon experience. In the same year the weekly minimum for women in the telephone and telegraph field in B.C. ranged from $11 to $15 per week.[118] Not unexpectedly, such variation made supervision all the more difficult.

The precise level at which wages should be fixed provoked acrimonious debate right from the beginning. Commissions constantly encountered employers who argued "that the hours of labour should be determined by the state of the trade"[119] or "that most of their employees were not self-supporting, but lived with their parents, and were not under such heavy expenses."[120] Opposition to guidelines included the threat to replace women by boys and men.[121] There were also cases "where employees have been recommended by the inspector for an increase and have been dismissed in consequence."[122]

Revealing its half-hearted acceptance by the business community, efforts to avoid the legislation were all too common. Overworked and understaffed, government inspectors could only give cursory and infrequent attention to the great majority of establishments within their jurisdiction. At times it must have been only too easy to accept employers' assurances and explanations. Reform was a tedious and exhausting business for even the stout-hearted. Whatever their personal doubts, however, inspectors persisted in chronicling a wide range of abuses beginning with the failure to display minimum wage rates on the premises. Reluctance to abide by the legislation sometimes took imaginative forms. The B.C. Department of Labour ran into pseudo-schools which claimed "to teach some industry or occupation," often with tuition fees.[123] Employees in a barber "school" were typical victims; they collected only a percentage of what customers paid, an amount rarely equal to the minimum wage.[124] The continuing shift to piecework and subcontracting in many trades throughout the decade made wage rates all the more difficult to calculate and enforce. Unfortunately, redress was not easy even when offenders were identified. In most provinces it remained the victims' responsibility to sue for back wages. Such a recourse could be intimidating, not to mention expensive. Matters were improved when Ontario and B.C. began collecting arrears, but even then retaliation was an ever-present fear.[125] The situation was particularly desperate for newcomers whose limited understanding of local customs and language made them prime targets for exploitation.[126] Since fines were relatively low (in 1929 a $50 maximum in Quebec and $100 in Saskatchewan), employers had all the more incentive to avoid directives.

Offenders were of every type, but largely Canadian-born Minimum Wage Commissioners often claimed to discover a similarity among them. Not untypical was the B.C. report in 1929 which characterized such "deviants" as "usually foreigners, or owners of business, who through lack of systematic management, can see no way to reduce their overhead expenses except by cutting wages."[127] The elimination of the "unCanadian" and the inefficient would restore occupations, so it was hoped, to their rightful condition of equity. Guidelines would enlighten, discipline, and, in a word, modernize out-of-step employers without bringing businessmen as a group into disrepute. Such reasoning helped commissioners come to terms with the contradictions of a capitalist economy. Lest they shift

attention from the individual offender to the system itself the
commissions everywhere were reluctant to prosecute illegal operators in the courts in the 1920's.[128]

The commissions' success was a matter of some debate even in
the post-war decade. Many critics believed that the rates themselves were insufficient for a decent standard of living. Father
Léon Lébel, testifying before the House of Commons' Committee on Industrial and International Relations in 1929, condemned Quebec's model budget as "lower than [that of] any of
the organizations which they had consulted."[129] The Alberta
Federation of Labour criticized decisions taken after consultation with employers and wage-earners. Concluding that girls
were too often intimidated in these conferences, the AFL pointed
out that "The only cases where employees differed with their
employers . . . were cases in which the employees were protected
by being members of a trade union."[130] The OBU's *Canadian
Labor Advocate* was still more severe, charging that insufficient
wage levels drove "women of the working class into prostitution. . . ."[131]

The base rate was not the sole flaw. A more serious difficulty
lay in the permissible exceptions. Handicapped and aged
workers could be exempted by permit; special permission could
be granted for longer hours; and up to 50 per cent, and in some
instances more, of the employees could be classified as
"trainees" and thus liable to lower wages. It was only too easy
for an unscrupulous employer to hire, fire, and rehire workers to
ensure their continued classification as apprentices.[132]

Despite minimum wage legislation, the overall position of
female workers remained poor. Abuses survived in a wide range
of occupations. Government intervention could moderate unsatisfactory conditions but it rarely eliminated them completely.
A young factory hand, testifying before the 1935 Royal Commission on Price Spreads, for instance, was asked "Do you
know what the minimum wage was for experienced workers?"
Her reply indicted Quebec's Wage Commission: "I do not know,
I never heard about it."[133] Another study for the same commission discovered that minimum wage legislation had had little effect in the men's clothing industry.[134] Evidence on every side
confirmed that piecework, contract shops, and employer tactics
often outmanoeuvred even sincere efforts on the part of government investigators to bring about an improvement in working
conditions or salaries.

Despite the generally sorry picture, there were gains. Wage standards, however inadequate, had been established. As the Commission on Price Spreads discovered in examining variety chain stores:

> The variety chain evidence shows in an interesting way the effect of the absence of Minimum Wage Laws on sweated conditions. One chain operating across Canada paid 88 per cent of its full-time female clerks in the Maritime Provinces, and 72 per cent in Quebec below $10 per week. There was no minimum wage order covering them at that time. In Ontario, the Prairie Provinces and British Columbia, where there were such orders, only 5, 3, and 0 per cent, respectively, of female clerks received below this figure.[135]

Certain employers, humane, fair-minded, or publicity-conscious, had been encouraged to raise wages. Some working women did collect back pay. While such benefits did not negate the continuing disadvantages facing women in a discriminatory labour market, they muted them.

In the 1920's single women became an acceptable part of the paid work force for all but the most reactionary. The welcome for married women was much less certain. In the final analysis, acceptance of any kind was in large measure predicated on the continuation of women's inferiority in the labour force. Although some optimistic spirits anticipated that the disappearance of invidious distinctions between male and female labour was an inevitable outcome of modernization, discrimination found as comfortable a home as ever in the 1920's. Women had become merely the white-collar privates and NCOs whose deferential support was an essential component of the new corporate state. Yet the seeds of some more critical reassessment of women's role in the workplace had also been sown. The all-too-familiar hardships of blue-collar labour energized a new generation of women workers. Untouched by the glamourized optimism which so distorted understanding of work in offices and stores, some blue-collar women took full measure of modern society and found it wanting. Over the long term their outrage would be essential in building a collective tradition of protest and in expanding women's awareness of their oppression. Not all, of course, had the strength, the stamina, or the insight to enter the struggle directly. Unknown numbers turned, as had their mothers and grandmothers, to marriage as the most accessible and attractive escape from bad jobs and bad bosses. Some female wage-earners found limited relief in minimum wage legislation. No solution finally overcame the familiar disadvantages women encountered in the paid labour force. The "Girl of the New Day," wherever she toiled, soon discovered that she must wait still longer for a better dawn to break. In the 1920's sexist discrimination remained an integral feature of economic organization, however modern.[136]

NOTES

1. See, for instance, W. Calderwood, "Pulpit, Press and Political Reactions to the Ku Klux Klan in Saskatchewan," in S.M. Trofimenkoff, ed., *The Twenties in Western Canada* (Ottawa, 1972); H. Glynn-Ward, *The Writing on the Wall*, introduced by P.E. Roy (Toronto, 1974); V. Strong-Boag, "Canadian Feminism in the 1920s: the Case of Nellie L. McClung," *Journal of Canadian Studies*, 12, 4 (Summer, 1977), 58-68; James Struthers, "Prelude to Depression: The Federal Government and Unemployment, 1918-29," *CHR*, LVIII (1977), 277-93; Marie Lavigne and Jennifer Stoddart, "Ouvrières et travailleuses Montréalaises 1900-1940," in M. Lavigne and Y. Pinard, eds., *Les Femmes dans la société Québécoise* (Montréal, 1977); S.M. Trofimenkoff, *Action Française* (Toronto, 1975).

2. This is all the more misleading as it is increasingly apparent that women in the "male" professions had substantial problems in the 1920's. See, for instance, Strong-Boag, "Feminism Constrained: The Graduates of Canada's Medical Schools for Women," in L. Kealey, ed., *A Not Unreasonable Claim. Women and Social Reform in Canada* (Toronto, 1979).

3. Available labour force statistics are probably somewhat misleading at the higher age levels as many older women participated in the paid work force as day charwomen, laundresses, boarding house keepers, or pedlars on a part-time basis and were likely to be missed.

4. "Report of the Windsor Free Employment Bureau," Annual Report of the Ontario Department of Labour, *Sessional Papers of Ontario* (henceforth SPO), 1928, #10, 42.

5. It is of course difficult to know how much home work was performed by the husband of the working woman in the 1920's, but modern studies give no cause for optimism. See, for instance, Martin Meissner, "Sexual Division of Labour and Inequality," in M. Stephenson, ed., *Women in Canada* (Toronto, 1977).

6. Annual Report of the British Columbia Department of Labour, 1927, 72.

7. A useful discussion of the informal recruitment network which stresses the role of the foreman is Daniel Nelson, *Managers and Workers. Origins of the New Factory System in the United States 1880-1920* (Madison, 1975), Chapter 5. Informal networks were perhaps most essential for the non-native-born. See, for special reference to women, C. Baum, P.A. Hyman, and S. Michel, *The Jewish Woman in America* (New York, 1977), *passim*.

8. Canada, Royal Commission on the Textile Industry, *Final Report*, 1938, 157. See also the similar situation in a bakery in "Christie-Brown Plant Has Undergone Thorough Clean-up Since Change," *Financial Post*, 14 August 1925.

9. For a description of economic development in the period, see W.A. Mackintosh, *The Economic Background of Dominion-Provincial Relations* (Toronto, 1964), Chapter 5; A.E. Safarian, *The Canadian Economy and the Great Depression* (Toronto, 1970), 27-39; and L.G. Reynolds, *The Control of Competition in Canada* (Cambridge, Mass., 1940), Chapters I-V *passim*.

10. The outstanding examples of this type of literature in the period were Marjory MacMurchy, *The Canadian Girl at Work* (Toronto, 1920); Ellen Knox, *The Girl of the New Day* (Toronto, 1919); and Alice Parkin Massey, *Occupations for Trained Women in Canada* (Toronto, 1920).

11. MacMurchy, *Canadian Girl*, vi.

12. Knox, *New Day*, 105.

13. See, for instance, "Heads a $1,000,000 Corporation," *Maclean's*, 1 May 1921, 65-6; and "Art Collecting as a Profession for Women," *Saturday Night*, 5 April 1919. Both are typical examples of coverage given to the workplace.

14. *Labour Gazette* (December, 1920), 1618.

15. Knox, *New Day*, 107.

16. *Labour Gazette* (March, 1921), 373-6.

17. See Robert Stamp, "Teaching Girls their 'God Given Place in Life,' " *Atlantis*, 2, 2 (Spring, 1977), 18-34; Mgr. Albert Tessier, "Les écoles ménagères au service du foyer" (1942), and L'Association des femmes diplômées des universités (Montréal), "Les Idées directrices des Instituts familiaux et leurs consequences: extraits" (1964), in M. Jean, ed., *Québecoises du 20ᵉ siècle* (Montréal, 1974).

18. Mr. F.S. Rutherford, "What Technical Schools Have Done to Meet the Recommendations of the Royal Commission on Technical Education," *Labour Gazette* (May, 1928), 473.

19. Annual Report of the Ontario Department of Education, SPO, 1928, #17, 14.

20. Saskatchewan's city bureaus in 1926-27, for instance, supplied

1,949 female requests for housekeeping positions, 2,080 for domestic, 3,010 for scrubbing, and 385 for cooking. Such women made up 75.84 per cent of all applicants to the employment offices. Urban vacancies for women in the same year in the domestic service category made up 94.18 per cent of all requests for help. Annual Report of the Saskatchewan Bureau of Labour and Industries, 1926-27.

21. See Suzann Buckley, "Some Schemes for the Emigration of British Females to Canada, 1884-1931," paper presented at the meetings of the Canadian Historical Association, Quebec City, 1976; for a later period, see R. Pierson, "Home Aid," *Atlantis*, 2, 2 (Spring, 1977), 85-97.

22. See, for example, the girlhood experiences recalled in N.L. McClung, *Clearing in the West* (Toronto, 1935); Elizabeth Goudie, *Woman of Labrador* (Toronto, 1973); Laura Salverson, *Confessions of an Immigrant's Daughter* (Toronto, 1939); Madge MacBeth, *Boulevard Career* (Toronto, 1957); and T.F. Casgrain, *Une Femme chez les hommes* (Montréal, 1971).

23. See Ontario, Royal Commission on Unemployment, *Report*, 1916, 180.

24. On the importance of transiency, see Michael Katz, *The People of Hamilton, Canada West: Family and Class in a Mid-Nineteenth Century City* (Cambridge, Mass., 1976); and David Gagan and Herbert Mays, "Historical Demography and Canadian Social History: Families and Land in Peel County, Ontario," LIV (1973), 27-47. These studies examine the nineteenth century but there is little reason to suppose matters changed much in the first decades of the twentieth century, especially for those workers with few marketable skills. See, for instance, the working experience of Phyllis Knight in P. Knight and R. Knight, *A Very Ordinary Life* (Vancouver, 1974). Note that my use of the word "transiency" would include both changing jobs and/or locale. The other studies focus on residential shifts which often, in fact, include occupational changes.

25. In 1921 and 1931 the service category contained 71.15 per cent and 82.23 per cent of all ten- to thirteen-year-old working "women" and 42.24 per cent and 41.46 per cent of all working women over sixty-five.

26. See Enid M. Price, "Changes in the Industrial Occupations of Women in the Environment of Montreal during the Period of the War, 1914-1918" (M.A. thesis, McGill, 1919).

27. "Report of the Toronto Employment Bureau," Annual Report of the Superintendent of the Trades and Labour Branch of the Ontario Department of Public Works, 50.

28. Annual Report of the Quebec Department of Public Works and Labour, 1921, 131. See also Strong-Boag, *The Parliament of*

Women (Ottawa, 1976), *passim*, regarding the efforts of some middle-class mistresses to deal with the unpopularity of domestic service.

29. Annual Report of the Ontario Department of Labour, SPO, 1925, #16, 13.

30. *Ibid.*, 1921, #16, 40.

31. "Report of the Ottawa Bureau of the Employment Service of Canada," SPO, 1924, #16, 40.

32. Annual Report of the Ontario Department of Labour, SPO, #10, 30.

33. See strike of Toronto waiters against the hiring of waitresses, *Labour Gazette* (April, 1922).

34. For a description of conditions, see E.E. Hancox, "What Hotel and Cafeteria Life Means to the Worker," *The Worker* (Toronto), 31 October 1925; and F.P. Grove, *Search for America* (Montreal, 1928), Chapters III-VII.

35. The life of the young waitress, Florentine, in Gabrielle Roy's *The Tin Flute* (New York, 1947) provides a realistic portrayal of the opportunities for human contact.

36. On the importance of manufacturing in Montreal, see Lavigne, Stoddart, "Ouvriéres et Travailleuses Montréalaises," 127-32.

37. See, for example, J. Rouillard, *Les Travailleurs du coton au Québec 1900-1915* (Québec, 1974). On the continuation of this pattern into the 1970's, see Pat and Hugh Armstrong, *The Double Ghetto* (Toronto, 1978).

38. See, for example, "Samples of Wages and Hours of Labour for Miscellaneous Factory Trades," *Labour Gazette*, Supplement (January, 1930), 40-95.

39. "United Garment Workers Union Helps Boss to Impose Worsened Conditions," *The Worker*, 28 September 1929. These new machines and procedures were part of the continuing introduction of the "scientific management and industrial efficiency" movement into Canadian operations. For a valuable study of this development in the pre-World War I period, see Craig Heron and Bryan D. Palmer, "Through the Prism of the Strike: Industrial Conflict in Southern Ontario, 1901-14," *CHR*, LVIII (1977), 423-58.

40. The use of "incentive" practices appeared in the nineteenth-century factory but their introduction appears to have been intermittent and uneven. For a helpful discussion of some of the issues related to these practices, see Nelson, *Managers and Workers*, Chapter 3. For evidence of their increased use in Canada in the 1920's, see the strike files of the federal Department of Labour for the period.

41. "In a Dress Factory," Working Women's Section, *The Worker*, 12 September 1925.

42. See "Working for Eaton's, 1934," in M. Horn, ed., *The Dirty Thirties* (Toronto, 1972).

43. See "Report of Inspectress Eleanor Gurnett," Report of the Ontario Department of Labour, SPO, 1925, #16, 49.

44. "Report of Inspectress G.E. Hornell," *ibid.*, SPO, 1927, #10, 51. For a discussion of changes in the factory environment, see Nelson, *Managers and Workers*, Chapter 2.

45. Nova Scotia, Royal Commission on Wages, Hours of Labour and Work Conditions of Women in Industry in Nova Scotia, *Report*, 1920, 11. See also conditions in Montreal in T. Copp, *The Anatomy of Poverty* (Toronto, 1974), Chapter 3.

46. For a useful reminder of the uneven application of mechanization and the continuing importance of hand labour for an earlier period but which is also relevant to some degree for the 1920's, see R. Samuel, "Workshop of the World: Steam Power and Hand Technology in mid-Victorian Britain," *History Workshop*, 3 (Spring, 1977), 6-72.

47. "Report of the Women's Minimum Wage Commission," Annual Report of the Quebec Department of Public Works and Labour, 1930, 70.

48. Annual Report of the Ontario Minimum Wage Board, SPO, 1923, #89, 27.

49. Mrs. E. Scott, Annual Report of the Ontario Department of Labour, SPO, 1930, #23, 69.

50. Series s323-331, M. Urquhart and K. Buckley, *Historical Statistics* (Toronto, 1965), 559; for some of the arguments in favour of automatic switchboards and their effect on operators, see R. Young, "Automatic Telephony" (1921), in F.S. Grant, ed., *Telephone Operation and Development in Canada, 1921-1971* (Toronto, 1974), 12-21.

51. See conditions revealed in the Report of the Royal Commission Regarding the Dispute Respecting Hours of Employment between the Bell Telephone Company of Canada Ltd., and Operators at Toronto, 1907. While physical conditions have improved, it appears that modern personnel practices maintain the psychological stress which was so much a feature of the employment from the beginning. See Elinor Langer, "Inside the New York Telephone Company," *New York Review of Books*, 12 March 1970, 16, 17-18, 20-4; and "The Women of the Telephone Company," *ibid.*, 26 March 1970, 14, 16-22.

52. J.N. Schacht, "Toward Industrial Unionism: Bell Telephone Workers and Company Unions, 1919-1937," *Labor History*, 16 (1975), 12.

53. On training of operators, see Mr. N.G. Fitchpatrick, "Training Plans for Traffic Employees," in Telephone Association of Canada, *Proceedings of the 7th Annual Convention*, 1927, 135-8. For an indication of how little attention was paid to the possibility of training women for higher positions, see TAC, *Proceedings of the 5th Annual Convention*, 1925, 62-92.

54. For a description of some of these programs, see Mr. E.F. Helliwell, "Employee Relations," in TAC, *Proceedings of the 3rd Annual Convention*, 1923, 115-29. For an analysis of the U.S. Bell system which appears comparable to that in Canada, see Schacht, "Toward Industrial Unionism," 12-14.

55. Regarding the expansion of the chain stores, see Clifford H. Cheasley, *The Chain Store Movement in Canada*, McGill University Economic Studies, no. 17, n.d.

56. University Women's Club of Winnipeg, "The Work of Women and Girls in the Department Stores of Winnipeg," 1914.

57. MacMurchy, *The Canadian Girl at Work*, 12.

58. *Vocational Opportunities in the Industries of Ontario. A Survey. Department Stores*, 1920, 4-5.

59. *Ibid.*, 31.

60. *Ibid.*, 5.

61. See conditions described by 'YL' (Montreal), "Conditions in the Departmental Store," Women's Section, *The Worker*, 6 February 1925.

62. Fourth Annual Report of the Trades and Labour Branch, Ontario Department of Public Works, 1920, 49.

63. M.P. Marchak, "The Canadian Labour Force: Jobs for Women," in M. Stephenson, ed., *Women in Canada* (Toronto, 1977), 148.

64. MacMurchy, *The Canadian Girl at Work*, 15.

65. For some of the debate which surrounded this program, see "University Women in the Business World," *Financial Post*, 24 December 1926, 10; and the arguments between Margaret Thompson, head of Western's Department of Secretarial Science, "Pays to Use Best in Buying Brains," and Mrs. E. Cooper, Chief of Stenographic Division of Maclean Publishing, "College Training Not Key to Success," *ibid.*, 10-11.

66. For an illustration of such stereotypes, see R.M. Dawson, *The Civil Service of Canada* (London, 1929).

67. There were comparable efforts after World War II. See R. Pierson, "Women's Emancipation and the Recruitment of Women into the Labour Force in WWII," *Historical Papers* (1976), 141-73.

68. This general trend is an extension of the pattern already observed for Montreal and Toronto in the important study by Marie Lavigne and Jennifer Stoddart, "Analyse du travail féminin à Montréal entre les deux guerres," Thèse de la Maitrisse en Arts (Histoire), Université de Québec à Montréal, 1973, chapitre V.

69. First Annual Report of the Ontario Minimum Wage Board, SPO, #73, 1921, 6.

70. *Labour Gazette* (April, 1929), 407.

71. The number of women who were forced into prostitution, part-time or full-time, as a result of inadequate salaries is unknown. Some contemporaries did believe, however, that such a fate was

not infrequent. See "The Life of Factory Girls. A Day's Impressions in Toronto," *Maritime Labour Herald*, 13 October 1923.

72. Women's work in the pre-industrial community most often took place in the context of the patriarchal family, her own or her master's. This family model, with its implicit provision for physical and moral protection, shaped the attitudes of early factory owners to their girl workers. See, for instance, J.W. Scott and Louise A. Tilly, "Women's Work and the Family in Nineteenth-Century Europe," *Comparative Studies in Society and History*, 17 (1975), 53.

73. For a good example of this type of discipline, see G. Kealey, ed., *Canada Investigates Industrialism* (Toronto, 1973), 222-32.

74. "Report of Mr. Louis Guyon," Annual Report of the Quebec Department of Public Works and Labour, 1918, 75.

75. Mrs. Louisa King, *ibid.*, 93.

76. *Labour Gazette* (February, 1921), 131. See also "A Community House for Women Workers," *Financial Post*, 22 October 1920.

77. "Conditions in a Cigar Factory in Montreal," Working Women's Section, *The Worker*, 24 October 1925.

78. See Nelson, *Managers and Workers*, 111.

79. Unfortunately, no critical history of Eatons' and its labour policies yet exists. It is possible, however, to read hagiographic accounts such as W. Stephenson, *The Store that Timothy Built* (Toronto, 1969), for the details which will allow a more critical analysis of its development. On the 1920's, see especially Chapter 3.

80. *Vocational Opportunities in the Industries of Ontario*, 9.

81. See S. Jamieson, *Times of Trouble* (Ottawa, 1968), Chapter IV.

82. W. Tite, "Married Women in Industry," *Canadian Congress Journal* (October, 1924), 41.

83. H.A. Spence, "Minimum Wage Laws for Women," *ibid.* (March, 1925), 37.

84. See, for instance, the experience of Pauline Newman, Fannia Cohn, and Rose Pesotta (who organized for the International Lady Garment Workers in Canada) in Alice Kessler-Harris, "Organizing the Unorganizable: Three Jewish Women and their Union," *Labor History*, 17 (1976), 5-23.

85. See Lavigne and Stoddart, "Ouvrières et travailleuses," 141; and the discussion over whether women should be permitted on committees in "Fourth Convention of National and Catholic Unions," *Labour Gazette* (October, 1921), 1262-7. On the slow shift in attitudes by the successor of the Catholic body, the Confédération des Syndicats Nationaux, see Mona Josée Gagnon, *Les Femmes vues par le Québec des hommes* (Montréal, 1974), chapitre 6.

86. *Labour Gazette* (March, 1921), 418.

87. *Ibid.* (February, 1924), 170-1.

88. "Woman Rules," *The Worker*, 14 November 1929.

89. Unfortunately, no critical assessment exists of any of these individuals or groups. The hagiographic treatments by Catherine Vance of Bella Hall Gauld, *Not by Gods but by People* (Toronto, 1968), and by Louise Watson of Annie Buller, *She Never was Afraid* (Toronto, 1976), do suggest, however, how central a role such women played in the Canadian Communist Party.

90. This is in sharp contrast to the relative passivity depicted in Suzanne Cross, "The Neglected Majority: The Changing Role of Women in 19th Century Montreal," in S.M. Trofimenkoff and A. Prentice, eds., *The Neglected Majority* (Toronto, 1977).

91. See, for instance, Kessler-Harris, "Organizing the Unorganizable."

92. PAC, Department of Labour Papers, vol. 329, folder 22(66), clipping, "6000 Clothing Workers to Lay Down Needles in Friendly Warning," *Montreal Star*, 11 July 1922.

93. *Ibid.*, vol. 333, folder 24(81), S. Gariepy to Deputy Minister of Labour, 29 December 1924.

94. *Ibid.*, vol. 334, folder 24(11), "Score King Government," *Toronto Telegram*, 6 February 1925.

95. *Ibid.*, vol. 337, folder 26(63), "Union Workers Appear in Court," *Montreal Star*, 20 July 1926.

96. *Ibid.*, vol. 332, folder 23(97); vol. 335, folder 25(53); vol. 341, folder 28(106); vol. 342, folder 29(4), "Strikers Still Out: Pickets on Duty at Plant," *Hamilton Spectator*, 1 February 1929.

97. *Ibid.*, vol. 338, folder 26(79), "Strikers Are Hurt in Fight," *Free Press* (Winnipeg), 27 October 1926.

98. *Ibid.*, vol. 328, folder 20(331), W. Pearson to Deputy Minister of Labour, 18 September 1920.

99. *Ibid.*, "Statement to Employees," 31 August 1920.

100. *Ibid.*, "Statement from Mrs. L. Tuff," 13 September 1920.

101. *Ibid.*, vol. 333, folder 24(64), "Refused to Sign Forms Presented," *Ottawa Journal*, 27 September 1924.

102. *Ibid.*, "National Catholic Central Trades and Labour Council."

103. *Ibid.*, "Match Factory Head Given a Warm Reception by Girls and Kept from Eddy Plant," *Ottawa Evening Journal*, 20 October 1924.

104. Canada. Department of Labour, *Statistics*, 1929, 67-8.

105. See the description of the female types in Molly Haskell, *From Reverence to Rape. The Treatment of Women in the Movies* (New York, 1974), Chapter 2; and Alexander Walker, *Sex in the Movies* (Harmondsworth, 1968). For a useful Canadian study, see M. Vipond, "The Image of Women in Mass Circulation Magazines in the 1920s," in Trofimenkoff and Prentices, eds., *The Neglected Majority*.

106. The question of what constituted "femininity" for working-class women is difficult since few records from the women themselves

survive. The "structural" approach suggested by W. Roberts, *Honest Womanhood* (Toronto, 1977), is valuable so long as it is remembered to include marital or family influences together with the "demographic and occupational" factors Roberts notes (p. 5).

107. For a moving description of this solution in an American setting, see Wm. O'Neill, ed., "The Long Day," *Women at Work* (Chicago, 1972).

108. "In a Dress Factory," *The Worker*, 12 September 1925.

109. *Ibid*. Compare this with a folksong heard in New York's sweat-shops (from Kessler-Harris, "Organizing the Unorganizable," 7):

> Day the same as night, night the same as day.
> And all I do is sew and sew and sew
> May God help me and my love come soon
> That I might leave this work and go.

Such Jewish folksongs were doubtless common in Canada.

110. Patricia Branca, "A New Perspective on Women's Work: A Comparative Typology," *Journal of Social History*, 9 (1975), 147. This readjustment in focus for the study of working women is part of an increased awareness that working people live lives distinct from the traditional accounts of labour unions and political parties. For women in particular this meant lives more closely tied to family demands and cycles. See the introduction to R.G. Hann *et al., Primary Sources in Canadian Working Class History 1860-1930* (Kitchener, 1973), for a reminder of the need for a "new labour history."

111. In the 1920's fears about the effect of paid work on a woman's ability to "mother" were especially evident. See Strong-Boag, " 'Wages for Housework': Mothers' Allowances and the Beginnings of Social Security in Canada," *Journal of Canadian Studies* (February, 1979).

112. Nova Scotia. Royal Commission . . . 1920, 6.

113. Annual Report of the Minimum Wage Commission of Ontario, SPO, #73, 1921, 5.

114. J.W. Macmillan, "Minimum Wage Administration," *American Economic Review*, 18 (1928), 248. Compare these arguments with similar ones presented in the state of New York in the 1930's in R.P. Ingalls, "New York and the Minimum Wage Movement, 1933-1937," *Labor History*, 15 (1974), 179-98.

115. Macmillan, "Minimum Wage," 250.

116. Annual Report of the Minimum Wage Board of Ontario, SPO, #89, 1923, 21.

117. *Labour Gazette* (July, 1925), 647.

118. Annual Report of the Quebec Department of Public Works and Labour, 1928-9, 71; Annual Report of the B.C. Department of Labour, 1929.
119. Annual Report of the B.C. Department of Labour, 1928, 47.
120. "Minimum Wages for Women in British Columbia in 1923," *Labour Gazette* (September, 1924), 76.
121. See Annual Report of the B.C. Department of Labour, 1919, 88, and the accusation in "Winnipeg Firm Employs Youths at $4 per Week," *OBU Bulletin*, 5 February 1925, 1.
122. Annual Report of the Saskatchewan Bureau of Labour and Industries, 1928, 39.
123. Annual Report of the B.C. Department of Labour, 1924, 51.
124. *Ibid.*, 1925, 50.
125. See the retaliation cases cited in Annual Report of the B.C. Department of Labour, 1929, 55-7.
126. See the examples cited in Annual Report of the Saskatchewan Bureau of Labour and Industries, 1928.
127. Quoted in "Minimum Wages for Women in British Columbia in 1929," *Labour Gazette* (September, 1930), 1031.
128. See the Ontario Commission's refusal to prosecute a particularly grievous offender in "Attempts to Evade Minimum Wage Orders," *Labour Gazette* (November, 1924), 913.
129. Canada, House of Commons, Committee on Industrial and International Relations, *Report*, 1929, 10.
130. Cited in the "Legislative Programme of the Alberta Federation of Labour," *Labour Gazette* (January, 1924), 28.
131. "Crucifying Canadian Women," *Canadian Labor Advocate*, 27 November 1925.
132. See the case cited in "Attempts to Evade Minimum Wage Orders," *Labour Gazette* (November, 1924), 913.
133. Canada, Royal Commission . . . Price Spreads, *Evidence*, vol. 8, 4362.
134. F.R. Scott and H.M. Cassidy, *Labour Conditions in the Men's Clothing Industry* (Toronto, 1935), 48.
135. Canada, Royal Commission . . . Price Spreads, *Report*, 1935, 122.
136. I should like to thank Suzann Buckley, Gregory and Linda Kealey, Michael Piva, Douglas Ross, and Jennifer Stoddart for their comments at various stages in the preparation of this article.

Readings in Canadian Social History

In print in the series: